THE BOOK OF **NOTS** IN SCIENCE & RELIGION

*A Believer's Guide
to Reality*

Abraham Rempel

Produced by:

FriesenPress

Suite 300 – 852 Fort Street
Victoria, BC, Canada V8W 1H8

www.friesenpress.com

Distributed to the trade by The Ingram Book Company

Contents

Prologue 1

1. I call my old friend 7

2. The Earth is not a planet 13

3. Humans are not immortal 23

4. Paul was not an apostle 37

5. The New Testament is not Scripture 47

6. The Earth is not very old 61

7. Jesus was not God 79

8. Jesus was not a sacrifice for sin 99

9. Humans did not evolve 119

10. The Earth is not a planet II 133

11. Saturday is not the Sabbath 155

Mesologue 181

12. We are not Gentiles 199

13. The universe is not serene 219

14. Satan is not a real being 239

Epilogue 253

Bibliography 259

Index 265

This book is a memorial to my mother
who lived by her faith, taught me to believe,
and said that one day I would write a book.

Mary Rempel Dick
November 1,1922 – February 8, 2010

Listen, my son, to your father's instruction
and do not forsake your mother's teaching.
(Proverbs 1:8)

For to the one who has, more will be given,
and he will have an abundance,
but from the one who has not,
even what he has will be taken away.
(Yeshuah the Messiah)

The future of this world,
this Eden that was entrusted to us,
is ours to shape if we dare to finally begin
searching, learning, and implementing truth over fiction.
(Shmuel Asher)

Our being has escaped
like a bird from the snare of the trappers;
The snare was broken, and we have escaped.
(Psalm 124:7)

PROLOGUE

Identifying myself is not something that I am very keen to do, perhaps because there isn't much to identify. I was born in 1945, a Canadian, and retired after twenty-six years in the financial sector – long enough to learn that the world is a sorry place to do business. I have a university degree in Classical Studies from Brock University, and spent one academic year in a Lutheran seminary. I have never held a position of importance in a college or church. My wife, Barbara, and I have two grown children whom we dearly love, as they do us. My legal name is Rudolphe Abraham Rempel.

My religious upbringing is Mennonite Brethren, or more broadly, Anabaptist. It's a heritage I cherish – the one with the least amount of unsavory baggage to come out of the Protestant Reformation. My parents were born in Russia, and for what it's worth, my believing mother once told me that I had been "given to missions". Some who know me consider me devout, some even saintly. I can live with that, but at the same time, I have a keenly secular mind and a no-nonsense approach to what I believe. At times, I don't even think of myself as religious.

I spent many long years studying the Bible in private with intensity. This took place in three distinct periods, and curiously, they came about sixteen years apart. I began my biblical studies in 1970 when I started to 'believe' as an adult in my early twenties and as a church member of the Mennonite Brethren. The next period of intensive study began in 1986 as a prelude to my nine-year association with the Worldwide Church of God. The third (three times and you're out) commenced around 2002 with my discovery and participation in the Messianic or Hebrew Roots movement. Those associations have all come and gone. This is with sadness, yes, but not without a deep sense of gratitude and thankfulness. My devotion to biblical studies remains as strong as ever.

I was just as keenly a student of history and science throughout those years and remain so to this day. I can hardly overstate the pleasure I find in my secular studies, nor understate my appreciation for minds that can think clearly and wisely no matter what their profession of faith or lack of it. As the late and venerable scientist, Stephen Jay Gould, understood, it's a nineteenth century myth that there's an ongoing dichotomy or warfare between science and religion. The myth is attributable to Darwinism's overt clash with religion, and although Gould was an evolutionist and agnostic, he was equally honest and insightful. Gould did not think of religion and science as fixed and opposing categories, and neither do I. There are secular truths as well as religious truths, and in my mind, they are often complementary.

I can't truly say that I've ever had a conversion experience. At one or another time, I thought I did, but now realize that my religious upbringing was too powerful not to be overwhelming. It got the better of me, so to speak, and I've had to spend nearly a lifetime overcoming the intellectual, psychological and spiritual impact of what I received as a child. Admitting to ingrained and misguided beliefs was no small matter, but I realized early on that I could either walk away from my early religious experience with indifference, and possibly face a lifetime of internal strife, or concede its influence and work with it, and to explore it with dedication. I chose the latter with no regrets and much enjoyment.

So too in matters of science. In my early teens, I became acquainted with the story of evolution. At that age, with a keen imagination and sponge-like mind (and the encouragement of an uncle who was a church minister), I quickly absorbed the story in all its fascination. Long ages of time, the similarities of a human hand and a bat wing, the discovery of a female skeleton dubbed Lucy in 1974 – all had an allure that captivated my mind. In 1969 a man actually walked on the moon, the Hubble Space Telescope was launched in 1990, and now there's talk of a one-way trip to Mars with human passengers. All in all, absolutely engrossing! For me, the story of science, with its attesting miracles, was no less beguiling than what I had read about in the Bible.

One would think that every living being wants to know the truth and avidly seek it out, but from somewhere deep in the human psyche, the truth is more often than not actively resisted. Conformity, peer pressure, reputation and self-preservation are all factors. So are economics and the mighty dollar, since countless salaries are earned from both science and religion. The very thought that we are being misled by those two domains is in itself resisted. There is something about truth or reality that threatens us as human beings. Consequently, internal barriers go up, minds close, groups rally in self-support, and the status quo is preserved.

A superb example of resisting truth is central to my book. It's an immediate test. From our ordinary and daily experience to sending satellites into space, we know the Earth as a stable platform in a revolving universe. We see it with our very own eyes – how the sun, moon, planets, stars and manufactured satellites all circle the heavens each and every day. The sciences of meteorology, maritime travel, time keeping and many others are inextricably linked to the rising and setting of the sun, moon and stars. Yes, NASA uses fixed-Earth coordinates to launch its satellites into space. By all experience and practical application, it's the Earth that is stationary and the sky that is moving. Yet, not wanting to admit that the sky's rotation is for real, the scientific priesthood calls an illusion, reminding us *ad nauseam* that the Earth is rotating on its axis every twenty-four hours. Granted, the effect would be the same, but not the underlying truth. Again and again, when the geocentric nature of the universe is broached, minds instantly snap shut and refuse even to consider the possibility. The usual dodge is to associate geocentricity with egocentricity, and deny that the Earth is a very, very special place.

A test that might be considered purely religious is the chapter, "Jesus was not God." That the Almighty Creator became an individual human being and singular personality at a specific time in history must surely be the foundational truism of Christianity. I dare say that "Jesus is God" is repeated as often as "the Earth rotates on its axis." Both statements depend on repetition for their continuance as truisms. In like manner, no amount of repetition in denying that Jesus was God is likely to be very effective. For the vast majority of Christians and unbelievers alike, that axiom is so deeply rooted in their consciousness that all but a few will only scratch their heads in bewilderment. *Caveat lector* (reader beware), the path to recover our religious sensibilities and powers of cognition will not be an easy one.

Central to my book is an attempt to answer the question of who we are as human beings and what it is that we can become. In that context, I make two concessions to what seems very orthodox. I am allowing that Yeshuah was the Messiah and that he was raised bodily from the dead. In a book that declares one "not" after another, and where so many lies are exposed, something must remain to inspire our confidence and invigorate our identity as human beings. At its core, this book is as affirmative as any other you care to read, and by far more than most.

As far as Yeshuah's messiahship, at the very least he was a man uniquely sensitive to his time and place. No man before or after has demonstrated an equal ability to set aside his own interest for the sake of his people and their plight. He delivered the highest example for all time by his willingness to lay down his life for his friends and in actively serving rather than wanting to be served. Regardless of if he did all the miracles or spoke all the words attributed to him, by all that we know or can surmise, his was the gift of loving the Master and Mighty One with all his heart, all his soul and all his mind. To this end, he was appointed.

As for Yeshuah's resurrection, it's difficult to comprehend a real afterlife without a physical body, and the idea of living forever as a disembodied spirit is not very appealing. To be sure, believing in Yeshuah's bodily resurrection may press our rational abilities and defy experience. To say that Yeshuah now resides in Heaven is as inexplicable as the cow jumping over the moon (not quite: the latter is absurd while the former is not.). Yet no one can say with finality that there was no resurrection or that there never will be. Who can dismiss the notion of an afterlife based on lack of experience or its perplexity to the human mind? When all that is said, the concept of living fully and forever in a resurrected and physical body can stand on its own merits as a long-surviving and intractable hope for the future of humankind. In my mind, and the minds of countless others, nothing has ever surpassed the Good News of Yeshuah's bodily resurrection from the dead. I'll go for broke on that one. It's too good not to be true.

My experience is not uncommon. Untold numbers of people have either chosen or been forced to re-examine themselves and their beliefs at many levels. This book examines our commonly held beliefs in science and religion. Our beliefs regarding politics, economics and the media are also being challenged. Assuredly, it's not only religion that is suspect. Indeed, many have jumped from the religious frying pan into the scientific fire, unaware that much of popular science is as false and empty as the religion it aims to replace. Hence the title, *The Book of Nots in Science & Religion*. I put science first because for many it's the more sacred of the two at this time in human history.

In writing this book, I came to a conclusion that surprised me. My initial intention was only to present the "nots" of false beliefs in science and religion, but as I continued to write during the three years it took, the "nots" became interrelated and compelled a startling conclusion. I did not anticipated that the book would present a singular answer to the threat of humankind's threatening extinction with the added promise of a very happy future. This book presents nothing less than a formula for humankind's ultimate salvation and the pathway to a new heaven and Earth.

I must make some apologies. First, I am not an expert in any of the subjects or themes in this book, and those themes cover a very wide range in both science and religion. Despite my diligent research and best effort at careful wording, it is a forgone conclusion that some level of error has crept in. Even as a competent generalist, I can't claim that everything in the book is exactly right. It's my first book as well, so its shortcomings are inevitable, and I'm still learning.

I chose the format of a dialogue between two individuals for that very reason. As an informal conversation between two people, the format avoids any pretense of being a textbook or academic paper. The two individuals are interacting and communicating as best they can, in a casual setting, and enjoying their camaraderie. The central figure was once a dear friend in my life, Harry Vandergriendt, who is now deceased. These conversations never actually took place, although we did have many in our relationship. I trust my readers will be drawn in by the book's informal style and be able to identify with its characters in a way that they would not with a textbook or formal treatise. My book is meant to be enjoyed.

I quote Scripture texts frequently. The quotations are from a variety of translations, usually without the chapter and verse supplied. The wording has been changed by removing the Thees and Thous for example, sometimes to clarify the meaning, but never for the sake of a private interpretation. I wanted to avoid clutter, and let the texts speak for themselves. Bible readers with a concordance can easily find the text for themselves.

There are many people to thank, especially authors who have influenced and inspired me. They are Steven M. Collins, Yair Davidy, Geradus D. Bouw, Shmuel Asher, James R. Brayshaw, Douglas J. Del Tondo and John Vujicic. All of them are authors and, with one exception, are email associates who have been patient and helpful with my questions. There's also John Mayer, George Nathan and Kathleen Batstone for their invaluable editing. Finally, I'm grateful for the many YMCA friends who have encouraged me in the course of writing this book.

Finally, I am grateful for my readers. I am convinced that our future is in the hands of men and women like myself who honestly seek for the truth, recognize it when it comes, apply it to their lives, and make a difference – one person at a time.

1. I CALL MY OLD FRIEND

I wasn't thinking about eschatology when I called Harry. I only knew his wife had died a few weeks earlier.[1]

Hi, Harry.

Hi?

It's your long ago friend, Abraham.

Avi? It's good to hear from you. It has been a long time.

Yes. Sorry, Harry, but I heard your wife died.

Yes, she did, Avi.

Are you okay?

We had a good life together, and I'm happy.

The comment made me remember why I wanted to talk to my old friend. I had always known Harry as a happy person. He was called Happy Harry by his friends. Truthfully, Harry never had close friends, but he was well liked. What made him happy was his religion, or so people thought. Harry never referred to himself as religious either, but accepted his nickname. I fumbled around for something to say, and finally said:

Are you happy because Anne is now in Heaven?

---

1   *Eschatology* is the study of the end times, the last events before the Earth in its present state passes away.

As soon as I said it, I prepared myself for an unwelcome response. Harry never minced words, and was always ready with a long answer. I felt silly and held my breath. Harry surprised me by being evasive.

Avi, you're fishing aren't you?

That made me laugh.

You're such a straight shooter.

Did you want me to shoot something?

I paused. Harry was putting me on the spot. There was silence for several long seconds before I answered my friend carefully.

All right. I was testing you. I remember how you were never very conventional, and always had an opinion about nearly everything. It didn't matter if it was religion or any other topic, you were never a person I could put in a box. I'd miss it if you didn't say something unorthodox.

Harry didn't hesitate in the slightest.

I've changed, Abraham. You're only partly right about me not being conventional in my beliefs. In the past thirty years, I've had to rethink many of the things that I once took for granted. What happened was, I started to read books... history books, science books, some in philosophy, and many on Biblical themes. I read book after book after book after book, and I changed. To my surprise, I discovered that many of my most cherished beliefs were still only conventions. I'm astonished at how much the world is trapped in traditional ideas that have no connection with reality.

But Avi, I don't want to disappoint you. Now I'm more confident than ever in what I do believe, and I'm sure that my beliefs are not just my personal opinions. My long-standing willingness to be unorthodox has lead me to more and more of what the truth really is.

Suddenly, I had an urge to lash out with sarcasm. I wanted to say, "Sure, sure Harry, you and your opinions. You always think you're the only one with the truth." I fought back the urge, and before Harry could say more, I exclaimed:

Do you believe we can really know what the truth is?

Yes, I was just going to say that. The things I have laboured over for so long, and come to understand as well as I do, are really true. Absolutely. Yes, we can be sure about our beliefs, and that our beliefs are real. I'm certain of it.

I don't see much of that certainty around me, Harry.

You're right. There's uncertainty everywhere. Many people don't know what to believe any more. Many others are stuck in their traditions. I'm convinced that may be ending for some people. I'm not the only one who is starting to get connected with reality. Here and there, believers are beginning to see the light, so to speak. Something is happening.

Do you know what it is?

Harry was quiet for what seemed like a long time before he answered.

I can't say it's any one thing. A lot happened throughout the twentieth century: the study of ancient languages, archeological discoveries, biblical criticism, new technologies, and the development of the Internet. In just the last sixty years, there has been an exponential increase in knowledge.

I want to believe that our everlasting Father has heard the groaning of His people after centuries of oppression. Those who cry out to the Mighty One of Jacob are slowly being set free. Our people all over the world are seeing through the deceptions that have imprisoned them for so long. There is potential now to reassert our ancient faith in a way that will make the world take notice. Believers in the Most High are on the verge of being respected again, for who they are. I believe that.

That is a mouthful!

Yes, it is, Avi, and I pray that it will happen because we are running out of time. This present age is surely drawing to a close.

I waited a bit before I said:

Can we get together again?

It would be a pleasure, Abraham.

There was a pause, and I began feeling unsure about meeting with Harry again. In the past, he had often made me feel inadequate, and I didn't want to be confronted by his dogmatisms again. My own convictions were too uncertain, mostly inherited, and not much had changed from my childhood. However, I was prepared to take the risk. I liked Harry, and never doubted that he genuinely liked me. Besides, over the years I had accepted not being certain in many ways, not just in religious matters. I had become skeptical about science and politics too. I wasn't going to turn down seeing my old friend, even if I ended up feeling inadequate again.

Good. I want to know.

In the next instant, something strange happened. There was a lightness in the air when Harry spoke again. At first, I thought he was trying to ease my uncertainty. However, if Harry was aware of my insecurity, he never affirmed it in the slightest. Instead, he let me know what to expect of our meeting, and what we would talk about. I sensed that Harry had a very organized mind, and was already laying out a plan. I felt a little giddy.

Abraham, I'd like to talk about the status of my deceased wife, whether she is in Heaven or not. We talked about that a long time ago, as you remember. First, though, we need look at the big picture. The One who we want to know is The Creator of the heavens and the Earth, so that's where we need to start. In a manner, that's also where we'll end. After all, our everlasting Father has a plan for humankind with a start and a finish. We'll deal with a variety of topics, including our individual responsibility. That is, if you are interested.

Harry wasn't making it entirely easy. He wanted a commitment.

Are you interested, Avi?

I'm interested.

We will be talking about some very basic traditions that almost everyone believes. So be prepared to talk about what is "not" true. If that sounds negative, it's our wrong beliefs that keep the real truth from emerging. By the way, it's not just wrong religious beliefs. Science has its lies too. You will be surprised by how many things are not true. Very likely you'll be shocked. Still interested?

Harry was building my confidence. My mind was racing. What if I had been lied to by both science and religion? Small wonder my convictions had never been very strong. I had based my confidence on wrong things! Now I wasn't going to be threatened by that sudden realization. Something intuitive was happening. I wanted to know where I'd been wrong. It wanted to know where the truth really lay. What a happy thought! In that moment, I answered Harry with confidence.

Yes, my old friend. I'm very interested.

Avi, two days from now is a Sabbath. Would you like to meet then?

I can do that.

Come early, whenever you like.

Okay.

We stopped talking. I felt good about beginning a new life. I would change to the best of my ability. I wouldn't be hesitant about examining my traditional beliefs. None of that mattered because I wanted to know what really is true.

At the same time, it nagged at me that the truth could be bitter sweet. I wasn't sure why I felt that way, but I knew it was coming and accepted it. It may have been the first time I was ever willing to set aside my inner feelings for the sake of knowing something that was beyond my personal self. Whatever the cost would be to me personally, the reward would be so much greater. I was sure about that.

Suddenly, not knowing if Harry was still on the phone, I blurted out my question.

Harry, what are we going to talk about two days from now?

Fair question. I'll tell you up front: it will be a test. Our first topic will determine how open-minded you are. It could also show that your mind is completely shut. Next week, I will be asking you to think the unthinkable.

Go on, please.

We are going to talk about the Earth not being a planet. The Earth is quite different from the planets like Venus, Mars and Jupiter. The Earth does not orbit the sun or rotate on its axis. The Earth is unique and fixed in place near the centre of the universe. Everything else rotates around the Earth just as we experience it.

I held back on what I was thinking. My mind already wanted to snap shut, but I was determined to hear the matter out before I made any judgment.

The big picture?

Yes, the big picture.

I'm looking forward to seeing you again.

Thank you, Abraham. Me too.

2. THE EARTH IS NOT A PLANET

Harry lived in a small house on the corner of a busy street. The house was surrounded by mature cedars, old junipers, and barely visible. Inside the yard were shade trees, flower beds, open spaces, and a small artificial pond. I found Harry there, sheltered from the outside world, sitting and reading in his mini-paradise. My urge was to sit down without saying anything, but Harry noticed me, stood up, shook my hand, and made me feel included. It was just before eight o'clock in the morning.

Avi, you came early.

You said I should.

Harry looked at me, and the fondness I remembered was still there. Without any small talk, he invited me inside. He wanted me to see his library while he made tea. The library was not large, but the selection of books was purposeful. Each book I took down and paged through was carefully highlighted and annotated. The books had been methodically read and re-read. Many were reference books with various diction- aries including Hebrew and Greek lexicons. Some were clearly unusual, showing an inquisitive and searching mind. Others were standard textbooks in theology, history and science. Harry was self-taught, and I marveled at his belated love of learning. This was not the Harry I had known in the past.

When Harry called me back outside, I asked the obvious question:

Why did you start reading? I remember how you read the Bible avidly, but very little else.

Well, in part it was out of frustration. Too often I realized I didn't understand what I was reading. I also began to suspect I was reading into the Scriptures what I thought was there, and missing what the text was actually saying. Certain inconsistencies began to bother me. My reading began slowly with simple Bible dictionaries and grew from there. As for my secular reading, it began with a visit to the public library. On one occasion when I was browsing through the stacks, a strange sense of peace came over me, and I have been reading ever since. Reading so much is not for everyone, but it suits me very well.

We sat quietly for a few moments and sipped our tea. I was anxious to get started.

Harry, you said the Earth is not a planet. I have been thinking about it, or I should say "trying to think about it", because it seems so improbable. That the Earth orbits the sun was one of the great discoveries in the history of science. Surely, we can't go back to thinking that the Earth is at the centre of everything![1]

Harry didn't hesitate and answered me directly.

In practice, we have never stopped treating the Earth as a fixed place at the centre of the universe. All our star charts are based on a fixed Earth. The positions of the stars and planets have been plotted for thousands of years without ever assuming the Earth to be in motion. For example, the easiest way to explain eclipses is by means of what is called the *Celestial Sphere*, a descriptive model with the Earth at its centre, and the sun, moon and stars revolving around it. Navigators at sea calculate their position by the stars based on a fixed Earth. Even NASA uses fixed Earth calculations to send satellites into space! It's actually often impractical to treat the Earth as a moving body, and always has been.

Avi, here's a simple depiction of the Celestial Sphere. It is an imaginary but highly practical depiction of the visible universe. Picture yourself at the centre of the sphere with all the heavenly objects imprinted on its inside surface. The sun, moon, planets and stars are all the same distance away from yourself in the sphere, but otherwise it matches what we actually observe. The Celestial Sphere works extremely well as a tool in astronomy, navigation and other applications. Again in the common parlance, it's 'imaginary' because the sphere is rotating and not the Earth. Here's the depiction:

---

1   *Planet* comes from a Greek word meaning "wandering stars" in reference to the visible planets like Venus and Mars. The modern definition means any body that orbits the sun or a star. It must also be massive enough for its own gravity to make it round. By that definition, Pluto is no longer a planet.

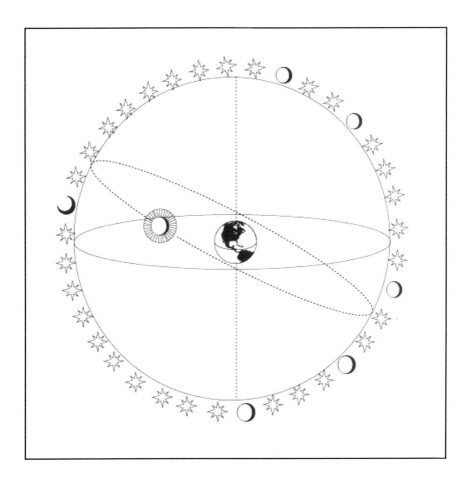

Harry, I've never heard this before, that NASA uses fixed Earth calculations to send its satellites into space. So if it's true, why aren't scientists more open and honest about it?

Well, scientists get away with it by what they call the *Equivalency Principle*. They say that whether the Earth rotates on its axis every twenty-four hours or the universe rotates around the Earth every twenty-four hours, the calculations are the same. That gives scientists the right to do fixed Earth calculations without having to abandon their belief in a moving Earth.[2]

---

2   The great astronomer, Sir Fred Hoyle, wrote: "We know the difference between a heliocentric theory and a geocentric theory is one of relative motion only, and that such a difference has no physical significance." See, *Astronomy and Cosmology - A Modern Course*, W. H. Freeman & Co., San Francisco, 1975, p 416.

If you think about it, Avi, we don't perceive the Earth to be actually moving. We talk about sunrise and sunset quite naturally. We watch the stars rising and setting on the horizon. We see our satellites circling the Earth every ninety minutes. Nothing in our experience indicates that what we see isn't real. We certainly don't feel the Earth moving, and it's counterintuitive to think it is. It amazes me that people continue to insist that the Earth is moving. That's just an idea in our heads.

While watching the stars the other night, I purposely tried to visualize it was the Earth turning, not the stars. I immediately started feeling dizzy and had to shake it off. It was the same sensation we feel when a ship is leaving port and the land seems to be moving. Similarly, I'm told people get seasick when they can no longer see the shoreline. Earthquakes also take away our sense of stability, which by itself is quite frightening. In practice, we need the assurance of a solid and immovable Earth. Our psyche is dependent on a fixed Earth for a sense of certainty and permanence.

I blurted out,

There must be some proof one way or the other!

If there was proof, we wouldn't be having this conversation. In four hundred years since Copernicus, no evidence for the Earth's orbital motion has ever been detected. Many logical arguments have been presented, but not a single scientific measurement. With the coming of powerful telescopes and artificial satellites, much has been learned about the Earth's place in the cosmos, but not one thing to verify the Earth's physical motion has ever come forth. Many well qualified scientists have candidly admitted as much, and hence we are having this dialogue. There is no proof that the Earth is moving.[3]

At that point, I was a little shocked by Harry's forthrightness. Harry was never domineering in any discussion. His patience and consideration were always present. Then I thought, if I could blurt out my need for proof, then Harry had the right to make an appropriate response. He was being as honest as I was. Harry wasn't out of character as he continued.

The only real proof would be if we could step outside of the universe and observe what is actually doing the moving, but all our experiments are earth-bound. Even the information coming from satellites many billions of miles away is still received and

---

3   By the end of the 19th century a number of experiments had been performed with the intention of either proving or disproving the Earth's supposed motion through space. One of the most significant was when George Bidel Airy demonstrated (by filling a telescope with water as Ruggiero Boscovich had proposed a century earlier) that it was the stars, including the sun, that were in motion and not the Earth. The experiment known as *Airy's Failure* is seldom or never mentioned in modern text books for obvious reasons.

interpreted from here on the Earth. It seems that humanity's ability to leave the Earth is limited to the moon. I doubt if human beings can survive a trip to Mars and return alive. Our scientists can only peer into space from their humbling position on this Earth, and that limits their ability to understand how the universe functions.

There was one experiment, however, that really shook up the scientific community. It was the experiment conducted Michelson and Morley around the year 1900. The two men believed they could measure the speed of the Earth relative to the medium through which the Earth is passing in its path around the sun. To their utter amazement, and to the consternation of the whole scientific world, the Earth showed hardly any motion at all. The experiment has been repeated countless times with better equipment, different locations and different seasons. Yet, the resulting measurement of the Earth's motion has always been close to zero. Michelson and Morley reluctantly concluded that space has no substance or medium through which the Earth is passing. They and the rest of the world could not accept the simpler and more obvious conclusion that the Earth really isn't moving![4]

Am I doing okay, Avi? Shall I continue?

Yes, please do.

It took a man like Albert Einstein to save the world from having to go back to an Earth-centered universe. Einstein postulated that the speed of light is always the same whether the Earth is moving or not. This was quickly shown to be false.[5] Einstein ignored it. He liked to conduct thought experiments, and according to Einstein himself, his greatest gift was his imagination (The man did little if any experimental work in a laboratory.). The upshot is that modern cosmology came from the mind of Einstein. That includes the Big Bang theory with its black holes, ultra vast distances in time and space, and the idea of an expanding universe. To that fanciful conception, we can add that the universe has no centre or boundary and that everything is moving with nothing at rest.

These conclusions are entirely theoretical and based on some very obscure and extremely difficult mathematics. Hence, the Earth is now thought to be a small planet, orbiting an inferior star, situated at the outer edge of a rotating galaxy – among the billions of other rotating galaxies – all in relative motion to each other, and situated in a universe expanding at nearly the speed of light. That's Albert Einstein's legacy.

---

4   Their conclusion contradicted other known scientific laws that depend on there being some medium in space – the propagation of light for example. It's even absurd and demonstrably wrong to suggest that space is filled with a perfect vacuum or nothing at all.

5   Georges Sagnac (1869-1926) – and many scientists since then – proved in a laboratory that light travels at different speeds depending on its direction eastward or westward. This is called the *Sagnac Effect*.

Harry sat back with a slight look of tiredness. He looked at me inquisitively, perhaps wondering if I was following or agreeing. His mood was pensive, but I knew he wanted to say more. I took the initiative.

I like what you're saying, Harry, but can we take a break? I'd like some more tea if I may.

Harry's mood didn't change. He hardly even smiled when he said yes, and told me he'd be right back. In a matter of minutes, he returned with tea, a kettle, and a book. There was an electric outlet nearby for the kettle. The mood remained sombre as we waited for it to boil. Then I took the initiative again.

Was there something you wanted to add, Harry?

Yes. The great scientists of the past were not exactly stupid men. Many were at least nominal Christians and believed in a created universe having order and laws that could be discovered. They were inquisitive, courageous and brilliant. That goes for Einstein too, although his religion was pretty abstract. They weren't closed-minded either. Einstein himself theorized about an Earth-centered universe. With his encouragement, Lense and Thirring experimented using a rotating sphere with a fixed object at its centre. They were quite willing to assume that the rotation of the stars around the Earth would result in certain forces. Einstein did not object. His exact words were...

Harry opened his book at the appropriate page.

> One need not view the existence of such centrifugal forces as origi-
> nating from the motion of [the Earth]; one could just as well account
> for them as resulting from the average rotational effect of distant,
> detectable masses as evidenced in the vicinity of [the Earth], where
> [the Earth] is treated as being at rest.[6]

Harry looked at me in his easy manner.

Avi, that quotation comes from a paper Hans Thirring wrote in 1921. Thirring wanted to know what effect the mass of the rotating stars would have on the Earth. He found that the effect was identical to the natural phenomena that we normally explain by the Earth's rotation on its axis – the Coriolis Effect in particular. The concept of a rotating universe has been addressed in the secular literature on many occasions. It was especially

---

6   Albert Einstein, quoted in Hans Thirring, "On the Effect of Distant Rotating Masses in Einstein's Theory of Gravitation", *Physikalische Zeitschrift*, 1921, p 22, 29. In keeping with the theme of Thirring's paper, in the quote above, K' is substituted with "the Earth."

so in the heyday of relativity when many scientists weren't concerned about which was in the motion, the Earth or the rest of the universe. The literature is there for anyone to investigate.

For the most part, those scientists didn't care about the Bible or religion. They were pursuing their scientific interests without any prejudice one way or another. Nowadays, most people think that only Bible believers are geocentrists, but that's not true. A quotation I like very much comes from Dr Gerardus Bouw:

> There have been other mathematical expositions showing that the physics of the geocentric universe is the same as the heliocentric.... Rosser expanded on the Lense and Thirring papers explaining how the outer reaches of the universe could not only be moving many, many times the speed of light, but also how the universe would not fall apart, even if it were trillions of times per second. *All of these physicists (and there is not a geocentric Christian in the bunch) conclude that there is no detectable, experimental difference between having the Earth spin diurnally on an axis as well as orbiting the sun once a year or having the universe rotate about the Earth once a day and possessing a wobble centered on the sun, which carries the planets and stars about the Earth once a year.* In none of these models would the universe fly apart, nor would a stationary satellite fall to Earth. In every one of these models, the astronauts on the moon would still see all sides of the Earth in the course of twenty-four hours, the Foucault pendulum would still swing exactly the same way as we see it in museums, and the Earth's equator would still bulge. In other words, each of these effects is due to either the centrifugal force, Coriolis force or some combination of the two and can be totally explained in any geocentric model. (*Emphasis added*)[7]

I can tell you, Abraham – with conviction – you can explain the universe and all its motions just as easily without having to assume that the Earth is moving. In practice, we do that anyway, with no scientific laws being broken or contradicted. It's that simple.

I looked at my old friend and thought to myself, "Harry doesn't need my support, but I feel like giving it." My response came eagerly.

---

7   *A Geocentric Primer* by Gerardus D. Bouw, p 115. Dr Bouw is a Christian physicist and has a website at geocentricity.com. He has been very helpful to me personally. *Geocentricity* is the modern term for the model which ties the parts of the cosmos together into a whole, and describes the integrated motion of all the heavenly bodies in keeping with the known laws of physics.

I feel it, Harry! This may sound strange, but I felt as you were talking that I stopped moving. Now it's the rest of the universe that's in motion.

Harry stood up slowly to his full six foot, two inch height, and took a few steps to the little pond. After a few minutes, he came back.

Never underestimate your ability to perceive what is really true. There's an old saying, "The simplest explanation is usually the correct one." It was once used to support the Copernican model, but the Copernican model was never any simpler, and modern theories about the cosmos have become unbelievably complicated. It's by far easier to explain the universe by having the Earth at its centre. Good for you.

As prepared as ever, Harry handed me a neatly drawn diagram with the label, "A Geocentric Model."

Abraham, here is an Earth-centered model based on the work of Tycho Brahe in the sixteenth century, one of history's most respected astronomers. Based on his amazingly accurate observations – without the aid of a telescope – and his confidence in the Bible, he depicted the sun as orbiting the Earth and carrying all the planets with it. In other words, the planets orbit the sun as the sun orbits the Earth. Simple enough, and Tycho's model works very well to this day.[8]

---

8   Heliocentricists (those espousing their sun-centered beliefs) consistently aim their fault finding at the Ptolemaic, earth-centered model of the 1st century AD. Most, if not virtually all of them, are not even familiar with the Tychonian model of the 16th century, and its practical application. Heliocentricists are instead content with proclaiming the short comings of the older and more complex Ptolemaic model.

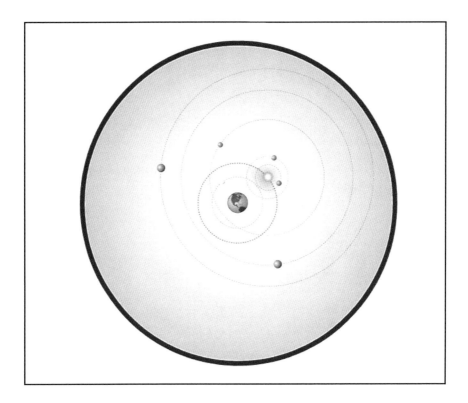

Harry stopped talking and I knew it wasn't for effect. He was looking at me with a long and cautious gaze. Was he wondering if he could trust me? Was he holding something back that still needed to be said? His look became even more focused. I knew he wasn't going say any more and his gaze went inward.

For the first time that morning, I studied my friend carefully. I could see his quiet confidence, thoughtful energy, unfettered good will, and easy pleasure in conversation. He had all the attributes of an unusually gregarious man, but what made him so reclusive and solitary? It came to me slowly at first, and then with a sudden rush. It was sorrow. Harry was grieving in a way that had nothing to do with his wife's passing, and beyond what was personal to him. Yes, Harry was happy toward others, but inwardly he was still sorrowful. I broke the silence.

I'm sorry that we've been out of contact for so long.

Harry answered quietly without looking at me.

Me too, Avi. I was happy with our friendship. You were like a son to me.

It wasn't you're fault. I just got tired of our religious conversations. Nothing conclusive ever came from them, and I became more and more disappointed. I guess I gave up on you. Can you accept my apology?

I never blamed you, Avi. I had to be alone for a while.

Thanks, Harry. You were like a father to me.

When I stood up to shake hands with my friend, I marveled at our relationship. Harry was now eighty-five. I was sixty-five, and we were still like a father and son to each other. I knew that I loved Harry, and there was never any doubt that he loved me.

What will we be talking about next week?

My friend, we'll get right to the question you asked me two days ago, about my wife being in Heaven. Many people believe they go somewhere when they die. Supposedly, they continue to be conscious and active in another dimension, and it's quite common to refer to an immortal soul. Our topic next Sabbath will be that the human soul is not immortal.

I found myself blurting again,

Harry, you will to have to explain this Sabbath stuff to me. Today is a Wednesday and yet you referred to it as a Sabbath. I'm a little confused.

I will in time. Just come again seven days from now, please.

Okay, good enough.

I was about to go when, for the first time, I felt a little awkward. Something still needed to be said, and Harry perceived it.

The ancient Hebrew salutation was, "May the Eternal One be with you." Both parties would give each other the same blessing. So, may the Eternal One be with you, Abraham.

May the Eternal One be with you, Harry.

3. HUMANS ARE NOT IMMORTAL

We began just as we had ended.

May the Eternal One be with you, Harry.

May the Eternal One be with you, Abraham.

I was so pleased to be with my friend again. Our camaraderie was blossoming, and I was sure the Creator was teaching us. I truly loved my friend, so I freely asked:

Will we go to Heaven when we die?

No, Avi.

That is the hope for many people, is it not?

Yes, it is, but it is a misplaced hope based on a misunderstanding of death and of our Father's plan of salvation. The greatest miracle of all time is that a man was raised from the dead and made immortal. Nothing can ever give humanity more hope than that miracle.

If the truth is so knowable, why are we even discussing it?

That's well asked, Avi. Our traditional belief, that we go to Heaven when we die, is a belief common to all religions. The Greeks thought they would go to the *Elysian Fields* for example. In Buddhism, it's *Nirvana*, for Catholics, it's *Purgatory*, for Muslims, it's *Jannah*, and for North American Indians, it's the *Happy Hunting Ground*. Almost without exception, all religions have a belief in an afterlife immediately following death – living beings instantly going from one state of consciousness to another state of consciousness without interruption.

Avi, notice I said 'immediately', because there is one notable exception. Nowhere in

23

the Hebrew Scriptures is it ever taught that there is consciousness following death. In the Tanak[1] all activity and consciousness ceases at death. The dead don't know anything or have any thoughts and feelings. The dead have no memory of the past. The dead don't worship the Almighty Father. Life simply ends at death, according to the Hebrew Scriptures. Such a view of death is only found in the Hebrew Tanak, and nowhere else as far as I know.

The one passage in Ecclesiastes – all by itself – pretty much says it all:

The living know that they shall die: but the dead know not any thing, neither have they any more a reward; for the memory of them is forgotten. Also their love, and their hatred, and their envy, is now perished; neither have they any more a portion forever in any thing that is done under the sun... There is no work, nor device, nor knowledge, nor wisdom, in the grave, where you are going.[2][3]

How true, Harry! We don't go straight to Heaven at death. We really do die.

I waited for a while, and then added,

We talked about that many years ago. The dead can't look down from Heaven and see their loved ones. As comforting as it may be, parents can't see their children from Heaven, and husbands can't see their wives when they are dead.

Harry nodded before elaborating.

The need for comfort at the time of death is undeniable, and there is comfort! However, there is also a need to grieve for the shortness of our lives. I often let it sink into my being, that my life is temporary. Someday, and always so soon, I will stop living and breathing, and be forgotten. As the prophet said, "The grass withers, and the flower fades." I have allowed the shortness of my life and its end to become a part of my consciousness. Rather than have an unreal perception of what I am, I want to be connected with my mortality. That's how the Creator made me.

---

1   The Tanak is a name used for the Hebrew Scriptures. The name is an acronym for the three traditional subdivisions: The Torah (Five Books of Moses), the Nevim (Prophets), and the Ketuvim (Writings) - hence TaNaK.

2   Ecclesiastes 9:5, 6, 10.

3   Theis author uses various translations, and alters some texts. The word 'God' is deliberately voided - being only a word, and not a name or attribute. *The Almighty One* is the Hebrew version of 'God.' The word *The Almighty One,* however, has a meaning and can be translated as Mighty One or Almighty. When translations use *thou*, the author substitutes it with *you*, etc.

You must still take comfort in an afterlife, Harry.

In a way, that's true. It is easier to accept my mortality knowing it's not the final end. I can still hope at the same time for a much better life to follow, but it doesn't take away from how fleeting this mortal life is. Nor does the hope of eternal life make this life any less important. We will to come to it, Avi. What we do in the here and now will determine our future – one way or another.

It was my turn to be silent and let Harry's words take effect. I had felt no despair when Harry spoke about his mortality. I was sure he did not want to die or that he found any comfort in death. Harry's honesty about his mortality was intense and at the same time reassuring.

I feel it too, Harry. This present life is profoundly important. There is always a tendency in religion to trivialize this life in comparison to the next one. Come to think, it sounds like religious control, and preventing people from having a real life experience. Why, there's even something unnatural about being told I have an immortal soul. It's just not right.

Very good, Avi, very good. That's so perceptive. The doctrine of an immortal soul contradicts not only the Tanak, but also our human experience. We should want to live our lives to the full. Furthermore, we know intuitively our lives will come to an end.

Then where did the idea of an immortal soul come from?

The word *soul* has a very long past. Historians tell us that the belief in an immortal soul came from ancient Babylon and Egypt, was adopted by Greek philosophy through Plato and Aristotle, and incorporated into church dogma through Origen, Tertullian and Augustine.[4] The doctrine of an immortal soul is now so deeply entrenched in the religion of Christianity that it has become virtually synonymous with eschatology. That's

---

4   "The Egyptians were the first that asserted that the soul of man is immortal…This opinion some among the Greeks have at different periods of time adopted as their own" (from *Euterpe*, the second book of Herodotus' *History*).

"The belief that the soul continues its existence after the dissolution of the body is…nowhere expressly taught in Holy Scripture…The belief in the immortality of the soul came to the Jews from contact with Greek thought and chiefly through the philosophy of Plato its principal exponent, who was led to it through Orphic and Eleusinian mysteries in which Babylonian and Egyptian views were strangely blended" (*The Jewish Encyclopedia,* article, "Immortality of the Soul").

"For some things are known even by nature: the immortality of the soul, the instance, is held by many… I may use, therefore, the opinion of Plato, when he declares: 'Every soul is immortal'" (Tertullian, A.D. 155-220, *The Ante-Nicene Fathers*, vol. III).

the history in a nutshell.

As strange as it may seem, it became heresy to believe in a mortal soul. In 1513, at the Lateran Council, it was ruled:

> Whereas some have dared to assert concerning the nature of the reasonable soul that it is mortal, *we, with the approbation of the sacred council do condemn and reprobate all those who assert that the intellectual soul is mortal*, seeing, according to the canon of Pope Clement V, that the soul is... immortal... and we decree that all who adhere to like erroneous assertions shall be shunned and punished as heretics. (*emphasis added*)[5]

Many did not agree. Martin Luther certainly didn't. Neither did William Tyndale. In 1530, Tyndale responded vigorously:

> And ye, in putting them [the departed souls] in heaven, hell and purgatory, destroy the arguments wherewith Christ and Paul prove the resurrection... And again, if the souls be in heaven, tell me why they be not in as good a case as the angels be? And then what cause is there of the resurrection?[6]

We should recall, Avi, that very early in church history many of the church fathers were schooled in Greek philosophy, and believed that philosophy was a valid source of truth, comparable with the Scriptures. Most of them, if not all, were Gentiles. The Jews of the time were influenced by Greek philosophy as well, but never to the extent of putting philosophy on par with the Hebrew Scriptures. At least nominally, the Jews held fast to their faith in the Torah or the five books of Moses. It was the Gentile church fathers who gave the doctrine of an immortal soul its impetus, and made it so important in their understanding of an after-life.

If the truth be known, the doctrine of human immortality is far more deeply rooted. This false doctrine is truly primordial. I have identified three great lies in the Bible. We'll eventually talk about all three, but it was the very first lie that human beings have an immortal soul.

I gave Harry a little non-patronizing pat on the shoulder. My friend had the

---

5 Caranza, 1681, p 412.
6 Responding to Sir Thomas More's objection to his belief that "all souls lie and sleep till doomsday." William Tyndale, *An Answer to Sir Thomas More's Dialogue* (Parker's 1850 reprint), Bk. 4, Ch. 4, p 180, 181.

knack of arousing interest that went well beyond mere curiosity. He was suggesting that there are lies in the Bible, something very intriguing indeed.

You have my attention, Harry.

Harry returned my look without assertiveness. In his mind, the truth would speak for itself.

Avi, we can go right back to the beginning at a time soon after Creation. There in Adam's lifetime the soul's immortality was first postulated, and it came from the mouth of a lying serpent. It was in the Garden of Eden that the serpent said to Eve, "You shall certainly not die." Eve was deceived, and she ate from the tree of the knowledge of good and evil. Eve ate the fruit even though The Creator Himself had said to Adam, "In the day that you eat of it you shall certainly die." Those are two statements in blatant contrast; one from the Creator and the other from a serpent. Eve chose to eat from the forbidden tree, believing the serpent rather than the Creator, and therein lies the origin of the doctrine that humans have an immortal soul. Eve succumbed to the oldest lie ever told to human beings.

The continuing dialogue between Harry and myself was distinguished by regular and long pauses. Often when something was said, it was followed by a time of thoughtful quietness. It was mutual. Even though I was learning and needed to let Harry's teaching take root, he also seemed to want to reflect on what was being said. Neither of us felt rushed, or allowed our minds to scatter in other directions. There was an intense concentration in our dialogue. We were exceptionally aware that there was truthfulness in our time together, and were equally keen to absorb that truthfulness. We needed those times of quiet. After a while, Harry interjected.

Avi, I'll give you a heads up on the three great lies in the Bible. Again, all of them can be found from the beginning in what the serpent told Eve. The serpent said to the woman, "You shall certainly not die. For the Almighty One knows that in the day you eat of it your eyes shall be opened, and you shall be like the Almighty One, knowing good and evil." The three great lies then are: You shall not die; you shall be like the Mighty One; and you shall know good and evil. These are cardinal lies that have deeply infiltrated human thoughts and beliefs. I'll explain the last two lies at another time, but right now we are dealing with the false doctrine of the immortal soul.

Harry readjusted himself in his chair.

Avi, we might as well say who the real liars are, and stop pretending we're not being lied to in the same way. You touched on it already when you mentioned religious control.

I'm telling you truly, the religious leaders of our day are lying to us every bit as much as the proverbial serpent lied to Eve. I'm talking about priests, clergy, pastors, rabbis, imams or whatever other title they go by. I mean the professional elite, whether Catholic, Protestant, Jew or Muslim. All of them have a long history of setting aside the truth for the sake of controlling as many of the Eternal One's people as they possibly can. They want what others can give them for themselves, for their own reputation, good standing and livelihood.

This not a polemic, Avi. Most of them cannot be trusted. Very few will speak the truth for fear of losing their self-image, cherished reputation and source of income. They will all toe the line of whatever establishment they come from, without exception.

If that sounds like vitriol, think again. The prophet Jeremiah said, "Our fathers have inherited nothing but lies, worthless things in which there is no profit." The Messiah said, "Thus you nullify the word of the Almighty for the sake of your tradition." Both prophets were speaking to the religious leaders of their time with unsparing honesty. We should be asking ourselves if our leaders are any different. Aren't they? Here's what another author has written:

> You Christian professional theologians, Clergy, Scholars and Teachers have become scoffers in the face of The Most High Eternal Creator leading not some, but virtually ALL of His good people astray. You have done violence to His true Torah and to His created ones on a scale that must make Noach's time pale by comparison... *You have become worse than the Scribes and the Pharisees you so vehemently rage against. (emphasis added)*[7]

Here's the tip off, Avi. If 'ministers' are earning a salary, asking for money or appealing to the law of tithing, then they're false shepherds and fleecing the sheep. It's just that simple, whether we like it or not. Some ministers may be less guilty than others, and many are themselves victims of a covetous and oppressive system, but if they want your money for their ministry, it's a dead giveaway who they're working for.

One more thing needs to be said. At the heart of their deception is the desire to impose their will on others rather than promote the will of the Creator. To add deception upon deception, they teach that their followers should do the same. They teach that the Almighty's commandments have been set aside, leaving humankind to follow their own selfish inclinations. It's all about the self-will of the leaders and their followers. Avi, it's willfulness that defines religion and the world's religious systems.[8]

---

7   Dr Shmuel Asher, *The Greater Exodus*, Amazon CreateSpace Publishing, 2012, p 254-255.

8   Nothing demonstrates the willfulness of religion more than the religious wars following the Protestant

Harry continued.

I believe that many difficult passages in the Bible can be understood by the average reader. We don't need to depend on religious authorities if we stick with the most basic and common sense meaning. Interpretations that we can identify with are much more likely to be true than interpretations that are outside of our everyday experience. That's a big thing with me. We need to stay with what can ordinarily be understood.[9] With that in mind, let's look at what the Scriptures say about the immortal soul.

My friend, I'm not going to explain these so-called difficult passages to you. Based on certain texts, it is believed that Enoch didn't die, that Abraham is already in Heaven along with Isaac and Jacob,[10] Yeshuah preached to the dead in Hell, and the thief on the cross went into paradise the same day. Such texts have been well studied and easily explained. Anyone familiar with those stories can verify the real truth for themselves with a little effort.

That's fine, Harry. I can explain those passages too.

Harry continued without pausing.

Many foundational truths are found in the early chapters of Genesis. From the beginning, we are told the true nature of a human being:

And YHWH, the Mighty One, formed man of the dust of the ground, and breathed into his nostrils the breath of life; and man became a living being.

And immediately after Adam sinned, the Eternal One said to him:

Reformation in which the Catholics and Protestants were equally guilty. Those wars were preceded by the Muslim military dominance of the Middle East and much of Europe, and the Christian crusades against them. All are very sad attempts by one religious group to impose its will on the others.

9   Sir Isaac Newton (1643-1727) was also a great biblical scholar. Stephen D. Snobelen in his paperchapter, *Isaac Newton, Socinianism and "The One Supreme God,"* writes " Newton believed that the Scriptures are reasonable and composed in the tongue of the common people. Moreover, he was committed to the hermeneutic of interpreting more difficult passages with those more easily understood" (p 272). Newton was firmly against the doctrine of an immortal soul.

10   The context for many of the 'difficult' passages is in the certainty of a future resurrection. In typical Hebrew fashion, Yeshuah spoke about Abraham, Isaac and Jacob as if their resurrection had already been accomplished. He expressed the same future assurance with the thief on the cross, saying, "I'm telling you today that you shall be with me in Paradise." He was proclaiming the resurrection on that day with absolute certainty.

For you are dust, and to dust you shall return.

The Hebrew word *nephesh* means 'that which breathes' or 'living being.' The Creator breathed life into the dust of the ground and what He breathed into became a living breathing creature. In other words, humans *became* souls – they did not *receive* souls. Truthfully, Avi, we'd be better off not using the word *soul*. It's a poor substitute for *nephesh*.[11]

Now here's the real cruncher. It may be difficult to accept, but animals are living, breathing creatures too. The same word nephesh is used to describe animal life. After the Great Flood, the Creator promised:

I will remember my covenant that is between me and you
and every living creature of all flesh.
And the waters shall never again become a flood to destroy all flesh.

There, in Genesis 9:15 and many other passages, *nephesh* is used for animal life. Humans are *nephesh*, and so are animals. Just let me read another few verses from Ecclesiastes:

I said in my heart,
"Concerning the condition of the sons of men,
the Almighty One tests them,
that they may see that they themselves are like animals."
For what happens to the sons of men also happens to animals;
one thing befalls them: as one dies, so dies the other.
Surely, they all have one breath; man has no advantage over animals...
All go to one place: all are from the dust, and all return to dust.[12]

Avi, I wish I could shout it from the roof tops, "Animals are living beings too." Right now, it might sound strange to you, but before our talks come to an end, you will know how real it is, and you too will want to shout it from the roof tops that animals are living beings just like us.

Harry looked to me cautiously.

I'll continue talking about our mortality as humans, but not before drawing attention

---

11 "The translation is unfortunate; soul in common speech reflects a complex of ideas which go back to Greek philosophy as refined by medieval scholasticism" (Dictionary of the Bible, John L. Mackenzie, Simon and Shuster, 1995, *Soul*).

12 Ecclesiastes 3:18-20

to the definition of life. Living beings are creatures that breathe. More specifically, they are creatures that have blood. According to our Creator, the life of all creatures is in their blood.

> **This is because the life of any creature is in its blood.**
> **So I have said to the people of Israel: Never eat any blood,**
> **because the life of any creature is in its blood.**
> **Whoever eats blood must be excluded from the people.**

Harry bowed his head with reverence.

Returning to the simple texts that are easy to understand – there are so many of them.[13] They are among the clearest and most precise statements in the Hebrew Scriptures, and their meaning cannot be missed by an honest reader. Those teachers who insist that humans have an immortal soul are lying, and violating what their own common sense is telling them. The simple texts confirm that the everyday perception that we have about our life is the real perception: we are mortal beings and our life is temporary. As the great prophet Isaiah said:

All flesh is grass, and all the goodliness thereof is as the flower of the field.[14]

I know that, Harry! We talked about this years ago, and it always stuck with me. It seems to me that the only way anyone can continue believing in an immortal soul is by ignoring the Scriptures, and the long standing witness against the belief. There is no end of sound biblical scholarship on this topic!

Thank you, Avi. The Hebrew Scriptures are clear in this matter, and so is the historical record. We can see it from the writings of Justin Martyr, a second century Christian with a close connection to a congregation in Ephesus. The congregation he attended was keeping the Torah of Moses, making it a first century church and still fairly pristine. Justin Martyr put his teaching in the mouth of an old man, who was apparently a member of the same congregation:

---

13 "The soul that sins, it shall die" Ezekiel 18:20. "Then shall the dust return to the earth as it was: and the spirit shall return unto the Mighty One who gave it" Ecclesiastes 12:7. "The spirit of the Mighty One is in my nostrils." Job 27:3. "The living know that they shall die: but the dead know not any thing, neither have they any more a reward; for the memory of them is forgotten. Also their love, and their hatred, and their envy, is now perished; neither have they any more a portion for ever in any thing that is done under the sun... There is no work, nor device, nor knowledge, nor wisdom, in the grave, whither thou goest." Ecclesiastes 9:5, 6, 10. "The dead praise not the Mighty One." Psalm 115:17. "If his sons are honored, he does not know it; if they are brought low, he does not see it" Job 14:21.
14 Isaiah 40:6.

It makes no matter to me whether Plato or Pythagoras, or, in short, any other man held such opinions... Now the soul partakes of life, since God wills it to live. Thus, then, it will not even partake [of life] when God does not will it to live. For to live is not its attribute, as it is God's; but as a man does not live always, and the soul is not for ever conjoined with the body, since, whenever this harmony must be broken up, *the soul leaves the body, and the man exists no longer*; even so, whenever the soul must cease to exist, the spirit of life is removed from it, and *there is no more soul*, but it [the spirit] goes back to the place from whence it was taken. (*emphasis added*)[15]

We can see from Justin Martyr's writing that Plato's doctrine of an immortal soul was being refuted by the Scriptures in the second century A.D. Justin was adamant that the soul should not be called immortal. So was Martin Luther about fourteen hundred years later. He vigorously opposed the declaration of the Lateran Council in 1513, condemning "all who assert that the intelligent soul is mortal."

Luther, with a greater emphasis on the resurrection, preferred to concentrate on the scriptural metaphor of sleep. For just as one who falls asleep and reaches morning unexpectedly when he awakes, without knowing what has happened to him, "we shall suddenly rise on the last day without knowing how we have come into death and through death. We shall sleep, until He comes and knocks on the little grave and says, 'Doctor Martin, get up!' Then I shall rise in a moment, and be with him forever."[16]

Martin Luther used the term 'sleeping' as a euphemism for death. In that he was using a term from the Scriptures where 'sleep' is often used to mean death. It's appropriate because we awaken from sleep just as we will awaken from death, both being a temporary state. Some have wrongly called it 'soul sleep', but the soul doesn't really sleep. The soul dies, the spirit or breath of life goes back to the Creator, and the body returns to the dust. The prophet Daniel enunciated the sleep of death very well when he wrote,

And many of them that sleep in the dust of the earth shall awake, some to everlasting life, and some to shame and everlasting contempt.[17]

Harry, did the ancients believe in the resurrection?

---

15 Martyr, Justin. *Dialogue with Trypho*. Translated by Marcus Dods and George Reith. Chapter 6.
16 Kantonen, T. A., *The Christian Hope*, 1594, p 37.
17 Daniel 12:2

Oh, yes. That's for sure, in many ways beginning with an enormous respect for the human body. Their laws prohibited them from tattooing or mutilating themselves. They did not cut their bodies with knives for the sake of the dead, an act that expressed futility and hopelessness. Nor did the Hebrews practice cremation, except as a punishment for harlots, criminals and idolaters. The Almighty Himself buried Moses, so as not to leave his body exposed to the elements. Abraham took great care in burying his wife Sarah, buying a field and a cave for that purpose. Much later, the Messiah was anointed with spices and buried honorably in a rich man's tomb.

Not only did the Almighty's people respect the human body – living or dead – there are a number of examples when the dead came back to life. Elijah prayed to the Almighty Father and raised a young boy from death. Elisha raised the son of the Shunamite woman. The Messiah also brought the dead back to life, most notably his friend Lazarus, whose body was already corrupting. Job was confident that he would live again in his body. David believed that he wouldn't be abandoned in the grave, and Abraham looked forward to a future life.[18] The ancients associated life with a physical body. In their understanding, a spirit without a body was not a living being. For them, there had to be a physical resurrection.

One of the very best verses about a future resurrection is in Isaiah 26:19. The verse contains the central truth that we came from the dust of the Earth, we will return to the dust of the Earth, and from the dust of the Earth will we arise again:

Thy dead shall live; My dead bodies shall arise.
Awake and sing, you that dwell in the dust;
for your dew is as the dew of herbs,
and the earth shall cast forth the dead.

As a result of being born human, when the Messiah was raised, the permanence of death was abolished and immortality became an actuality.[19] By raising one man from the dead, it was demonstrated that all men can be resurrected physically and be alive again. Remember too, Yeshuah's body was changed from a temporary to permanent. In that sense, he didn't have a new or different body. Yeshuah was resurrected in his own body; the same body that was once his as a mortal man, but now his as an immortal man. It's a wonderful thing to know – in the resurrection, we will have a physical body like his, but our own body nevertheless.

I got it, Harry! A spirit without a body cannot function. A spirit can't be conscious of

---

18   Job 19:26, Psalm 16:10, John 8:56

19   : "But it has now been revealed through the appearing of our savior, Yeshuah the Messiah, who has destroyed death and has brought life and immortality to light through the Good News" (2 Timothy 1:10).

its environment or interact with it. Our spirits do not have their own personalities.

Yes, you are quite correct. The Scriptures do talk about the spirits of righteous men made perfect, but those are just spirits – not beings. Although our everlasting Father knows them as future beings that He will one day restore to life, in the meantime those future beings belong to the Father only as spirit. Therein we have the meaning of the Messiah's words at his death, "Father, into your hands I commit my spirit."[20]

It's so simple and easy to understand, Harry.

Yes, it is.

I continued.

This is great. We need a physical body in order to be a living being, and we will have physical bodies in the resurrection, different of course than the physical bodies we have now. We cannot be alive in any sense without a physical body, though. I'm convinced of that, and it makes too much sense to not be true.

Good.

What are we going to talk about next?

Abraham, I'm thinking we should talk about the Paul, who claimed to be an apostle, but really wasn't.

Okay, Harry. Questions are coming to my mind right away, but I'll wait for next week. It will give me time to think first.

How about coming tomorrow? I'm certain there will be a visible crescent tonight, making tomorrow a New Moon day. So if you can, please come tomorrow.

Harry looked at me in his usually pleasant manner. I knew he enjoyed our meetings, but his easy manner didn't mask the seriousness of his intention. Harry meant business all the time. I found it hard not to accept.

I'll be back tomorrow.

---

20 Reader take note: the words **breath** and **spirit** are interchangeable in the Hebrew language. There are no individual spirits attached to personalities existing in heaven or anywhere else. There has to be a physical body present for spiritual beings to have any real existence. Yeshuah could just as well have said, "Father, into your hands I commit my breath." (And then he breathed his last breath.)

I got up promptly, knowing we could continue in just a few hours.

When my friend stood up and I shook his hand, I tried to look deeply into his eyes. I couldn't. Harry had a profound affection for me in his eyes, and beyond that, there was a strength that I couldn't fathom. Harry was his own man, so to speak, and quite indifferent to how he was being perceived. He treated others in the same way, allowing them to be their own persons too, or at least capable of being their own persons. It was his vote of confidence enabling me to make up my own mind without any threat of manipulation. Our meetings were about me learning, not about Harry teaching.

May the Eternal One be with you, Harry.

And may the Eternal One be with you, Abraham.

4. PAUL WAS NOT AN APOSTLE

Shalom, Harry.

Dear brother, Abraham.

We stood there for a few moments. Despite Harry's almost infinite reserve, he was not without deep feeling, and was letting it show. Our friendship meant a lot to him too.

Come, sit down. The tea is ready. Did you sleep well, Avi?

Yes, I did. I feel well rested this morning.

Good.

We sipped our tea and enjoyed the morning. The early summer sun was warm and embracing. A light wind was stirring the cedars and shrubs. It fit the mood, and I spoke up.

I wasn't disturbed by your statement that Paul was not an apostle.

That's good. You may not know why yet, but this morning a great weight will be lifted from your shoulders. Better yet, your mind will be cleared from an intricately woven spiritual cobweb.

I like the sound of that.

Abraham, Paul's teachings are deeply ingrained in the minds of the Almighty's people, most of them, anyway. It is hard to overstate the damage that his teaching has done, and how we've all been infused by it. That goes for unbelievers too.

Why do you say that?

Paul's teaching followed a pattern. He would begin with a half truth, subtly make a wrong conclusion, declare he was not lying, and end by boldly claiming that his teaching came from the Almighty. Somewhere in that process, Paul managed to deceive almost everyone. Almost.

I'd like to be free from Paul's teaching. Where do we start?

We can start by defining apostleship, and that's easy. The remaining eleven apostles did it when they filled the office left vacant by Judas Iscariot. They gave the necessary qualifications.

Harry opened a Bible and read,

**Of the men therefore that have companied with us all the time
that the Master Yeshuah went in and went out among us,
beginning from the baptism of John,
unto the day that he was received up from us,
of these must one become a witness with us of his resurrection.**

The apostles wanted an eyewitness like themselves, someone who had been with them during the ministries of both John the forerunner and Yeshuah the Messiah – someone who had experienced all they had experienced. That experience defined for them the qualifications necessary for the office of apostleship. They had to be eyewitnesses. Rather than meeting this definition, Paul's claim to apostleship was based on the visions he received, and on the many years he spent alone in the desert of Arabia.

This is where it starts to get very interesting, Avi. We have all taken Paul's writings and Luke's account of Paul's ministry at face value, and have read them in an unsuspecting manner. I need to point out what Paul really said and did before it becomes clear. This is no more evident than in how Paul related to the apostles that the Messiah had personally called and appointed. Paul boasted that his gospel had not come from men, that it was not taught to him by men, and that he did not consult with the apostles. He asserted that after his conversion, "I did not go up to Jerusalem to see those who were apostles before I was, but I went into Arabia." After three years (according to Paul), he spent fifteen days with Peter, and then did not return to Jerusalem for another fourteen years. In giving his personal history, Paul claimed to have sat at the feet of Gamaliel as a student, but never at the feet of the apostles. By his own account, Paul studiously avoided contact with the disciples of Yeshuah, and chose instead to spend the first seventeen years following his conversion in self-imposed isolation in the Arabian Desert.

THE BOOK OF NOTS IN SCIENCE & RELIGION

This begs the question: Which witness is more reliable? In Acts 4:13 we read:

**Now as they observed the confidence of Peter and John
and understood that they were uneducated and untrained men,
they were amazed,
and began to recognize them as having been with Yeshuah.**

The Messiah had carefully chosen his disciples after a night of prayer, and then trained them during the entire time of his ministry, some three-and-a-half years. His disciples were eyewitnesses to the ministry of John the Baptist, and Yeshuah's teachings, miracles, death, and resurrection. The last thing that Yeshuah did was commission his disciples to be his witnesses to the nations of the world, and promise that he would be with them always. In contrast, Paul would say regarding the apostles:

**But from those who were of high reputation
(what they were makes no difference to me;
the Almighty shows no partiality) – well, those who
were of reputation contributed nothing to me.**

At the heart of Paul's gospel is a rejection of the Messiah's disciples and their apostleship. Therein lies the answer to the question: Which witness is more reliable?

Harry, that's just shocking!

Yes, it is. We all know Paul's story about how he rebuked Peter to his face in public. That was Paul's side of the story, but even that version doesn't hide the truth. By his own account, the men who had come to Antioch had been sent by James. James was the natural brother of the Messiah, and the recognized leader of the new faith in Jerusalem. We are not explicitly told what the issue was. It is highly plausible, however, that the Jerusalem leadership was concerned with Paul's teaching and not Peter's. In any event, Paul used the occasion to publicly rebuke Peter and those he had chosen to eat with by calling them hypocrites. In that deed, Paul was setting himself above Peter, James and the Jerusalem council. He was rejecting the very ones who had known the Messiah personally, and had been appointed by him as his apostles. The truth shines through in Paul's own account.

My friend bowed his head.

I want to make an important digression, Abraham. The issue at hand may have been food, and why Peter chose to eat with the ambassadors from Jerusalem. At the Jerusalem council, it was agreed that new converts should not eat meat sacrificed to idols and specifically not eat blood. To that Paul had agreed, and took the council's ruling with him in written form. Later, Paul dismissed those requirements, saying that idols are nothing and the meat offered to idols could be eaten as long as it didn't offend. It's even possible that Peter had asked for support from James when he saw what was happening in Antioch. This is not a minor digression. We are going to talk more about this subject.

Harry looked at me in a way that was not happy.

After the rebuking incident, Paul would boast how he was not a whit behind "the very chiefest apostles."[1] Paul was surely including Peter in his boast. Peter had been called Cephas or 'stone' by the Messiah for his inspired confession of faith. Peter had been promised the power to bind or loose in accordance with heavenly authority.[2] Three times, Peter had been given the commission to feed the flock by the Yeshuah. Peter had delivered the first sermon when about three thousand were converted, and he had settled the dispute at the Council of Jerusalem in Acts 15. It's unlikely Peter thought of himself as the chief apostle,[3] but Paul did, and boasted that he was at least Peter's equal.

There is an extant document from the second century A.D. called *The Letter of Peter to James*. This document was highly valued by early believers although it never made it into the accepted cannon.[4] In this letter, Peter worries that the books containing his sermons will fall into the wrong hands, and has reservations how his writing should be preserved for the Gentiles. He is concerned that his teaching will be distorted into many opinions, and says:

> And this I know, not as being a prophet, but as already seeing the beginning of this very evil. For some from among the Gentiles have rejected my legal preaching, attaching themselves to certain lawless and trifling preaching of the man who is my enemy.[5]

That Peter was referring to Paul is an easy conclusion to make. It becomes even more certain as Peter continues:

---

1 Much of what follows is based on 2 Corinthians 11.
2 In Matthew 18:18, Yeshuah gave the authority to "bind and loose" to all his disciples – not only to Peter.
3 Peter was a converted man, having learned the Master's teaching, "The first will be last and the last first."
4 Other extant works that merited the attention of the early believers in the Messiah are: *The Gospel of Nicodemus, The Gospel of the Hebrews, The Epistle of Barnabas* and the *Clementine Homilies*. These documents and others can easily found on the worldwide web.
5 *The Letter of Peter to James*, Chapter 2, also from the *Clementine Homilies*. Peter's opponent here is often understood to be the apostle Paul. The distinguished American scholar, Bart D. Ehrman has that view as well as that Simon Magus is a cipher for none other than Paul himself. See his book, *Peter, Paul and Mary Magdalene: The Followers of Jesus in History and Legend.*

And these things some have attempted while I am still alive, to transform my words by certain various interpretations, in order to the dissolution of the law; as though I also myself were of such a mind, but did not freely proclaim it, which God forbid! For such a thing were to act in opposition to the law of God which was spoken by Moses, and was borne witness to by our Lord in respect of its eternal continuance; for thus he spoke: "The heavens and the earth shall pass away, but one jot or one tittle shall in no wise pass from the law." And this He has said, that all things might come to pass. But these men, professing, I know not how, to know my mind, undertake to explain my words, which they have heard of me, more intelligently than I who spoke them, telling their catechumens that this is my meaning, which indeed I never thought of. *But if, while I am still alive, they dare thus to misrepresent me, how much more will those who shall come after me dare to do so!* (emphasis added).

From this letter by Peter, we know that Peter continued to be faithful to the Law or Instructions of Moses, and to instruct the Torah to the new converts or *catechumens*, and that certain lawless teachers were distorting his instruction. There is a striking parallel passage in II Peter 15-17:

Bear in mind that our Master's patience means salvation, just as our dear
brother Paul also wrote you with the wisdom that the Almighty gave him.
He writes the same way in all his letters, speaking in them of these matters.
His letters contain some things that are hard to understand,
which ignorant and unstable people distort,
as they do the other Scriptures,
to their own destruction.
Therefore, dear friends, since you have been forewarned,
be on your guard so that you may not be carried away
by the error of the lawless and fall from your secure position.

Some scholars believe this passage to be a later insertion, and others that it has been poorly translated. Originally, the passage may have been written as a warning against Paul, explicitly saying it was Paul who was unstable and distorted the Scriptures, allegedly by virtue of the wisdom he had received from the Almighty, to his own destruction. Paul's 'wisdom' came through visions, and not from the Apostles or the Torah.

The central theme in *The Letter of Peter to James*, is that Peter's teaching is in conformity with the Scriptures, namely the Instructions of Moses, and that Paul's teaching is subtly and dangerously different. Both passages warn that the distortions are going to worsen over time. Neither passage succumbs to the abusive "let him be accursed" language that Paul so frequently employed. Nor does Peter boast about his apostleship.

Harry stopped speaking with a crushing silence. I was sure he was not trying to make me feel responsible for what I had heard. I just mulled it over in my mind. Then the significance of it all occurred to me.

You know, Harry, Paul wrote more than a third of the *New Testament*. It leaves us with the impression that Paul was the apostle of transition; a transition from Old to New, from Law to Grace, and from the Jews to the Gentiles. That's how we understand Paul's relationship with the other apostles. He was defiantly rejecting them for the sake of his gospel.

That's right, Avi. That's why Paul said, "For such men are false apostles, deceitful workers, fashioning themselves into apostles of the Messiah." Paul had, paradoxically, fashioned himself into an apostle, even as he maligned the true apostles and those appointed by the Master Yeshuah.

Was he really referring to Peter and the rest of the apostles, including James, as deceitful workers?

I don't know who else. In the same context, Paul asked, "Are they Hebrews... are they Israelites... are they descendants of Abraham?" He was undoubtedly speaking about the old guard, and as you say, defiantly. Paul was introducing a new order, and to that end, he had to make himself the chief apostle. I believe when he spoke against the 'Judaizers' and 'they of the circumcision,' he was referring to Peter, James, the Jerusalem council, and the rest of the apostles. That was his way of sidelining their witness.

Paul went still further when he said, "But though we, or an angel from Heaven, should preach unto you any gospel other than that which we preached unto you, let him be accursed."

Paul asserted himself above every other authority, even the authority of Heaven. No one else should be listened to as far as Paul was concerned. "If any man thinks himself to be a prophet, or spiritual, let him take knowledge of the things which I write unto you, that they are the commandment of the Master." Only Paul's gospel came from the Almighty – according to Paul. Finally, and unbelievably, Paul would say, "Follow me as I follow the Messiah." This was far removed from what Yeshuah the Messiah said, that the sheep hear his voice and follow him. Paul made himself into the final and absolute authority in all manner of doctrine and practice. The rest were all to be rejected.

Avi, I am by far not the only one saying such things about Paul. I came across these excerpts just recently:

> ... *Paul is in effect the first Christian heretic*, and his teachings, which become the foundation of later Christianity, are a flagrant deviation from the 'Original' or 'pure' form extolled by the leadership. Whether James, the 'Lord's brother,' was literally Jesus' blood kin or not (and everything suggests he was), it is clear that he knew Jesus... personally. So did most of the other members of the community or 'early Church,' in Jerusalem, including of course, Peter. When they spoke, they did so with first hand authority. Paul had never had such personal acquaintance with the figure he'd begun to regard as his 'Saviour.' *He had only his quasi-mystical experience in the desert and the sound of a disembodied voice. For him to arrogate authority to himself on this basis is, to say the least, presumptuous.* It also leads him to distort Jesus' teachings beyond recognition, to formulate, in fact, his own highly individual and idiosyncratic theology, and then to legitimize it by spuriously ascribing it to Jesus.
>
> As things transpired, however, the mainstream of the new movement gradually coalesced, during the next three centuries, around Paul and his teachings. *Thus, to the undoubted posthumous horror of James and his associates, an entirely new religion was indeed born, a religion that came to have less and less to do with its supposed founder.* (emphasis added).[6]

Harry abruptly got up.

Let's go for a walk.

We walked for a short while before Harry stopped and looked at me. His manner was as kindly as ever, and he wasn't prying into my being. He could see that I was not distressed or unsettled by what had been said, and that what had transpired between us was constructive and wholesome. For my part, I wasn't even aware that what I was hearing came from Harry. My ears had been opened.

Abraham, you can't hide the truth! This is especially obvious with Paul. Just consider what he said and how he said it. He used expressions such as, "I speak as if insane," "I will boast also," and that he served "with my flesh the law of sin." Most telling was his frequent

---

6   Bajgent, Michael and Leigh, Richard, *The Dead Sea Scrolls Deception*, Corgi Books, London, 1991.

insistence that he was not lying. He said it too many times to be credible. Paul claimed he would not build on another man's work, and yet his letters went to churches that he hadn't establish or even visited. He even said, "I robbed other churches." He said that no one should judge a brother, and yet, without being present, he assigned a brother to Satan, "for the destruction of his flesh." He himself was "ready to punish all disobedience." He called Peter a hypocrite in public, and cursed anyone who taught a gospel different from "my gospel." He admitted to being "still judged as a sinner," that not everyone regarded him as an apostle, and that "all Asia has left me."

Yeshuah never spoke about himself in like manner, or used that kind of language, nor did the apostles that he appointed. Rightly did Yeshuah say, "It is not what goes into a man that defiles him, but what comes out of him," and "it is by your words that you will be judged." Paul gave himself away by his own words.

We walked on for a while before Harry continued.

There are warnings everywhere within the *New Testament*. Yeshuah said repeatedly that many false teachers would come in his name, that the evil one would sow weeds among the wheat, and that we should be aware of wolves in sheep's clothing. Yeshuah warned:

> **For false messiahs and false prophets will appear**
> **and perform great signs and wonders to deceive,**
> **if possible, even the elect.**

Moses gave the same warning:

> **If a prophet, or one who foretells by dreams, appears among you**
> **and announces to you a sign or wonder,**
> **and if the sign or wonder spoken of takes place, and the prophet says,**
> **"Let us follow other gods" (gods you have not known)**
> **"and let us worship them,"**
> **you must not listen to the words of that prophet or dreamer.**
> **YHWH your Mighty One is testing you to find out**
> **whether you love him with all your heart and with all your soul.**

Yet Paul said, "Through mighty signs and wonders, by the power of the spirit of the Almighty; so that from Jerusalem, and round about unto Illyricum, I have fully preached the gospel of the Messiah."

That's it, Abraham. Many authors in our time are exposing Paul as an impostor. They point out how boastful, abusive and contradictory he often was; how his letters are much more authoritarian than they are affectionate, as if written by a man who was full of envy and pride, a man who only wanted to make a name for himself and gain a following. More than anything else, Paul wanted to be the chief apostle.

Thankfully, not everyone has been deceived. In the book of Revelation, Yeshuah says,

I know your works, and your toil and patience,
and that you cannot bear evil men,
and have tried them that call themselves apostles, and they are not,
and have found them to be false.

Before we go on Avi, where are your thoughts going?

I wasn't astonished.

You've rightly anticipated, Harry. Accepting that Paul was a false apostle has a deeper consequence. After all, Paul's letters make up most of the *New Testament*. His letters have been canonized and accepted as Scripture for at least fifteen hundred years. From that it's obvious that the *New Testament* can't be called scripture in the normal sense. That's what I've been thinking.

Good, Abraham. I was sure that you would see it right away. So let's deal with that.

5. THE NEW TESTAMENT IS NOT SCRIPTURE

As we continued walking, I noticed an increasing somberness in Harry's demeanor, and it puzzled me. My friend was so courageous in his pursuit of the truth, and so driven by his desire for understanding. It was obvious he found that part of his life so very exhilarating. Truth for Harry wasn't an intellectual pastime. He lived and breathed it with pleasure. Then why the somberness?

The somberness had come, in part, from accepting his rejection. Although every-one liked Harry, few cared to know why or were drawn to him. Harry inspired respect and even admiration, but that was as far as it went. The reaction was invariably to leave Harry alone. I was the exception.

Harry had an amazing capacity to accept others into his life. Anyone could walk right in. He never allowed his great learning, seemingly unlimited knowledge and disciplined focus to inhibit his relationship with others. Harry was like a good hotel and open for business every hour of the day. He could even love his enemies and invite them in.

I was beginning to understand Harry's sorrow. At the heart of it was the rejection of the truths that he had found so abundantly in his own life. The world around him didn't care a whit about the truth of anything, and it was bringing him endless grief. Inadvertently, Harry had become a man of sorrows.

My puzzlement was understandable. Harry made it all so easy for me. I was free to accept or reject what I was learning. I didn't have to prove myself to him. I could be my own person. The choices I needed to make were clear. There didn't seem to be any reason to be sorrowful about anything. I was feeling empowered!

We had walked at a robust pace, and soon we were again sitting in the seclusion of Harry's backyard.

Harry, you seem a little dour today.

I said it in a pleasant way.

I am, Avi. It's not easy to say that the **New Testament** is not Scripture, or that the Bible is not wholly inspired. It's a conversation stopper that usually gets me nowhere in a hurry.

What is Scripture, then?

Harry paused to choose his words carefully.

To answer the question, let's begin with terminology. What we call the Bible has been divided into two books, the so-called **Old Testament** and the so-called **New Testament**. That's misleading. For most believers, it means that an old contract has been torn up, and a new contract made in its place. That's wrong. From here on, I'll use the terms 'Hebrew Scriptures' and 'Greek Scriptures.' I will also refer to the Greek Scriptures as the 'Christian Scriptures' or 'Gentile Scriptures.' I will still refer to the Hebrew Scriptures as 'the Tanak'.

The Messiah did say that a teacher should bring forth things both old and new, but he never called the ancient Hebrew Scriptures 'old.' He simply referred to them as "the Scriptures." The authors of the **New Testament** followed his example. In every instance, the term **Scripture** refers to the Hebrew Scriptures. In effect, that defines the word **Scripture**. To answer your question, the Scriptures are what we mistakenly call the 'Old Testament.'

Most of the authors of the Greek Scriptures called their writings 'letters.' Later, some of their writings were called 'Gospels', which means Good News, but none of those authors ever claimed they were writing Scripture. They used the term **Scripture** in reference to the Hebrew Scriptures, and would have been appalled by the claim that they were writing Scripture themselves. In their minds (as much as we can know their minds), they were recording the events surrounding the life of Yeshuah the Messiah and recording his words, or writing letters of encouragement and instruction to those who had believed in him. However, at no time did they ever call what they wrote Scripture, or presume they were writing Scripture. The term **Scripture** was consistently applied to the Hebrew Scriptures by the authors of the Greek Scriptures.

Are we okay so far, Avi?

Sure. There are one or two verses that are used to show that the Christian writings are Scripture, but that's a prejudice. People can always find a reason to believe what they want to believe.[1] At the same time, it's hard to undo sixteen hundred years of tradition.

It would help, Abraham, if the canonization of the Greek Scriptures was better known. It seems that Athanasius was the first to list the twenty-seven books that we now have, and to refer to them as Scripture. In a letter of 367 A.D. he wrote,

> These are the springs of salvation, in order that he who is thirsty may fully refresh himself with the words contained in them. In them alone is the doctrine of piety proclaimed. Let no one add anything to them or take anything away from them...[2]

Athanasius was no saint, however, despite the title allotted to him by history. As one historian described him, Athanasius was an "uninhibited faction fighter, had his opponents excommunicated and anathematized, beaten and intimidated, kidnapped, imprisoned, and exiled to distant provinces."[3] As the Bishop of Alexandria, Athanasius could incite the mobs of his city to murderous acts against his enemies. That begs the question, was this violent bishop a man capable of discerning true doctrine or deciding on a canon?

We talked about this matter last week – about the use of political power. Athanasius was a very powerful man in the same way the great reformers of the sixteenth century were powerful. They used the state to advance their religious influence. All in turn used their power in murderous ways: Luther in the massacre of the peasants in 1525, and Calvin for having Servetus executed. Such unrighteous deeds mark those men as impostors regardless of their reputation. I can tell you truly, Abraham, that such men can never enter the Kingdom of Heaven. As Yeshuah said, "The meek shall inherit the Earth."

I knew that what Harry was saying was true.

Those religious leaders, and many others, greatly influenced the long process of canonization. Hundreds of books and letters were written for several centuries following Yeshuah's lifetime. Many of them were read in early congregations and considered authoritative, but never canonized, including books such as, *The Gospel of Nicodemus*, *The Gospel of the Hebrews*, and *The Epistle of Barnabas*. Other books are still disputed,

---

1   Anecdotally, Benjamin Franklin described his conversion to a vegetarian diet in the first chapter of his autobiography, and then he justified his frequent relapses by saying: "So I din'd upon Cod very heartily and continued to eat with other People, returning only now and than occasionally to a vegetable Diet. So convenient a thing it is to be a reasonable Creature, since it enables one to find or make a Reason for every thing one has a mind to do."

2   The 39th Festal Letter of Athanasius.

3   Rubenstein, Richard E., *When Jesus Became God*, Harcourt, Inc., 1999, p 6.

such as Hebrews, Second Peter, and Second and Third John. There is uncertainty also about when the *New Testament canon* was actually ever closed.[4] Many of the books that were never canonized have found favour again among Christian readers. As one modern scholar has said:

> The canon of the New Testament was not closed historically by the early church. Rather, its extent was debated until the Reformation. Even then, it was closed in a sectarian fashion. Therefore the question must be asked, *is it then heresy for a person to question or reject a book of the present canon ? There have been repeated reevaluations of the church's canon.* This happened during the initial sifting period. It happened again during the Renaissance and Reformation period, *and it is beginning to happen again now.* In such instances the fringe books of the canon have been repeatedly questioned. If an individual believer should come to question or reject a book or books of the accepted canon, should that person be regarded as a heretic, or accepted as a brother whose opinions are not necessarily endorsed? (*emphasis added*).[5]

I made a deliberate effort to keep silent. Harry was trusting me, and I wasn't going to spoil it, but my mind reeled as his words sank in. I concentrated on my breathing, keeping it regular.

Over the years, I had never questioned my trust in the Bible. I had always considered it as the ultimate source of truth. If all else failed, then at least the Bible was true. Word for word and line by line, I had accepted it with complete confidence. I had doubted my understanding of it, but never its truthfulness.

I looked over at Harry. He seemed unconcerned, and there was nothing threatening in his manner. A sense of relief came over me. I was sure that I could trust him, at least in his attitude towards me. I breathed a prayer, and asked,

How deep does this go, Harry? Should we just throw the *New Testament* in the trash can?

We don't want to reject the Christian Scriptures outright, Avi. That would be a very serious mistake. However, we need to be honest about what kind of a testament it actually is. The problems of authorship, transmission and selection need to be realistically

---

4   Athanasius' festal letter (367 AD) is generally viewed as the document which fixed the canon in the East, and the decisions of the Council of Carthage (397 and 419 AD) as having fixed the canon in the West.

5   Sawyer, M. James, *Evangelicals and the Canon of the New Testament*. See bible.org.

appraised. No matter how much we retain from our Christian Scriptures as valuable and true, we must give up believing in them as infallible documents. They are not word-for-word inspired letters and records.

I have another quotation I'd like to read to you. Take note that it comes from an unorthodox source.

> The Arian Catholic Church does not accept biblical infallibility; there are over a thousand recognized errors in the New Testament (not accounting for translational errors) ranging from Luke's geographical mistakes to contradictions over the conception, birth, crucifixion and resurrection of Jesus. *The bible should be read with caution and interpreted with logic and reason.* One must remember that it was written and re-written by people who were awe-struck, people who had relatively little understanding of the world around them and people who had an anti-semitic, anti-gnostic, trinitarian or other political agenda! *While much of the original scriptures were the inspired word of God, the bible that we know today is a fifth, tenth or even fifteenth generation transcript and translation of these words*; the original New Testament manuscripts, bar a few fragments have long since been destroyed in favour of the redacted versions. *Most of the New Testament has been subjected to numerous redactions, selectively assembled, and many of the books included have been amended in various ways...* in the fourth century following the council of Nicaea, at least 300 Gospels were tragically burned and it was made a penal offense to possess an unauthorized Gospel. (*emphasis added*).[6][7]

Avi, I have resolved that we may never know who the authors of the Christian Scriptures were, or what was actually written in the original documents. I give much credence to our modern scholars in their assessment of the Greek Scriptures. Yeshuah's disciples could not have written or even dictated any of the documents found in our Bibles. If the disciples wrote anything at all, it has been outright lost or severely tampered with. That much is certain based on many decades of close scrutiny by biblical archaeologists, geographers, linguists and other academics. All that scrutiny tilts in favor of the

---

6 See arian-catholic.org under *Virgin Birth - Separating Myth from Fact.*
7 This appraisal comes from an unorthodox source, but is not unique to the Arian Catholic Church. Although the Arian traditions resurfaced after the Reformation, the substance of this appraisal comes from modern scholarship in the study of languages, ancient manuscripts, archeology, history and many related disciplines. Similar conclusions are now widely accepted regarding the inerrancy of the **New Testament** canon.

scholarship, not against it. In the end, we have to be honest about it.

I nodded to my friend. Intuitively, I knew that Harry's insight was enriching my understanding, and that I was better off because of it. I asked,

How should I understand the Christian Scriptures?

Yeshuah gave us the key to understanding the character of what came to be known as the **New Testament**. He knew exactly how his message would be transmitted to future generations, and he said it so clearly that it's a wonder how it was missed.

I'm listening, Harry.

Yeshuah said it repeatedly. First, he warned that many false teachers would come either in his name or posing as messiahs. Remember, **messiah** means 'anointed.' In our terms, many will come in the name of 'Jesus' claiming to bring the same message he brought, or professing that Yeshuah was the Anointed One. There will be many of them – not just a few – many. This was both a warning and a prediction.

Yeshuah was giving his disciples the heads-up for their own time. In the parable of the sower, the "evil one" came immediately to take away the seed that was sown. Immediately. In other words, many false teachers would come after Yeshuah and without delay. That Yeshuah's warning became true very quickly is apparent within the Christian Scriptures since in it are many references to false teachers, false prophets, false apostles, false witnesses, false brethren and so on. In Yeshuah's acute foresight, he knew his teaching would be promptly followed by every false teaching imaginable. That is exactly what happened!

Then Yeshuah taught something truly remarkable. In another parable, a man sowed a field of wheat, and then while everyone slept, his enemy came and sowed weeds in the same field. When his servants came and asked if they should pull out the weeds, he said no, because in pulling the weeds they might uproot the wheat. Then Yeshuah made this remarkable statement. He said, "Let both grow together until the harvest." The good seed and the bad seed were to grow together in the same field.

Another parable followed, the one about a mustard seed that grew into an enormous tree, so large that birds nested in its branches. Birds in the Scriptures can represent intellectual thoughts, human reasoning, false teaching and fantasies.[8] Birds can also

8 "Now as the fowls of the heavens signify truths of the understanding, and thus thoughts, they also signify their opposites, such as phantasies or falsities, which being of man's thought are also-called fowls, as for example when it is said that the wicked shall be given for meat to the fowls of heaven and to the wild beasts, meaning phantasies and cupidities (Isaiah 18:6; Jeremiah 7:33; 16:4; 19:7; 34:20; Ezekiel 29:5; 39:4). The

mean abominations.[9] In the Revelation of John, it is said that Babylon has "become a habitation of demons, and a hold of every unclean spirit, and a hold of every unclean and hateful bird."[10] That verse sounds very much like the parable of the mustard seed, like the huge tree in which birds had come to rest.

Harry looked over at me and became a little somber again.

Avi, let's keep it simple and not elaborate too much. That warning and the parables perfectly describe the Christian Scriptures and historical Christianity. Both are a field in which the wheat and the weeds are growing together. Christianity has been called a spiritual Babylon often enough, and I don't care much about repeating it, but that mixture of good seed and bad seed, right teaching and false teaching, truth and lies began in the *New Testament* and ended with historical Christianity.

Here's something very interesting. It's exactly how Peter the apostle thought about it. From his preaching as recorded in the *Clementine Homilies*, Peter explicitly said, "For the Scriptures have had joined to them many falsehoods against God."[11] He repeated the assertion in another homily:

> If, therefore, some of the Scriptures are true and some false, with good reason said our Master [Yeshuah], 'be ye good money changers,' inasmuch as in the Scriptures there are some true sayings and some spurious.[12]

In the *Homilies*, Peter used the term 'money changers' several times. In Homily XVIII, Chapter 20, he elaborates:

> Wherefore every man who wishes to be saved must become, as the Teacher said, a judge of the books written to try us. For thus He spake: 'Become experienced bankers.' Now the need of bankers arises from the circumstance that the spurious is mixed with the genuine.[13]

Lord Himself also compares phantasies and false persuasions to fowls, where He says: The seed that fell by the wayside was trodden under foot, and the fowls of heaven came and devoured it (Matthew. 13:4; Luke 8:5; Mark 4:4, 15), where the fowls of heaven are nothing else than falsities." See *Birds, Fowl* at biblemeanings.info.

9 At last upon the bird of abominations shall be desolation (Daniel 9:27).

10 Revelation 18:2, American Standard Version.

11 Homily II, Ch. 38.

12 Homily II, Ch. 51.

13 Reader take note: in the Homilies, Peter is referring to the Hebrew Scriptures. Closely following Peter's time, the Ebionites also believed the Torah of Moses had been tampered with, and things added contrary to the the Almighty's original Instructions. There will be more of this theme in a later chapter.

Of course, Peter didn't know anything about a *New Testament*, and we don't even know if he ever preached such things, but the parallel is too close to what Yeshuah said about the wheat and the weeds growing together to be avoided. It's a stark warning for us that the seeds of truth and falsehood can be mixed, and that we need to be good money changers or be able to tell the difference.

Abraham, there's another defining characteristic about the Christian Scriptures that I want you to consider. I'll give you a point by point summary.

One: The Christian Scriptures were written in Greek. No ancient manuscript of the Christian Scriptures written in a Hebrew dialect has ever been found. None. All of the ancient manuscript copies, nearly six thousand in total, are in Greek.

Two: This is really a sub-point, but the quotes from the Hebrew Scriptures in the Christian Scriptures are also in Greek. That is, the authors were quoting from a Greek translation of the Hebrew Scriptures. This is why Yeshuah and his disciples appear to be quoting from a Greek text, and not from a text in their own language.

Three: Similarly, those authors and the early church fathers used a Greek translation of the Hebrew Scriptures. Today we call it the Septuagint, although it's not likely that such a unified text ever existed.[14] In reality, the authors of the Christian Scriptures and the church fathers used a variety of Greek texts when they wrote the books in it or expounded on the Hebrew texts. Their textual resource was the 'Septuagint' or some version of a Greek translation.

Four: Koine Greek was the *lingua franca* of the Roman Empire, the most common and widely spoken language during the formative years of the Christian church. The church fathers wrote their letters and commentaries in koine Greek. In every way, the Good News and its accompanying Epistles were disseminated to the Gentile world through the Greek language.

Five: The church fathers were nuanced by Greek culture and learning. Along with the Greek language came an acceptance of Greek ideas and Greek philosophy. Many of the fathers such as Justin Martyr, Clement of Alexander and Origen thought of themselves

---

14 The Septuagint, as the Greek Bible came to be called, has a long and complex history. The story of the seventy Jewish scholars who came to Alexandria in Egypt in about 300 BC to translate the Hebrew Scriptures into Greek has been dismissed as a legend, and the Greek-Septuagint text of today is not the same as the Greek text(s) in vogue from 200 BC to 100 AD. The Septuagint of today is largely Origen's (185-254 AD) which he transcribed using the Greek language of his time. Origen went as far as inserting specific *New Testament* passages into his version of the Septuagint, leading scholars to ask if there ever was such a thing as an authentic version of the Septuagint.

primarily as philosophers, and tried to reconcile Greek philosophy with the truths of the Hebrew Scriptures and the emerging Christian Scriptures. In their minds, Greek philosophy was the means to understanding biblical truths, and a platform to build on.[15] Greek philosophy was not something that needed to be examined in the light of the Hebrew Scriptures, or repented of.

Six: The church fathers soon began to distance themselves from Jerusalem and Judaism. They took the destruction of Jerusalem in 70 AD as the Almighty Father's indictment against the Jews, and began to view the Church as the New Israel. The political centre of Christianity shifted from Jerusalem to Antioch, Alexandria and Rome. From then on, the Church would view the Hebrew Scriptures from a Greek or Gentile perspective, very often in defiance of anything Jewish or Hebraic.

What's so important to understand? Every language possesses its own inner structure, unique idioms, innate meanings, and brings with it a certain way of thinking. These elements shape the thinking of those who write in that language, convey their intentions, and define the meaning of what they are writing. In essence, every language has its own mindset.

Abraham, I believe that the Christian Scriptures convey meanings and ideas that would never have been possible if those Scriptures had been written in Hebrew. This is the heart of the matter: the *New Testament* is truly a Gentile document with a Greek mindset. Sure, the Greek language made it possible for the Good News to be spread widely and quickly – something impossible with the Hebrew language. However, along with the Greek language came a Greek mindset that radically altered what the Good News was all about. That's what's so important to understand.

We both sat quietly for a little while, breathing it in.

Avi, many of the doctrinal ideas and beliefs that are so common today come from the Greek mindset of the Greek Scriptures.

Can you give me an example?

We've already had a few, and the first was the example of Paul. In essence, Paul taught that we can be saved by faith, as do all Christians today. That is, it's our faith that will save us and not our deeds. It's hard to understand where that thinking came from if it wasn't

---

15 I clearly remember the day one of my Lutheran professors, a very learned man, when referring to certain elements in Greek philosophy said, "You can build on that." It staggered me then to think that anyone could build a doctrinal structure on a platform of Greek philosophy. Yet this is precisely what he and many other learned men have done since the beginning of church history.

from the Greek mindset. The Greeks loved philosophy, the realm of ideas and the ability to reason. Theirs was a cerebral world where right thinking was more important than right action. That's Paul's legacy to the Church: intellectual consent to the right beliefs. Need I say how headlong Christianity has fallen into Paul's Greek mindset with all the persecutions and anathemas against those with false doctrines? That's the consequence of Paul's declaration – from a Greek mindset – that we can be justified by faith.

As one author has written:

> In fundamentalist Christian circles, it is often more important to believe and espouse "the right thing," than to live the right way. This is why we are so obsessed with creeds, doctrinal statements, Systematic Theologies, orthodoxy vs. heresy, and creating "Evangelical" or "Sabbatarian" or "Trinitarian" theologies. *This mode of thinking is thoroughly Western, utterly Greek.* (emphasis added).[16]

Yeshuah didn't agree with Paul either. He said,

For the Son of man shall come in the esteem of his Father with his angels; and then shall he render unto every man according to his deeds.[17]

Another superb example is the one you already alluded to, concerning the so-called virgin birth.

Please continue.

The virgin birth of the Messiah is a religious myth and not a reality.

I looked over at Harry. There was not a hint of provocation in his demeanor. His statement was matter-of-fact, quiet and confident. I still couldn't rise to Harry's level of artlessness, and could still laugh at myself. I blurted out what I was thinking.

That's preposterous!

I wasn't rejecting what Harry had said. My mind I was agreeing with him, but my feelings weren't.

---

16 From the essay *The Hebrew Mind vs The Western Mind* by Brian Knowles.
17 Matthew 16:27

Harry, the virgin birth is so fundamental. A whole range of doctrines are involved!

That's true, and we'll get to it. The immediate question is concerning the reliability of the Christian Scriptures.

You mean there are things in the Christian Scriptures that aren't true?

Yes, exactly, and if we allow ourselves to be honest, some of what's written in the Greek texts isn't even believable.

And one of those is the virgin birth? You called it a myth.

The virgin birth is a prime example of something essentially implausible. Just think about the history of the doctrine and it extensions. It ends up as a rather pathetic doctrine.

Go on.

As far as we know, the belief that Mary was a virgin when she gave birth to her son was widely accepted by the beginning of the second century AD. As a historical development, there is no mention of the virgin birth in the Nicene Creed of 325. At the Council of Constantinople in 381, the belief became a dogma, and at the Lateran Council of 649, its denial was anathematized. The same council articulated that Mary, "bore Him without any corruption, her virginity remaining intact after His birth."[18] In 1854, Pius IX dogmatized Mary's immaculate conception, meaning that Mary was born without the stain of sin, unlike all other humans. Finally in 1950, Mary's assumption into Heaven became an infallible doctrine, though the belief itself went back to at least the fourth century.

Abraham, virgin birth stories go back much farther than that. The belief may have originated in Egypt where the god Kneph impregnated Mutemua, the virgin Queen of Egypt by holding a cross to her mouth. Also in Egypt, Isis was the god-mother of Horus. Virgin birth stories abounded in the Ancient Near East, and include Krishna, Gautama Buddha, Plato, Alexander the Great, and Caesar Augustus. Whether those stories were actually believed or not, it was the way that the ancients exalted their champions or explained their exceptional powers.[19] They were not ordinary beings because they were

---

18 The status of being a postpartum virgin forced the authorities into a humorless attempt to prove that the hymen of the virgin Mary had not been ruptured during Jesus' birth. The text in Ezekiel 44:1-3 was found with the dubious reading, "The gates of the city were closed. Only the Lord could go in and out." Without a hint of shame or embarrassment, the text was said to show that Jesus could have been born without disturbing the gates of his mother's womb.

19 Proclus of Constantinople states: "If the Mother had not remained a virgin, her child would have been a mere man, and His birth not wonderful. If, to the contrary, she remained a virgin after His birth, how will the

born of gods. Try as we might to distinguish the virgin birth of Jesus from all the other virgin births, there remains an uncomfortable feeling that it's just one more myth of the same kind.

Harry, are you saying that a virgin birth would never have been accepted within a Hebrew mindset?

Yes, and that's historically true. There was a long debate between Christians and Jews about the verse in Isaiah 7:14, whether the word *almah* meant virgin or young woman. Each accused the other of tampering with the Scriptures, the Christians with the Septuagint and the Jews with the Masoretic text. However, the Dead Sea scroll of Isaiah proved that the original word was indeed referring to a young woman and not a virgin. The discovery didn't end the debate, but it did show conclusively that the explicit concept of a virgin birth was absent in the ancient Hebrew text. Nor would such a concept have ever appealed to the ancient Hebrews.

Hold on. Mary's virginity is plainly told in the Greek Scriptures – twice over. The Holy Spirit would cause Mary to conceive, and Joseph did not have relations with Mary until after the child was born. Stripped of all the dogma that came later, the story of the Messiah's miraculous birth is undeniably there in the Christian Scriptures. Why should we doubt the story?

The story is only found in two places, in Matthew and Luke.[20] It is never referred to again in the rest of the Greek Scriptures, and never taught as a doctrine anywhere else. Paul said that Yeshuah was born of a woman, but with the very different assertion – that Yeshuah was a real human being.

In addition, the virgin birth stories of Matthew and Luke are not found in the earliest manuscripts.[21] They appear to have been added later, probably to validate an already popular belief. The virgin birth insertion is just one more example of the tampering of the ancient manuscripts in the process of canonization.[22]

Finally, the idea of a God-man is utterly foreign to the Hebrew Scriptures. Throughout

---

Son not be God, and the mystery indescribable?" (Gambero, 253).

20   Mary's virginity at the conception of Yeshuah is also a tenet of Islam. Muslims refer to Jesus with the matronymic "Jesus son of Mary," a term repeatedly used in the Quran.

21   The oldest manuscripts (P1 for Matthew and P4 for Luke) are fragmentary, which may also explain why the virgin birth is missing.

22   "The devil's apostles have filled the scriptures with tares, taking away some things and adding others... some have dared to tamper even with the word of the Lord Himself..." the first great Church historian Eusebius quoting the church father Dionysius (*Ecclesiastical History*, Book 4, p 23).

the law, the prophets and the writings, there is not the slightest hint of the Eternal One Creator incarnating Himself into a man, and the promised Messiah is never portrayed as anything other than a human being. That the Messiah was a divine being is a Greek idea and pagan concept that found its way into the Christian Scriptures. *Gnosticism* is alive and well in the so-called *New Testament*.[23]

I pondered briefly before I answered.

Harry, the story about the virgin birth isn't about a miracle, is it?

You're right. As a miracle, the story could be acceptable to a certain extent, but that is not why the virgin birth has been incorporated into our Bibles. The real intention was to explain how the Eternal One incarnated Himself. It's not just a matter of simply accepting the virgin birth as a miracle.

After that, I didn't feel like responding and wanted to ponder what Harry had just said. I looked over at him and he was pondering too. I wanted to make a more thoughtful response, and he was giving me the leeway to do that. I sat quietly and waited for my thoughts to gel before I said,

I agree with you, my friend. The *New Testament* is a Gentile document written with a Greek mindset. The Christian Scriptures are really the Gentile interpretation of who Yeshuah was and what he did.

But Harry, realistically, are Christians ever going to change? Do you really think that they can stop believing in Paul and the virgin birth?

Well, we need to separate fact from fiction. As I said earlier, we need to separate the wheat from the tares.

What's next, Harry?

My plan is to return to what popular science wants us to believe about the Creation. To be specific, I want to talk about the theory of evolution.

Avi, since today is a New Moon day, the next Sabbath will be seven days from now.

---

23 *Gnosticism* has been defined as "the acute Hellenization of Christianity." (*Helllenism* is another word for Greek culture.) Some Gnostics identified 'Jesus' as an embodiment of the supreme being who became incarnate to bring *gnōsis* (gnostic knowledge) to the Earth. Elements of Gnosticism are most evident in the writings of Paul and the Gospel of John.

May the Eternal One be with you in the meantime, Harry, and also with me.

Yes.

6. THE EARTH IS NOT VERY OLD

Shalom, Harry. I notice today is a Thursday.

Yes, the New Moon day was on the day immediately following the last Sabbath of the month, so the Sabbath only moved one day forward from Wednesday to Thursday. We are together today and will be for the next three Thursdays.

This is all new to me, Harry, but our meetings have always been restful and invigorating. I am beginning to appreciate keeping the Sabbath.

Good. That nicely leads to what we want to talk about today, about how in the beginning the Almighty Father created the heavens and the Earth. The question for us today is, when was the beginning?

Avi, I can tell you up front that the question about the Earth's age is all about credibility and trustworthiness. Who is really believable? It is apparent that in rejecting biblical truths, evolutionists have invented a story that is stranger than fiction. The story is unreasonable and lacks scientific evidence and common sense.

On the other hand, the person saying that the Almighty created the heavens and the Earth is making a perfectly logical and reasonable statement. In the realm of philosophy, no one has ever successfully refuted the argument from design.[1] Where there is design, there must be a designer. It takes very complex thinking to argue against there being a Creator, so complex that it makes no sense at all.

The point I'm making, Avi, is that you don't have to be a scientist or a university professor to be wise. Natural abilities and common sense don't come with a degree, and no college grants a certificate in natural ability. We should never allow ourselves to be

---

1 The teleological argument.

intimidated by the appearance of wisdom in the guise of higher learning.[2]

However, a little education can be very helpful. So let's talk about how it was mistakenly concluded that the Earth is 4.6 billion years old.

I'm keen.

Good. In a way, our modern legacy began with Copernicus. By removing the Earth from its place at the centre of the universe, he also removed the Earth from its place at the beginning of time. In 1774, Comte de Buffon speculated that the Earth must be at least seventy-five thousand years old. He also suggested that humans and apes are related. In 1830-1833, Charles Lyle proposed that the Earth must be very old and has been subject to the same natural processes in the past that are shaping the Earth's surface today. This process of slower, and progressive change is called *uniformitarianism*. The first technical analysis came from Lord Kelvin (William Thomson) around the year 1897. Kelvin assumed that initially the Earth was a molten blob and that it took about 20-40 million years to cool. Kelvin's personal preference was for the lower figure, that the Earth was only about twenty million years old.

The modern dating of the Earth's age began with the discovery of radioactivity and the decay rates of certain atomic elements. The discoverer of the radioactive half-life was the great scientist Ernest Rutherford at the very beginning of the twentieth century. His discovery led to the conclusion that the age of the Earth could be measured accurately by measuring the amount of decay in various materials. In 1913, Arthur Holmes proposed that the Earth was 1.6 billion years old based on the decay rate of lead. Holmes continued to revise this estimate throughout his life, producing a figure in 1959 some three times larger. In 1956, Clair Patterson published his calculation based on meteorites and sediment from the ocean floor. His calculation was an astonishingly specific 4.55 ± 0.07 billion years, the figure that has been universally accepted.[3]

In little more than fifty years, the age of the Earth had grown from 20 million years to 4.6 billion. However, the Earth appeared to be much older than the universe itself, leaving a problem for cosmology. This inconsistency was resolved after the Hubble Constant[4]

2   According to a recent Gallop poll: 22% of people with a post graduate degree still believe that humans were created in their present form within the last 10,000 years; 49% believe that the Almighty guided the process; and only 25% of post graduates believe humans simply "evolved."

3   The numerically impressive figure of 4.55 ± 0.07 gives the estimate an air of credibility. With a figure so large, such a degree of accuracy is inconceivable, making the number look rather foolish.

4   The Hubble constant is one of the most critical numbers in the science of cosmology because it is necessary for estimating the size and age of the universe. Determining a true value for the Hubble constant is very complex, and requires two measurements. The first has to do with the redshift, or how fast a galaxy is speeding away from the Earth. The second is even more difficult, and is a galaxy's precise distance from the Earth

was revised many times until finally the age of the universe was settled at 13.75 billion years old, or about nine billion years older than the Earth.[5] Once these figures were arrived at, they were quickly adopted in all the various branches of science, and no further revisions were made. The age of the Earth and the age of the universe seem to be settled for now.[6]

Harry stood up and walked over to the little pond. He stood there for a few minutes without saying anything. I did not think he was waiting for a response from me. He started speaking again without sitting down.

Scientists tell us that they can't measure the age of the Earth directly. Supposedly, the Earth was molten at the beginning, and erosion and other forces have destroyed all of the earliest surface rocks.[7] Hence, the Earth's age must be measured indirectly by using fallen meteorites. Apparently, upwards of a hundred meteorites of different types have been measured using various radiometric dating techniques.[8] The resulting dates, we are told, have been very consistent and all very close to the figure established by Patterson in 1956, that is, 4.6 billion years.

Now please listen carefully, Abraham. I am not going to be so foolish as to deny that the Earth, or more specifically meteorites, are 4.6 billion years old according to radiometric dating. With all the testing that has been done, and the multiple techniques used, it would be futile for us to deny the resulting data. Subject to some still unknown factors, the Earth is 4.6 billion years old according to radiometric dating.[9] [10]

---

based on its brightness and other factors.

5   After seven years of results-taking, NASA's Wilkinson Microwave Anisotropy Probe (WMAP) has tightened the estimate on the age of the Universe down to an error margin of only 120 million years, that's 0.87% of the 13.73 billion years since the Big Bang.

6   "Seems to be." The Hubble constant is far from certain and contains "huge systematic errors." New studies put the age of the cosmos at 8.4 billion to 10.6 billion years. Perhaps even less. Since it's introduction as a formula early in the 20th century, the Hubble constant has been steadily revised downward. Hubble estimated the expansion rate at 500 kilometers per second. By the early 1970's estimates from Sandage and Tammann were hovering around 55 km/s.

7   Rocks that date to about 3.5 billion years have been found in the Canadian Shield, Australia and Africa. In 2008, a rock was found in northern Quebec, dating from 3.8 to 4.28 billion years.

8   There are various radioisotope dating methods. The major ones are uranium-lead, potassium-argon, rubidium-strontium and uranium-thorium. Together they give dates that are often consistent although for different lengths of time. The most accurate is the radiocarbon dating method which has a half life of only 5730 years. The shorter the time frame, the more reliable a method becomes.

9   There are anomalies. The Fourth Lunar Science Conference in 1973 revealed that one of the moon rocks dated to 5.3 billion years. Also, the potassium-argon dating method gave readings between 7 and 20 billion years for some of the Apollo 12 samples.

10   My readers should be aware that there is often a wide discordance between the various atomic or radioisotope methods. They do not always give the same results and often by a wide margin. Dating the 1980

Were you listening, Avi?

Yes. Twice you used the phrase, "according to radiometric dating."

Thank you. That's good. Now, tell me what I meant by that.

You were implying that radiometric dating is not the only way to measure the age of the Earth.

Harry sat down again and elaborated.

Abraham, there is something fundamentally different between radiometric or atomic dating and what we normally call 'years'. To begin with, atomic dating measures backward in time without a known starting point. That's not the way we usually measure time or distance. Normally we measure from one specific point to another, from a known starting point to a known ending point. From those two points, we can measure the time or distance between them. In atomic dating, we have a known ending point in the present, but no known starting point in the past. Try, for example, to measure the distance from New York City to an unknown location, or try measuring the time from September 11, 2001 to an unknown date. Obviously, it's impossible in both examples. It's not normal to measure time when the beginning point is unknown.

Next, the nature of time in the ordinary sense is very different from time in the realm of billions of years. In modern physics, we know this as 'relative time' where time is no longer uniform or absolute. Many modern physicists would even like to argue that time doesn't really exist.[11] Einstein went as far as saying, "People like us, who believe in physics, know that the distinction between past, present and future is only a stubborn, persistent illusion."[12] Time becomes more and more difficult to define when it is taken out of its normal context. Vast eons of time is not the time we know of in the ordinary sense.

Strangely, we know from very complex observations that time seems to slow down the closer it comes to a massive object such as the Earth.[13] In other words, time and gravity are related with time at its slowest on the Earth's surface – more specifically at the centre of the Earth. On Earth's surface, there are sixty seconds to the minute, but not far out in space. It has actually been observed that clocks run at different rates at different alti-

---

eruption of Mount St Helens, for example, yielded results from 340,000 to 2.8 million years!

11   Barbour, Julian. *The End of Time: The Next Revolution in Physics, 1999.*

12   As frequently quoted on the Web.

13   From the Pound-Rebka experiment and the time signals sent to and from the most distant satellites, Pioneer 10 and 11. The apparent slowing of Pioneer's speed away from the Earth can be equally well explained by a faster speed of light at that distance.

tudes with time running much faster in distant space. This might explain why meteorites are older than the Earth. The time imprinted in their atomic makeup is the time in space many millions of miles away. Since meteorites come from relatively nearby, it should be expected that their ages are similar, although slightly greater than the age of the Earth.[14] Meteorites not only come from a different place, they also come from a different time.

Harry stopped, gave me a look, and continued.

Someone might want to dismiss what I'm saying as weird science. Keep in mind, that I'm a geocentricist and believe that the Earth is at the centre of the Creation. For a geocentricist, space, matter, time and gravity are all centered on the Earth. Actually, what I'm saying agrees with much of current scientific theory. It's not weird at all.

What we are talking about is *time dilation* or the stretching out of time. As a proof for time dilation, we can point to two identical atomic clocks, one in Boulder, Colorado and the other in Greenwich, England. Significantly, the clock in Colorado is one mile higher in altitude than the clock in England, and runs five microseconds per year faster. That is, the farther a clock is from the centre of the Earth, the faster it runs!

The Scriptures speak in numerous places about how the Almighty Father stretched out the heavens in His act of Creation:

**It is I who made the earth and created man upon it.
I stretched out the heavens with My hands.**

**I, YHWH, am the maker of all things,
stretching out the heavens by Myself.**

**Surely My hand founded the earth
and My right hand spread out the heavens.**[15]

The picture in the Hebrew Scriptures is of the Almighty creating space as an act of expansion, pulling everything out and away from the Earth. Visualize Him cupping His

---

14 Most of the meteorites falling on Earth come from a belt of asteroids located between Mars and Jupiter. Due to the collision of their 'parent' asteroid' with another object, they were ejected into a new orbit, eventually falling onto the Earth. "Meteorites are a major tool for knowing the history of the solar system because their composition is a record of past geologic processes that occurred while they were still incorporated in the parent asteroid" (*Science Daily*, "Source Of Most Common Meteorites Discovered," July 14, 2008).
15 Is 45:12, 44:24 and 48:13. Se also Job 9:8, Ps 104:2 and Jer 10:12.

hands around the Earth and stretching everything outward, filling the void with space.[16] Space, or the universe, is what the Almighty created inside of His own absolute substance.

That's such a good picture, Harry.

Then go a little further. In stretching out the universe, the Almighty stretched space, time and light. In physics, we call it the space-time continuum. The stretching explains why we can see the stars even though they are immensely far away. The light from the stars that were once nearby has been stretched out to where the stars are now, many millions of light-years distant. It also explains why rocks seem so extremely old. Physicists know that the rate of decay for radioactive elements is directly related to the speed of light. It was not just light, but the entire electro-magnetic spectrum that was stretched out. That's why the radiometric rates of decay read as if millions and billions of years have passed by when in reality the rocks are only a few thousand years old. It comes from the stretching out of the heavens at the beginning of the Eternal One's creative work.[17]

There is good evidence, too, that the rate of decay changes over time. Slight variations have been reported in recent years, variations due to changes in the Earth-sun distance, solar flares and other environmental factors. Radio halos also give evidence that decay rates vary with time.[18] On a grander scale, some scientists believe that the decay rate could have been ten million times faster in the past.[19] Their studies are based on the decay in the speed of light, but apply equally to all forms of radiation. On that basis, the decay rates that are used to measure the age of the Earth are not what they seem to be.

Harry sat down abruptly.

---

16   Contrary to what is usually taught, the Almighty did not create *ex nihilo* or out of nothing. He created the heavens and the Earth within His own absolute substance. Many scientists have postulated in terms of the Planck constant, that the universe is very, very dense, and that the near vacuum of space is only a perception. Logically speaking, there can never be 'nothing' in absolute terms.

17   In science, this phenomena is also known as *accelerated decay*. Some have posited that both accelerated nuclear decay and an expansion of space occurred during the Great Flood.

18   Radiohalos are minute concentric rings of discoloration that occur in minerals such as granite and other igneous rocks. Physicist Robert Gentry has interpreted halos as evidence against a long cooling period for an originally molten Earth.

19   "In 1987, the Russian theoretical physicist, Dr. V. S. Troitskii..., postulated that a huge decay in the speed of light had occurred over time. Dr. Troitskii was talking about the speed of light having been 10 million times faster in the past compared to what it is today" (British journal *Astrophysics and Space Science* 139 (1987) 389-411, "Physical Constants and Evolution of the Universe").

Dr Troitskii work was preceded in a 1982 paper by Dr. Barry Setterfield of Australia, "The Velocity of Light and the Age of the Universe." In that paper he demonstrated that the measured speed of light has declined in a smooth curve for over 300 years. See setterfield.org on the web.

Where to go from here? What do you think?

It seems obvious to me that atomic time and actual Earth time are in some ways the same, or it is two different ways of measuring the same thing. In other words, the billions of years of atomic time all happened within the six thousand years of Earth time.

Harry, I'm using 'Earth time' to mean regular years, or the way we normally measure time. In that sense, we can definitely say that the Earth is not billions of years old.

This is marvelous, Harry! Now I know how to take it every time I'm told something is millions of years old. Those who say such things are not talking about Earth years, even if they think they are. This is so good.

I leaned back in my chair and let it sink in. Harry sensed it and left me alone with my thoughts. Again, a huge weight had been lifted from my mental shoulders. I had perceived science as a threat, and now Harry had again shown me that science was my friend. He hadn't been using any biblical language, and yet the truth was shining through. I was realizing how momentous this was.

Avi, let's describe the two views on the Earth's age, each in its own context.

The simple reading of the text in Genesis is that in the beginning the Creator brought forth matter and space and time, and then He worked on them for six days. The emphasis is on 'worked' because on the seventh day the Creator rested from all the work that He had done. Some people have tried to add additional time with a Gap Theory or say that the six days were not literal days. Their conception includes a satanic destruction imme- diately after the Creation, and the eons of time needed for all the life-forms to evolve. However, the text in Genesis reads easily and naturally that the Almighty worked on His Creation for six consecutive and literal days. I'm confident that's what the text means in Genesis chapter one. This is confirmed by scholars who have studied the ancient Hebrew, and specifically how the word 'day' is used in Genesis.[20]

I'll say this too, Avi. The Genesis text says and means six literal twenty-four hour days. Whether we believe or not that the work of Creation actually took six literal days is another subject, but no amount of lexical hoop jumping can change the meaning in Genesis or in Exodus 20:11. Day means day, and no longer period is implied by the text:

**For in six days YHWH made heaven and earth,
the sea, and all that in them is,**

---

20   See "A Defense of Literal Days in the Creation Week" by Robert V. Macabre, DBSJ 5 (Fall 2000): p 97-123 and available on the web. This paper is highly recommended by the author.

and rested the seventh day:
wherefore YHWH blessed the sabbath day, and set it apart.

Now balance that view with evolution when it is also described in simple terms. About 4.6 billion years ago, after the Earth had been formed by the converging of interstellar dust, the process of evolution began. As the Earth cooled from its molten state, it was bombarded by icy comets and an atmosphere was generated. Thereafter, the energy from volcanic activity, lightning and ultraviolet radiation caused chemical reactions that changed simple compounds such as methane and ammonia into more complex molecules. Beginning about 3.5 billion years ago, these complex molecules evolved into complex organisms such as bacteria. The earliest land plants evolved about 450 million years ago, animals about three hundred million years ago, upright walking apes about six million years ago, and finally humans about two million years ago. The mechanisms and processes that are involved in the evolution of life are unbelievably complex. Indeed, there is no real simple model of evolution other than to say it happened over a very long period.

Juxtapose those two explanations, Abraham. Which is easier to believe?

I can see where you're going on this, Harry. It's easier to believe that the heavens and the Earth were created in six literal days than it is to believe it just happened during billions of years through a process that defies any realistic explanation. Sometimes it's easier to believe in miracles.

That's right. Especially when the explanations come with so many unknowables, assumptions and fanciful conjectures, the explanations are themselves extremely doubtful, if not absurd. In the absence of genuine facts and hard evidence, it is easier to believe the account in Genesis.

I felt it before Harry finished. I felt affronted that something had been foisted on me by the duplicity of otherwise intelligent people. It's what I had been taught most of my life, and never encouraged to question. I was sure that some of my teachers had been knowingly and deliberately defying the belief in a Creator. There is an element – shared by many scientists, historians and educated men – of unbelief and defiance against the Biblical account of Creation. Their teaching has not always been innocent.

We've been lied to, Harry.

The bottom line is that much of human kind does not want to acknowledge a Creator or that we are created beings. The supposedly scientific mindset can be quite antagonistic. As one author said, "There is an active suppression of the truth going on to avoid an uncomfortable conclusion that we are responsible to our Creator."[21]

I nodded my head slowly. I was enjoying how interactive our conversation was becoming. I wanted it to continue.

Harry, I'm thinking that there must be some very compelling evidence that the Earth really is only thousands of years old and not billions. There has to be a realistic explanation if the billions of years are to make any sense. Those billions of years need a real context.

There certainly is evidence. Let's begin by talking about Bishop James Ussher (1581-1656). He deserves to be defended even if we don't accept that our Creator literally took six days to bring the Earth and humankind into being.

James Ussher is often made fun of by people who don't know he was one of the most highly educated and honored men of his time. He was by far not the only one to date the time of Creation from the chronologies in the book of Genesis. Bishop Ussher was preceded and followed by a long list of respected scholars such as Julius Africanus, Eusebius, the Venerable Bede, Maimonides, Joseph Scaliger,[22] Johannes Kepler, Isaac Newton and William Albright. The list is very long with most scholars dating the Creation to within fifty years of the year that Ussher is famous for, the year 4004 BC.[23]

Why are you bringing up Bishop Ussher?

Because he doesn't deserve to be maligned at all. The traditional view of Ussher is of a slightly unworldly scholar, at best a mediocre politician and administrator. In reality he was an effective bishop and archbishop, and politically well-connected. He was originally to be buried in the English town of Reigate, but at Cromwell's insistence he was given a state funeral and buried in Westminster Abbey. Ussher's date of 4004 BC continues to be accepted, and is the figure most often quoted. Modern scholars frequently confirm

21 Ross S. Olson MD, *Young Earth Creation: The Scientific Evidence*. Available on the Internet.
22 Most people are unaware that our commonly recognized and official historical dates are based on the biblical chronologies of Scaliger (1540-1609) and D. Petavius (1583-1652). They used the Bible as their basis for harmonizing the dates of world history from 3500 BC to 500 AD. Isaac Newton was against the chronology of Scaliger and Petavius, and published *The Chronology of Ancient Kingdoms Amended*, in which he re-dated key ancient events by shifting them several hundreds years forward. Many other scientists, philologists and historians have objected to the chronology of Scaliger and Petavius. But their biblically based chronology continues to be the basis for dating most historical events. It's a reality that most historians are unaware of or have chosen to ignore.
23 The major discrepancy is with those who use the *Septuagint* for their chronologies instead of the Masoretic text. The Septuagint chronologies are about 1500 years longer. The Septuagint's reliability has come into serious doubt in recent times, however. For example, the Septuagint has Methuselah living after the flood without being on the Ark.

Ussher's date.[24] No one should ever be ashamed of Ussher's legacy.

What evidence is there that the Earth is only a few thousand years old?

Abraham, the evidence is very convincing. There are other ways to measure the Earth's age that are much less technical, and yet still scientific. They confirm the biblical version of Creation with remarkable simplicity.

For example?

The most striking example is the layers in the walls of the Grand Canyon. We call those layers the geological column because they tell us about the Earth's physical structure and history. In the canyon, the layers are a witness against the very long ages that have been attributed to the Earth's history.

What is striking about the layers is that they show no signs of erosion. The layers are believed to result from the slow deposition of materials over tens to hundreds of millions of years, yet each layer is sharply distinct from the layers next to it, above and below. If those layers are separated by millions of years, they should have been distorted or even obliterated by erosion. The more reasonable explanation is that each layer was put down one after the other in rapid succession, so rapid that erosion could not take place. Therefore, the Grand Canyon is a witness to a very short period of time, and not to the millions of years that are attributed to the canyon's formation.

Avi, there is further contradictory evidence in the Grand Canyon. The layers prove that the geological column is a fiction. In the Grand Canyon there are Cambrian layers alternating with Mississippian layers. This could not have happened because those two strata are about three hundred million years apart. they alternate several times, with older layers on top of younger ones. There are also missing layers. There should be Ordovician and Silurian periods between the Cambrian and Mississippian periods. Those missing strata leave out two hundred million years of geological history. The same contradictory layering can be found in many other places in the world.

Similarly, there is evidence for rapid deposition in polystrate fossils.[25] Upright trees, thirty to fifty feet in height, extend through several geological layers lasting millions of years. Obviously, these trees did not remain standing for millions of years to be covered and fossilized. Such a phenomena clearly contradicts the idea of a gradually accumulated geologic column.

---

24 For example, Dr. Floyd Nolan Jones in his book, *The Chronology of the Old Testament*, 1993.
25 Polystrate means "many layers," and refers to fossils that cut through at least two layers of sedimentary-rock.

Avi, I'll talk more about the Grand Canyon again. There is much other evidence we need to examine.

For example, the Carbon-14 method has been used with great success in dating the Kennewick Man, Stonehenge, Hezekiah's Tunnel, the Dead Sea Scrolls, and even the Shroud of Turin. This is because carbon-14 has a short half-life, making it suitable for relatively recent dates. *Half-life* means organic matter will lose half its carbon-14 every 5730 years, and be 'carbon dead' after about a hundred thousand years.[26] Yet detectable levels of carbon-14 have been found in coal beds dating to nearly three hundred million years, and in diamonds dating to 1-2 billion years. Assuming the decay rate has always been the same, the Earth cannot be much older than 48,000 years based on coal, and 55,000 years based on diamonds. The amount of carbon-14 found in coal and diamonds indicates the Earth is much younger than 4.6 billion years.

By the way, Avi, many human artifacts have been found embedded in coal deposits. The most well-known are an iron pot, a gold chain, a ceramic spoon and a brass bell. Human bones and hand prints have also been found. Such articles are called OOPArt for "out of place artifacts." By the commonly accepted dates, there should be no human artifacts in coal seams that are 245 million to 290 million years old. OOPArt devastates the evolutional time-frame.

> There are other forms of OOPArt, and this is where it gets very interesting. Depictions of dinosaurs are frequently found in ancient artwork. The image on a Mesopotamian cylinder seal from approximately 3300 BC cannot be mistaken for anything other than a heavily bodied and long necked sauropod. The Nile Mosaic of Palestrina, dating to the first century BC, depicts Ethiopians pursuing what clearly appears to be a type of dinosaur. A carving found at the temple of Angkor Wat in Cambodia (200 AD) is recognizably a stegosaurus. There are dinosaur images in Shang Dynasty figurines, classical Greek vases, Roman mosaics, Mayan relief sculptures, and North American Anasazi and Havasupai petroglyphs. The conclusion: dinosaurs and humans were living together in the past. Dinosaurs did not become extinct sixty-five million years ago.[27]

---

26 After one half-life, half of the carbon-14 remains. After two half lives, a quarter is left. After three half lives, an eighth is left. After 10 half lives (50,730 years), less than a thousandth is left, and so on.

27 In a March 24, 2005 article, *National Geographic* reported, "A Tyrannosaurus rex fossil has yielded what appear to be the only preserved soft tissues ever recovered from a dinosaur. Taken from a 70-million-year-old thighbone, the structures look like the blood vessels, cells, and proteins involved in bone formation." No one can explain how living tissue can survive for 70 million years.

There are still more ways to measure the Earth's age. Many of them are easily under-stood and not highly technical. For example, oil and gas are found stored underground in relatively permeable rock. If these fluids had been trapped there for more than ten thousand years, the pressure that brings them to the surface would be far lower than it is today. Those pressures would have been dissipated by subterranean fissures and any porous neighboring strata. Oil and gas must have been trapped there only a few thousand years ago, and not sixty to six hundred million years according to radiometric dating.

Erosion rates are very well understood. The Himalayas are said to be eroding by about two hundred centimeters every thousand years. Mount Everest is thought to have been formed about sixty million years ago. However, even if the accepted erosion rate is too high and cut by half, that translates into at least sixty thousand vertical meters of erosion. That's enough time for Mt. Everest, with a current height of 8848 meters, to have been eroded thirteen times! The erosion that we do see on Mt. Everest indicates that the mountain chain was formed only a few thousand years ago.[28]

Scientists have accurately determined that the moon is moving away from the Earth at about four centimeters per year. By using standard scientific equations (taking into account that the force of gravity varies with distance), it can be shown that the moon is no more than 1.4 billion years old. That long ago, the moon and the Earth would have had to be in direct contact with each other in order to be as far apart as they are today. Obviously, the moon must be much younger than the standard equations suggest. To boot, any substantial difference in the Earth-moon distance from the present would have generated cataclysmic geophysical effects, most likely breaking the moon into pieces and circling the Earth with debris. The Earth-moon distance is very critical and cannot vary by much from its 384,430 kilometer average. Even in ten thousand years, the moon would recede from the Earth by less than one kilometer.[29]

There are so many ways to show that the Earth is young and only thousands of years old. Many are as simple as there being too little salt in the ocean, two few crater impacts on the Earth's surface, not enough stone-age skeletons, or that history is too short (how could two million years of human existence go by without any technological advance-ment, and then blossom in a few thousand years?). Some of the ways plainly show that the evolutionary time gap is non-existent. For example, the oldest known amber containing insects is, according to evolutionary dating, 146 million years old, but those

28 From *The Geological Column* by Sean D Pitman. Dr. Pitman's invaluable website can be found at detectingdesign.com.
29 There is something truly remarkable about the distances and sizes in the earth-sun-moon relationship. Their eclipses are nearly perfect. In a solar eclipse, the moon perfectly matches the apparent size of the sun. In a lunar eclipse, the shadow of the Earth perfectly matches the apparent size of the moon. The only explana-tion, realistically, is that they were designed that way.

insects reveal not the smallest change in their anatomical structures and are in every way identical to their modern counterparts. The same is true for the oldest feather, the oldest mushroom, the oldest small oak flower, the mosquito and biting black fly. Thus, tens of millions of years disappear as in a puff of smoke. The gap between the present and the past can only be thousands and not billions of years, realistically speaking.

Are we being realistic, Harry?

We are. Many scientists are not saying what they should be.

What do you mean?

They don't like to acknowledge their assumptions. If you enter a room and see an hour glass that's half full, there are a number of things you cannot assume. You can't assume when the last time the hour glass was turned, or if someone added or removed sand just before you entered the room. Nor can you assume that the sand has been seeping down at the same continuous rate. These kinds of assumptions are commonly made in atomic dating, but rarely acknowledged.

I looked over at my friend and was about to agree when I saw his deep pondering look. He was very much within himself, knowing something that was very troubling. I'd seen that look before when Happy Harry wasn't being happy. I held back and waited.

Scientists are coming around once again to the catastrophic nature of the Earth's history. The theory of **uniformitarianism** hasn't been supported by the evidence. That's why I want to talk about the Grand Canyon some more.

First, the Great Flood of the Scriptures can easily explain all the layers in the Canyon wall. It's easy to visualize how the twice daily tides with tidal wave after tidal wave sweeping the Earth could have laid down one layer after another in rapid succession. The waters spewing out from deep within the Earth's mantle, together with massive earthquakes and volcanic activity, would have caused immense turbidity currents and intense global vibrations. Moving water is a good medium for separating and sorting out particles of different sizes and composition. The layers would have settled out in a process known as **graded bedding**. The Great Flood is by far the best if not the only way to explain the layering in the walls of the Grand Canyon.

Second, geologists now say that the Grand Canyon was not formed by millions of years of erosion. At the current erosion rate, it would have taken only about 70,000 years for the Canyon to erode to its present form. Moreover, it is said that almost a thousand cubic miles of material has been eroded to form the Grand Canyon. Yet all that material has mysteriously disappeared. Most to the material that once filled the Canyon cannot be found within its vicinity. Erosion cannot explain how the Grand Canyon was etched into the Earth's surface.

One of the more recent explanations for the Grand Canyon's formation is through a process known as electrical arc scarring. Electrical *plasma* is another form of matter – aside from solids, liquids and gasses – that fills the universe. Electrical events in the plasma-filled universe can explain many of the land forms found on the Earth, moon, planets and planetary moons. Sinuous channels and neatly circular craters with steep walls can be explained as the results of arc scarring. That is why the Grand Canyon and its tributary canyons are so strikingly similar to the gigantic canyons of Valles Marineris on Mars. On both Earth and Mars, the canyons seem to have been cut cleanly into a raised flat surface with little damage to the surrounding area and no leftover debris. Bolts of lightning often cause similar damage on a much smaller scale. Electrical discharges in space, however, happen on a vastly larger scale. The Grand Canyon is one example of an unusually large catastrophic electrical event happening on the Earth.[30]

Harry stopped and looked at me. I anticipated what he was going to say.

This topic always leaves me with the deepest concern. Do you know why I find it so troubling, Abraham?

We're not talking about geological events over eons of time, are we, Harry? We're talking about the Earth as the place where humankind has been dwelling for the last six millennia.

That's right. All of these geological events happened within the span of human history. They have to do with humankind's past and future welfare.

Catastrophes are not random events, are they?

That's exactly the point. The Creator of Heaven and Earth allowed the Great Flood as the natural consequence of human wickedness when there was no longer an alternative. All humankind, accept Noah and his family, had gone beyond their allotted time for repentance, with ample warning.

---

30 Another example on the Earth is a canyon with its tributaries on Devon Island in the high Canadian arctic. The famous Meteor Crater in Arizona may be another since no meteor debris has ever been found. Other examples in outer space are the rilles on the Moon and Venus, and the electrically active Io, one of Jupiter's moons.

Harry, we're not talking about billions of years either.

No. All the talk about billions of years is a smoke screen to avoid the consequence of our actions. Humankind doesn't have billions of years to repent. The time is short.

There was pause before he continued.

Let's be honest about what we see in the geological column or in all those layers in the Grand Canyon walls. What we actually see is the worldwide destruction of innumerable species, both plant and animal. Evolutionists want to see a record of life evolving when the record only shows death. The Grand Canyon was ripped out of the Earth by a titanic cosmic or extraterrestrial force. That catastrophe and the Great Flood happened suddenly and over a short period. What we see in the Earth's geology is not a promise of life, but rather a vivid and unmistakable warning.

Avi, our everlasting Father has promised to never again destroy the Earth with another flood. The prophets, however, have made it very clear that another day of wrath is coming. We're going to talk about this soon, but let's not miss the obvious. We have been forewarned about the events still coming that will be catastrophic in nature and effect all of humankind. Indeed, every living human being.

Uncharacteristically, Harry did not pause for effect.

Abraham, the next time someone tells you the Earth is 4.6 billion years old, what will your response be?

I'm going to reply that those are atomic years, not calendar years.

That will do it. There's no way we can know if the atomic clock has always been ticking at the same rate. It's more likely that time has been stretched out in the process of Creation. Real history is measured in only thousands of years.

I have a straightforward question, Harry. Do you believe that the Earth was created in 4004 BC?

Harry looked at me with unusual appreciation.

Do you want me to be more definitive?

Yes.

Good, Abraham. I won't disappoint you.

First, I'll say this: the year 4004 BC is reasonably accurate for the history of human-kind. It fits with the facts of history as far as we know. Real history with language, written records, tangible artifacts, and manmade structures began about that time. Not long after came social conventions, trade and commerce, political institutions and empire building. It's pretty clear from most of the archaeological records that the history of human beings began around six thousand years ago or around the year 4004 BC.

It's not much of a problem when radio-carbon testing shows that ancient cities like Jericho and Catal Huyuk in Turkey were first settled in 8000 BC or earlier. It's a forgone conclusion that the radio-carbon dates are too long and need to be shortened for per-fectly valid scientific reasons. On the other hand, the genealogical records in Genesis may be deficient. There could be generations missing in those chronologies. Remember, not all biblicists have arrived at the same figure of 4004 BC. In any event, the different between ten thousand years and of six thousand years isn't material, at least in my mind. I'm not going to quibble over a few thousand years as far the history of humankind is concerned.

Here's the real issue: the year 4004 BC is relevant for the history of the Earth too. We've discussed some of the reasons for a recent Creation, and I'll give you two more. We know with considerable certainty that all the major life forms – animals especially – came into being at one time. Scientists call this phenomena the Cambrian Explosion. All life forms are utterly complex, even a simple cell, and yet they appear suddenly and whole in the geological record. The same goes if we look into the heavens. Globular clusters are considered to be among the oldest of all the astronomical objects, and yet they are perfectly spherical and sparkling clean as if they were created only yesterday. They have not been distorted by our galaxy's powerful gravity, nor have they accumulated any inter-stellar dust and debris. There are just too many indications that the Earth is only a few thousand years old, and not billions.

Listen up, Avi. We're taking about the difference between Creation and evolution. Evolution takes a very, very long time, but Creation does not. In the biblical record, the Almighty only spoke and it came to be. The act of Creation was apparently not bounded by time, and that's the important distinction. Even if the six days are allegorical, even if the year 4004 BC is only approximate, and even if the Earth is a few thousand years older according to the radio-carbon dates, none of that undermines the biblical account. Creation does not entail long eons of time.

For the record, I have no serious objection to Ussher's year of 4004 BC. We shouldn't be the least bit embarrassed by the biblical account of how the Earth and humankind came to be. So let's not be ashamed about it. Truly, it's the so-called science of evolution that is laughable, and its proponents who should be embarrassed.

Harry put his head back with his hand under his chin. After a moment of reflection he continued.

This isn't far-fetched. A respected solar scientist named John A. Eddy once wrote – I can remember it quite well – "given some new and unexpected results... and some time for frantic readjustment, I suspect that we could live with Bishop Ussher's value for the age of the Earth and Sun."[31]

Is that definitive enough for you, Avi?

I waited a bit, too.

Yes, but I am surprised. Believers have been laughed at for a long time on this matter with considerable effect. Maybe we should be responding in kind. To make fun of someone is not the answer, though. Thanks, Harry. You're a brave man. What are we going to talk about on the next Sabbath?

Well my friend, we are going to talk about such a fundamental issue that you may not want to come by again. I want to talk about – using the vernacular – that 'Jesus was not God.' Are you interested?

Harry looked at me so solidly that I wanted to start immediately. I wasn't in the least put off.

See you next Sabbath, Harry, and may the Eternal One be with you.

And with you, Abraham.

---

31 See *Vital Questions* by Philip Stott, p 107. It's an exceptionally good book to read.

7. JESUS WAS NOT GOD

The next Sabbath began with a slow drizzling rain, so Harry ushered me into his library and study room. He motioned me to one of the two comfortable chairs. It was so different from being outside in the garden. I felt confined.

I took the chair next to the window, in close proximity to Harry's desk chair with the teapot nearby. As soon as Harry sat down, I felt free again. The room seemed to have a vindicating energy to it. I felt Harry's presence and equally my own.

Harry poured the tea and started in his easy and unobtrusive manner.

Avi, if you and I were sitting with the Messiah and his disciples on the shore of the Sea of Galilee, we would be feeling just as we are feeling now. Nothing would ever have made us think that Yeshuah wasn't a man like ourselves, and we would be able to talk to him just as we are talking to each other right now.

There was no physical quality that distinguished Yeshuah from other men. Isaiah leaves us with the impression that he was not a handsome man or a man of exceptional stature.[1] The prophet said that Yeshuah had no stately form or majesty, suggesting that he was not physically attractive.[2]

Nor did Yeshuah make any exceptional claims for himself. He never said or ever reminded his disciples that his mother was still a virgin when he was born. Indeed, he acknowledged his birth mother along with his brothers and sisters. Some knew Yeshuah

---

1   In the Hebrew Scriptures, exceptional human size and strength are associated with spiritual weaknesses. The examples are Samson, Saul and Goliath. The Nephilim of Genesis 6 and Numbers 13 were also 'giants' or men of stature and renown. They were human beings nevertheless, and not the result of angels having sex with mortals, something that is impossible.

2   He grew up before Him like a tender shoot, and like a root out of parched ground; he has no stately form or majesty that we should look upon him, nor appearance that we should be attracted to Him (Isaiah 53:2).

as the son of a carpenter,[3] but at no time did Yeshuah ever correct the public perception of his birth and family background, or say that he didn't have a human father.

Abraham, let's deal with the second great lie in the Bible. Do you remember how I told you that I've found three of them?

Yes, the first was when the serpent told Eve that she would definitely not die if she ate from the fruit of the tree of the knowledge of good and evil. This was just after the Almighty One had said to Adam, "In the day that you eat of it you shall definitely die." What the serpent told Eve was a blatant lie.

Thank you, Avi. The three great lies were primordial. By primordial, I mean that they are all found in the serpent's statement in the paradise of Eden: "You shall certainly not die. For the Almighty One knows that in the day you eat of it your eyes shall be opened, and you shall be like the Almighty One, knowing good and evil."

In summary, the three lies are:

You shall not die.

You shall be like the Almighty.

You shall know (the difference between) good and evil.

The second great lie in the Bible is that Adam would be like the Almighty if he ate fruit from the forbidden tree. Adam was in for a rude awakening. When his eyes were opened, he discovered he was naked, vulnerable and mortal. He was ashamed of what he had done, and tried to hide himself from his Creator. He wasn't anything like the Almighty in his newfound awareness of himself.

Okay, so then let's jump forward about four thousand years to an incident recorded in the Good News of John. There we read, "The Jews answered him, 'For a good work we do not stone you, but for blasphemy; and because you, being a man, make yourself out to be the Almighty One.'"[4]

Here's an aside, Avi. Whoever wrote this book – and it wasn't John the disciple – was voicing his own anti-Semitism. This so-called 'gospel' was the last to be written, and the

3   It is highly unlikely that Yeshuah or his father was a carpenter. The Greek word for carpenter in the *New Testament* may be an Aramaic term that is used metaphorically in the Talmud to denote a scholar (Porter, 2004, p 81). Yeshuah was certainly a very literate man, and indications are that he was fluent in Greek.
4   John 10:33.

author was surely a Gentile. Accordingly, in this passage, Yeshuah was addressing the entire nation, and not specifically the Pharisees. We don't find such a polemic against the Jews in the earlier books of Matthew, Mark and Luke. It is evident from John's gospel that the Gentiles were starting to distance themselves from the Jews and condemning them as a nation.[5]

The Pharisees (some of them) were accusing Yeshuah of making himself out to be the Almighty One. In the common vernacular, 'Jesus was claiming to be God,' or that's what the Pharisees said he was doing. The scribes and Pharisees were often at odds with Yeshuah's teaching. In response, Yeshuah never minced words. He rebuked them with,

You are of your father the devil, and you want to do the desires of your father.
He was a murderer from the beginning, and does not stand in the truth because there is no truth in him.
Whenever he speaks a lie, he speaks from his own nature, for he is a liar and the father of lies.

Yeshuah left no doubt that the Pharisees could not be trusted. With an unconcealed vigor, he deplored their lying disposition – there was no truth in whatever the Pharisees said – including that he was making himself out to be the Eternal One.

It was a lie! Yeshuah could never have done anything like that! Who are we going to believe, Yeshuah or the Pharisees? Or perhaps the serpent who said that Adam would be like the Almighty if he ate from the tree of the knowledge of good and evil? Sadly, many people continue to believe that what the Pharisees were saying was true, that Yeshuah was truly claiming to be the Almighty himself.[6][7]

My friend Abraham, let's back up a bit. Do you think our Father wants us to be sensible, sound minded and reasonable?

That sounds trite, but yes, I do.

---

5   Dr A. Roy Eckardt was a leading scholar and pioneer in the field of Jewish-Christian relations. He contended that the **New Testament** provided a bedrock for antisemitism and ultimately for the Holocaust. Eckardt insisted that Christian repentance must include a re-examination of basic theological attitudes toward Jews and the **New Testament** in order to deal effectively with antisemitism.

6   Yeshuah never called himself the I AM. Modern day translators (modern day Pharisees) have deliberately capitalized the words to make them sound orthodox. They are compounding the same lie.

7   "It is the temper of the hot and superstitious part of mankind in matters of religion ever to be fond of mysteries, and for that reason to like best what they understand least" (Sir Isaac Newton).

I felt miffed at my friend's presumptive question.

Does that include being rational?

Who would want to disagree?

How about logical?

I swallowed my pride.

I see what you're getting at, Harry. Yes, logical too.

Thank you, Avi. There is nothing irrational or illogical about real faith. I believe in miracles because it's perfectly reasonable that the Almighty has absolute authority over what He created. He can stop the sun, make an axe float or raise the dead. Believing that He has such power is entirely reasonable, and it doesn't contradict what our minds tell us.

I understand you, Harry. It's irrational to believe that the Eternal One took on human form or became human Himself. That's logically impossible.

Exactly, The Creator of All can never be hungry, tired or weak. Those are the qualities of being human. Logically speaking, an infinite being can never be finite.[8]

Okay, Harry, but why can't the Almighty be irrational?

Because, Avi, our Almighty Father invites us to be rational with Him:

> **Come now, and let us reason together, saith YHWH:**
> **though your sins be as scarlet, they shall be as white as snow;**
> **though they be red like crimson, they shall be as wool.**[9]

In a way, the Almighty limits Himself to the same standard of what's reasonable. He wants us to be rational beings and promises in return to be rational with us. In other words, He won't be paradoxical, or be both Himself and a human being at the same time. We can count on Him being the Eternal One at all times. Therefore, we can reason with Him, which is what He invites us to do.

---

8   "Do you not know? Have you not heard? The everlasting Mighty One, YHWH, the Creator of the ends of the Earth, does not become weary or tired" (Isa 40:28). This verse by itself finalizes that Yeshuah was not the Almighty One.
9   Isaiah 1:18.

Why are you making this point?

Because the Almighty Creator has made us with the ability to be reasonable. He has given us the capacity to be rational and logical.[10]

What you are getting at Harry, is that we shouldn't believe things that are unreasonable or logically impossible.

That's right, Abraham. At one time in my life, I decided to trust my own mind and not go beyond what I can logically understand.

Including not believing that Jesus was God?

Yes.

I leaned back in my comfortable chair and looked outside. The drizzling rain had become a steady downpour. I started thinking how good it was that it was raining. I felt thankful, and my mind drifted along with a sense of well-being. My mind was at peace.

Avi?

It took me a while before I could respond.

Yes, Harry.

Let's examine the history once again. Not everything is as cut and dry as it seems to be from our vantage point nearly two thousand years later. In the first three centuries of what we call Christianity today, there were any number of different Christian groups and competing theologies, not one of which represented a majority. Commonly, Christians with radically different persuasions were actively involved in the life and worship of the same congregation. From the beginning, Christianity was remarkably varied in its beliefs and practices.

One competing theology came to be known as *Adoptionism.* In simple terms, adoptionists believe that Yeshuah was a flesh and blood human who had an earthly father

---

10   Martin Luther disdained the use of reason and thought it hindered a believer's faith. "Reason is the greatest enemy that faith has; it never comes to the aid of spiritual things, but - more frequently than not - struggles against the divine Word, treating with contempt all that emanates from God." Church leaders have typically disdained reason, but not for themselves. They fear that reason will liberate the laity from the authority of the Church.

and mother just like any other human being. In the classical definition, he was a human being *without remainder*. The 'without remainder' means that Yeshuah was a man and nothing more; he was *only* a human being. Adoptionists reject the belief that Yeshuah was the son of God from his birth or that he preexisted as a non-created being. Yeshuah's life began at conception, and he only became the son of the Most High by adoption when the Almighty chose him to be His son.[11]

The actual moment of Yeshuah's adoption was at his baptism when a voice from Heaven was heard to say,

Thou art My Son: this day have I begotten Thee.

Here's the hard part Avi, or should I say the easy part. That version of Luke 3:22 can no longer be found in nearly every modern translation. Almost all say, "Thou art my beloved Son; with thee I am well pleased." And yet, "This day have I begotten Thee" is ubiquitous in the ancient texts. It is quoted by the church fathers innumerable times. A footnote in the Revised Standard Version acknowledges the "other ancient authorities," and those are the words of Psalm 2:7:

YHWH said unto me, Thou art my son;
This day have I begotten thee.

It's easy to corroborate. I can quote one of our more celebrated modern scholars, Bart D. Ehrman:

> For this reading ("You are me, beloved Son, in whom I am well pleased.") constitutes a mere identification formula in which Jesus is recognized as the Son of God. It is only in the variant reading, **the one that is attested in virtually all the earliest witnesses**, that God is actually said to confer a new status upon Jesus ("Today I have begotten you"). Only in the theologically difficult reading is God said to "elect" Jesus... through a quotation of t**he royal adoption formula drawn from the second Psalm**.[12] [13]

---

11 The Ebionites were early adoptionists probably dating from some time after the destruction of the Temple in 70 AD. "They regard [Yeshuah] as plain and ordinary, a man esteemed as righteous through growth of character and nothing more, the child of a normal union between a man and Mary (Eusebius, *Ecclesiastical History,* Book 3, p 27).

12 *The Orthodox Corruption of Scripture,* p 66.

13 Ehrman goes on to say, "Among sources of the second and third centuries, it is virtually the only reading to be found; down to the sixth century.... The best attested reading of the early period, a reading known throughout the entire Christian world, virtually disappears from sight, displaced by a reading that is, as we shall see, both harmonized to that of another Gospel and less offensive doctrinally." The reading Ehrman is

The hard part is accepting that Yeshuah only became the son of the Almighty Father at the time of his baptism. Before that, Yeshuah had no special status. As Ehrman says, this is the more "theologically difficult reading."

Abraham, I'm going to quote more from Ehrman. Whatever we may think about modern scholars and their personal beliefs, what they say can still be objective and accurate. There is also a surprising unanimity in biblical scholarship. Few would entirely disagree with Ehrman:

> Together, these texts presuppose that at baptism *God actually did something to Jesus*. This something is sometimes described as an act of anointing, sometimes as an election [and sometimes as adoption]. In either case, the action of God is taken to signify his "making" Jesus the Christ. These texts, therefore, show that Luke did not conceive of the baptism as the point at which Jesus was simply "declared" or "identified" or "affirmed" to be the Son of God. The baptism was the point at which Jesus was anointed as the Christ, chosen to be the Son of God.

> ...Given Luke's indication elsewhere (Acts 4:25-26) that the text of Psalm 2 particularly applies to Jesus' anointing, it should now be clear that the voice in his account actually quoted these words as a proclamation of *the momentous election of Jesus as the begotten Son of God* at this, the beginning of his ministry. (*emphasis added*).[14]

Mainstream Christians rightly understand the earlier text of Matthew 3:17 as a threat to the seventeen hundred year old tradition that Yeshuah was more than just a man. Therefore, virtually all modern English translations of Matthew 3:17 are based on manuscripts of the third and fourth centuries, which read, "You are my beloved Son; with you I am well pleased." Still, the earlier texts read, "this day I have begotten you." One example is in Justin Martyr's quotation of Matthew 3:17 written in 142 AD: "You are My Son: this day have I begotten you." Some fifty years earlier, Saint Clement of Rome used the same wording in his *First Epistle to the Corinthians*. Many other documents confirm the original reading as, "this day I have begotten you." The phrase was used more frequently than not during the first four centuries of the Christian era. The fact that "this day I have begotten you" is hardly ever used in modern translations demonstrates how serious the threat is to mainstream Christianity and its traditions.

---

referring to is "Today I have begotten you," the reading which offends the orthodoxy of 'Jesus being God.' See pages 62-63.

14 *The Orthodox Corruption of Scripture*, p 67.

Harry put his hands on his lap and looked at me with unmistakable pleasure, or was it even merriment? Was Harry actually laughing?

It's funny, Abraham, how the most easily understood texts are ignored for the sake of the more difficult ones. There can be no mistaking the texts that plainly say Yeshuah was a man with human parents, although some of them have been altered. Twice Joseph is called Yeshuah's father in Luke 2:33 and 48. Significantly, in 48, it is Mary herself who calls Joseph the father of Yeshuah. In Luke 4:22 he is called Joseph's son. In John 6:42, he is "the son of Joseph" with the additional insight about Yeshuah, "whose father and mother we know." Again, there can be no mistake about the meaning of the texts – that Joseph and Mary were Yeshuah's biological parents. It is not surprising therefore (quoting Ehrman),

> In virtually every instance in which Joseph is called Jesus' father or parent, various scribes have changed the text in such a way as to obviate the possibilities of misconstrual.[15]

Of course, trinitarians everywhere will also insist the Yeshuah was entirely human. That's not an issue. What is at issue is whether or not Yeshuah was born as all other humans are from the sexual relationship of a man and a woman. Yet that is what the Christian Scriptures tell us when we take the numerous inferences at face value. No amount of textual changes can ever eliminate the unadorned and no-nonsense statements about Yeshuah's parents. Yeshuah had a father and mother just like every else.

The question can still be asked: What made Yeshuah different or unique? The answer has already been given in the text of Luke 3:22: Yeshuah was chosen by the Almighty Father to be His son. In that sense, Yeshuah was adopted by the Almighty for a special relationship and purpose. Therefore, we need to understand what really happened at Yeshuah's baptism.

In a word, Yeshuah was anointed at his baptism in the Jordan river. According to the texts, the spirit of the Almighty came down upon him in the form of a dove. Happily, we have Yeshuah's own description of the event and its purpose:

The spirit of YHWH the Almighty is upon me,
Because he anointed me to preach good tidings to the poor:
He has sent me to proclaim release to the captives,
And recovering of sight to the blind,

---

15 *The Orthodox Corruption of Scripture*, p 58. For example: "One important but fragmentary Greek witness of the fifth century and two Old Latin manuscripts read "Your relatives and I have been grieved"; while a number of ancient versional witnesses read simply "We have been grieved..."" p 56.

To set at liberty those that are bruised,
To proclaim the acceptable year of YHWH.
And he closed the book, and gave it back to the attendant,
and sat down: and the eyes of all in the synagogue were fastened on him.
And he began to say to them,
Today this scripture has been fulfilled in your ears.

According to Peter's confession of faith, Yeshuah was the Messiah, the anointed of the Almighty Father, the one appointed to be the savior of his people, and by extension the savior of the all the nations. It was for this purpose that the spirit of the Almighty Father came upon Yeshuah. It was through the anointing he had received at baptism that Yeshuah was able to perform the duties of his ministry. Certainly, no human being could have done what Yeshuah did without receiving from the Almighty the power to be the Messiah. As Peter said in Acts 10:

Beginning from Galilee,
after the baptism which John preached;
even Jesus of Nazareth,
how the Almighty anointed him with the... Spirit and with power:
who went about doing good, and healing all that were
oppressed of the devil; for the Almighty was with him.

Notice the phrase, "how the Almighty anointed him." That phrase is reinforced by other designations. In Luke 23:35, Yeshuah is acknowledged as the "anointed" and the "elect." In Luke's account of the transfiguration, the phrase is, "This is My son, My chosen." Some manuscripts read, "My son, the one who has been chosen." Notice also how a man was appointed in Peter's first sermon.

The Almighty One is now declaring to men
that all people everywhere should repent,
because He has fixed a day in which He will judge the world in righteous-
ness through a man whom He has appointed,
having furnished proof to all men by raising Him from the dead.[16]

Putting all the pieces together: The Eternal One appointed one particular man to be the Messiah, a man born physically by a woman; a man who when He raised him from the dead became an immortal being. That particular man was Yeshuah, from the tribe of Judah and the seed of David. Those fundamental realities are conveyed in the Christian Scriptures.

---

16 Acts 17: 30-31.

Harry opened a Bible and carefully read.

Which He promised beforehand... concerning his Son,
who was born of the seed of David according to the flesh,
who was declared to be the son of The Almighty One with power...
by the resurrection from the dead;
even Yeshuah the Messiah our Master.[17]

But now has been revealed by the appearing of our Savior,
Yeshuah the Messiah,
who has abolished death
and brought life and immortality to light.[18]

For this corruptible must put on incorruption,
and this mortal must put on immortality.[19]

That about sums it up.

A subtle but inwardly powerful change came into my peaceful reverie. I intuitively felt that Yeshuah had been a mortal man, as mortal as any other. Now in my mind, inscrutably, Yeshuah had become an immortal being. Truly, a mortal had been given eternal life.

I felt it well up from within me – the reality of the resurrection – that a human being had been raised from the dead.

Something is coming into my mind, Harry, or already has.

I paused before continuing.

It's the perception that a man can also be immortal. It's more than a perception, though; it's a reality.

May I add to that, Avi?

Sure.

---

17 Romans 1: 2-4.
18 2 Timothy 1:10.
19 1 Corinthians 15:53.

It's not just your perception. It's an awareness that has affected the consciousness of the entire human race. The thought of a man being raised from the dead has affected the minds of believers and unbelievers alike. It has not gone unnoticed. It's a reality imprinted on the world's consciousness.

That's a mouthful, Harry.

We all know the story of how a spirit that came from above fell on the disciples on the day of Pentecost in the book of Acts. That spirit came with the sound of a mighty wind and as tongues of fire. On that day there were present in Jerusalem, men from every nation and language on the Earth. Amazingly, all of them understood when Kepha got up and explained:

> **Men of Israel, hear these words: Yeshuah of Nazareth,**
> **a man approved of by The Almighty One to you**
> **by mighty works and wonders and signs**
> **which The Almighty One did by him in the midst of you,**
> **even as you yourselves know...**
> **whom The Almighty One raised up, having loosed the pangs of death:**
> **because it was not possible that he should be held by it.[20]**

Therein is the Good News in a few words. The Almighty Father had demonstrated His approval of Yeshuah – a mortal human being – by many miracles during his ministry, and when Yeshuah was put to death, the Creator confirmed His approval by raising him from the dead.

Here's the point I want to make. The outpouring of the Almighty's spirit in the book of Acts imparted a new reality into the minds and hearts of all those who have believed Kepha's message – past, present and future. The new spiritual reality is that Yeshuah became an immortal being. Even unbelievers have been affected by the new reality.

Abraham, the way I see it, we have two witnesses to our consciousness. The first is in what we call the Scriptures. The second is the witness that comes from within our own being. The Hebrew Scriptures are a record, in written words, of our experiences with the Eternal One, the Everlasting Father. The witness of Yeshuah the Messiah's resurrection, however, comes from within ourselves. This is what Yeshuah meant when he said:

> **But when the Comforter is come, whom I will send unto you from the**
> **Father, even the Spirit of truth, which proceeds from the Father,**

---

20 Acts 2:22,24. Notice again the expression "a **man** approved of by The Almighty One."

he shall bear witness of me.[21]

Harry then left me alone with my thoughts. It kept coming to me, over and over, that a flesh and blood man had been raised from the dead and made to be immortal. I breathed it in. If one person can be raised, then so can others. The thought was more than a comfort. It was filled with hope.

Harry, why do people want to believe that Yeshuah was 'God'?

Avi, there's such a range to the answer. It goes all the way from familiarity to excommunication. Certainly if something is repeated often enough, it's eventually taken for granted. In between there's peer pressure and fear of the unknown. No one wants to be different in their group or thought of as a heretic. Any overt denial of 'Jesus as God in human form' would be roundly censured by the Church. Worse yet, the denier would be condemned to purgatory or hell fire.

History and tradition are very powerful. The hypothesis that Almighty Father has incarnated Himself into a human being resulted in the doctrine of the Trinity. Using some very obscure language, the Council of Nicea in 325 AD declared that the Son was *consubstantial* with the Father. In 381, the Council of Constantinople affirmed the deity of the 'Holy Spirit.' Thereafter, all who rejected the Trinity were denounced as heretics. One historian has put it this way:

> The mystery of the Holy Trinity is the most fundamental of our faith. On it everything else depends and from it everything else derives. Hence, the Church's constant concern to safeguard the revealed truth that God is One in nature and Three in Persons.[22]

The same author goes onto say, "Minds that are not fully docile to the faith have, in greater or less measure, resisted the unquestioning acceptance of the Trinity." By that statement, it is readily seen that the orthodox church relies on the mindless naivety of its followers to maintain its doctrine of the Trinity. The above author even admits there is a certain logic against the Trinity, but repeats the age-old subterfuge that the human mind cannot comprehend the "mystery of the Triune God." The vast majority of Church's membership have not resisted its subterfuge.

In the end, it's because our traditions are very powerful and the desire to resist them equally weak. No one wants to be the odd man out, including those who lead – especially those who lead! Few of us have the willingness to question tradition, and even fewer the

21 John 15:26.
22 *Catholic Doctrine on the Holy Trinity* by Fr. John A. Hardon, S.J..

courage. We go right on believing that the Eternal One incarnated Himself because that's what we want to believe. The deception comes very easily. It's something the Christian church continues to take advantage of – or should I say, take advantage of us.

Thank you, Harry. It seems to me that the Church has had an easy time of it, bamboozling its followers with a lot of mystical and irrational language. Its leaders, too. You can't justify believing in something that doesn't make any sense by claiming it's a mystery too deep to understand. That's just another way of telling people not to think for themselves.

That's right.

Okay, so what's another reason for believing that Yeshuah was an incarnated being – that he came down from Heaven?

There's a more concrete reason for believing in the Trinity, Pre-existence, and Incarnation.[23] I believe the basis for those doctrines can actually be found within the Christian Scriptures. It took me a long time to admit this to myself.

How so?

For a long time I defended the more difficult passages by interpreting them in a non-Trinitarian way.[24] I tried to show that the English translators were biased or that certain expressions had been added to the original Greek texts. Those difficult texts have a degree of ambiguity, so I was fairly successful in convincing myself that the Christian Scriptures do not support the doctrine of Yeshuah's divinity or his pre-existence.

Did that change, Harry?

Yes. Whether I like it or not, certain passages in the Christian Scriptures are undeniably Trinitarian. So the question is, how did the belief in Yeshuah as a divine being find its way into the Christian Scriptures? Well, it turns out that it's not such a big mystery at all. The simple answer is that the scribes who preserved the Greek texts put their embryonic beliefs into the texts. I say 'embryonic' because the full-blown Doctrine of the Trinity took several centuries to develop into its present form.

---

23 The doctrine of Pre-existence is the belief that 'Christ' always existed along with the other two members of the Trinity. In other words, there was a pre-incarnate 'Christ' who took on human form at his physical birth. Before that, he existed in heaven along with the other two members of the Trinity. That's Church doctrine since 325 AD. Opposing groups and individuals have long maintained that Yeshuah's existence began at conception in the same manner as all other human beings.

24 The main 'difficult' texts are John 1:1-3, Colossians 1:15-20 and Philippians 2:5-11. Each of them have been subjected to judicious editing, translation and interpretation.

That's also the view of some of our most respected biblical scholars. Here's how Bart Ehrman said it:

> Did the scribes' polemical contexts influence the way they transcribed their sacred Scriptures? The burden of the present study is that they did, that theological disputes, specifically disputes over Christology, prompted Christian scribes to alter the words of Scripture in order to make them more serviceable for the polemical task. *Scribes modified their manuscripts to make them more patently "orthodox"* and less susceptible to "abuse" by the opponents of orthodoxy. (*emphasis added*).[25]

Elsewhere, Ehrman said it even better:

> And so, as we will now see, *they altered passages that might suggest that Jesus had a human father,* or that he came into existence at his birth, or that he was adopted to be the Son of God at his baptism. *They changed other passages to accentuate their own views that Jesus was divine,* that he pre-existed, and that his mother was a virgin. (*emphasis added*).[26]

Let's keep in mind that we no longer have the original Greek texts, the texts that we call 'autographs.' Those autographs may well have been lost or destroyed before the second century. It's well known that most of the Greek manuscripts actually date from the fourth century and beyond. That leaves more than two hundred years of transition between the original autographs and the emerging orthodoxy of the fourth century, the century that included the First Council of Nicea in 325 AD. "This was also a period in which various Christian groups were actively engaged in internecine conflicts, particularly over Christology."[27] What emerged was a 'Jesus' who was also 'God.'

Subsequent translators followed suit. There's no grammatical reason for the capitalization and personification of the word *Logos* in the opening verses of John. The only reason it's done, to quote Ehrman, is to make the translated texts "more patently "orthodox" and less susceptible to "abuse" by the opponents of orthodoxy." There's really no argument: the doctrines of the Trinity, Incarnation and Pre-existence are repeatedly supported by virtually every modern English translation. The opening verses of John are only one example among many.

---

25 Bart D. Ehrman, *The Orthodox Corruption of Scripture: The Effect of Early Christological Controversies on the Text of the New Testament,* Oxford University Press, 1993, p 3.
26 *The Orthodox Corruption of Scripture,* p 54.
27 *The Orthodox Corruption of Scripture,* p 27, 28 and 29 respectively.

However, I would be quick to add that the doctrine of the Trinity is nowhere clearly enunciated in the Gentile Scriptures. Nor was the full-blown doctrine of the Trinity in the minds of the scribes who copied and preserved the Greek manuscripts. Neither was the future doctrine of the Trinity anticipated by the original authors of the Gentile Scriptures – Paul and John for example. The doctrine of the Trinity, and its corollary doctrines, are historical developments that evolved over many centuries. We absolutely can't find them fully developed and explicit in the Christian Scriptures.

That's a fact. Here's a quotation from one author. I could easily quote a hundred more saying the same thing:

> What most Trinitarian scholars themselves normally recognize: namely, that the actual doctrine itself – as it is defined by the historic ecumenical creeds – is not one that is directly or formally taught to us in the Bible.[28]

It's striking that Yeshuah's mother, brothers and sisters, and his disciples never discuss or even mention Yeshuah's miraculous birth. We don't hear of it in the books written by John, Peter, James and Jude. Paul too explicitly says that Yeshuah was born of a woman and of the seed of David according to the flesh. Yeshuah never refers to his supernatural birth himself. One would think that if it really was true, Yeshuah and his disciples would have shouted it from the roof tops.

Also conspicuously absent is any claim coming from Yeshuah that he was the creator of the world, yet that is what several passages would have us believe. The most notable example is at the beginning of John where the world was created by the *logos* or some being other than the Almighty Father. Colossians 1:16 even says "for by him (Yeshuah) were all things created," or so it seems according to how the passages have been preserved and translated. Again, if Yeshuah really did create all things, he surely would have said it himself in a way that was unmistakable. All false modesty aside, he surely would have told his followers the truth.

The Hebrew Scriptures, however, tell us that the Eternal One created everything by Himself, and that He was alone when He did it.

**I am YHWH that made all things;
that stretched out the heavens alone;
that spread abroad the earth by Myself.**[29]

---

28   Patrick Navas, *Divine Truth or Human Tradition?*, Author House, 2007, p 4.
29   Isaiah 44:24.

I can conclude, therefore, that most of our modern translators, and the scribes who copied the Greek manuscripts, and the original authors of the texts, all brought their incarnational predilections with them as the Christian Scriptures took shape. Therefore, even if the Incarnation is not clearly enunciated in the Christian Scriptures, the doctrine is still there in its embryonic form.

Avi, two Sabbaths ago we talked about the tendency for certain cultures to deify their heroes in explaining their unusual greatness. The Greeks and the Romans did it frequently. The Hebrews had no conception of a god-man, but for the Gentiles the concept came naturally. We'll talk more about this at another time.

Well then, Harry, the Christian church was merely recycling an almost universal conception that a human can also be a god. That's the Gentile mind-set.

Yes. Bear this in mind. It's the first commandment of the Ten, that the Hebrews should have no other gods but their own Eternal One. They were strictly commanded not make idols and images to worship.

Harry, would you say that Jesus has become an idol?

Yes, I would. To demonstrate, I'd like to draw your attention to Isaiah 52:14:

Many were astonished at him.
His visage was marred more than any man,
and his form more than the sons of men.

The reference is usually understood as Yeshuah's brutal treatment at the hands of his Roman inquisitors. He was beaten beyond recognition. The same can be said about Yeshuah's public image, about how he is almost universally perceived. Yeshuah's true identity has been distorted beyond recognition. The man appointed by the Almighty Father as the Messiah has become something very different for nearly all of humankind. Yeshuah is now perceived as a deity, a being who preexisted in Heaven, one part of a trinity, and a creator. He wasn't even born in the normal way as a human being.

You know, Avi, if the Almighty and Eternal One could actually become a man, it would effectively take our humanity away from us. It would then be His humanity and not ours. We already have enough of feeling distant from The Creator without losing our sense of being uniquely created beings. The Almighty One has made us with our own special identity that is quite apart from His identity.

For my part, I wouldn't want the Almighty to be human in any way. That makes no sense to me, and takes away from my uniqueness as a created being.

Harry, there is something so pleasurable and comforting in knowing that Yeshuah was a flesh and blood man like ourselves.

Yes, there is. If the Almighty Father can make Himself and His purpose known through a man, it removes the distance we feel between Him and ourselves. By that very act of making Himself known through Yeshuah, the Father has confirmed our identity as human beings. He is then truly "with us" or "Immanuel" as Yeshuah was to be called.

Again, Abraham, if the Almighty Father could become a man, then He would cease to be the "Other." In the English language we say "holy," but in Hebrew the word means 'set-apart.' The Almighty Father will always be apart from us in His unlimited majesty, power and character. That is why we worship Him.

Harry, I think I'm following you in this. The Father doesn't want us to feel alone or separate from Him. He wants us to be secure in our own identity. We have our own substance, although we have our substance in Him.

That's right. The crowning achievement of Creation will be to change humans into immortal beings, beings that also have eternal life in themselves.

That's marvelous, Harry. Too wonderful for words.

Harry looked at me affirmatively.

In a way, it gets even better. The Eternal One, the Almighty Father, has exalted a man to a position second only to Himself. It's what the resurrected Yeshuah meant when he said, "All authority in Heaven and on Earth has been given to me." Simply put, The Eternal One has given a man the power to reign in place of Himself. The precedent for exalting a man to an all-powerful status is in Joseph's relationship with an ancient Pharaoh of Egypt. I'll read the passage in Genesis:

**Pharaoh said to his servants,
Can we find such a one as this,
a man in whom the spirit of The Almighty One is?**

**Then Pharaoh said to Joseph,
Inasmuch as The Almighty One has shown you all of this,
there is no one so discreet and wise as you:**

**you shall be over my house,
and according to your word shall all my people be ruled:
only in the throne will I be greater than you.**

**Then Pharaoh said to Joseph,
See, I have set you over all the land of Egypt.
Then Pharaoh took off his signet ring from his hand,
and put it upon Joseph's hand, and arrayed him in vestures of fine linen,
and put a gold chain around his neck;
and he made him to ride in the second chariot which he had;
and they called before him, Bow the knee:
and he set him over all the land of Egypt.**

**Pharaoh said to Joseph, I am Pharaoh,
and without you shall no man lift up his hand or his foot
in all the land of Egypt.**

Avi, there it is. The pharaoh made Joseph the supreme ruler in all the land of Egypt, second only to himself. In the same way, The Eternal One has made Yeshuah the supreme ruler in all of Heaven and Earth, second only to Himself.

I understand. That's marvelous. In essence, the Eternal One has given us the right and power to rule ourselves.

I looked over at Harry, and he was smiling.

You're coming very close to an ultimate truth, Avi.

It follows, then, that the Almighty will never impose His will on us. Ultimately, He wants us to rule over ourselves. That's the essence of giving a man, a human being: "all authority in Heaven and on Earth." The Almighty One is no tyrant!

That's good. I like that.

Harry stopped and allowed me to lapse back into my peaceful reverie. I really felt that the Almighty Father was not far away, that He was near. I was sure Harry was right about those inscrutable doctrines of the trinity, preexistence and incarnation. They take us away from what is real and true. Now I knew it with certainty that Yeshuah was truly a human being like myself, and I was grateful.

It seemed like a very long time before I spoke up again.

What will we talk about next Sabbath, Harry?

I've been thinking, Abraham, about how well you've done, and what a pleasant experience this has been for both of us. You haven't had any trouble with the Earth not being a planet that orbits the sun, or that we don't have immortal souls, or that Paul was not an apostle. You didn't balk about the **New Testament** not being Scripture, or about Yeshuah not being **God**. I'm confident that we can continue.

Are you alluding to something?

Yes. Our topic next Sabbath will go right to the heart of Christianity and expose a horrible perversion. I won't apologize for my less than tactful language because the issue at stake is so utterly transparent. It's one of those black and white issues that leaves no room for interpretation. Christians have universally believed a perverse lie.

I have been hesitant about it, Avi, but the time is right, and I know you'll understand.

All I can say is that you have been building up my faith and not destroying it. I'll be here next week anticipating an unmixed blessing. I trust you, Harry.

I trust you, Abraham. This is a big, big issue. I can't name anything else that is more devastating for Christianity as a religion.

Okay, but, I'm not going to brace myself for the unthinkable. I'm well past that point.

Good.

May the Eternal One be with you, Harry.

May the Eternal One be with you, Abraham.

8. JESUS WAS NOT A SACRIFICE FOR SIN

The next week we began as we had left off. Like before, I was so please with Harry's companionship and the thoughtfulness of our conversation. I was sure Harry felt the same, if not even more.

May the Eternal One be with you, Harry.

May the Eternal One be with you, Abraham.

The weather, the secluded back yard and the tea pot were in conjunction once again. It was the third Sabbath of the month. All was good, except me. I hadn't come with a mind as free as I wanted and was feeling dour. I began our conversation.

It's good to see you, Harry. I was so looking forward to today.

I waited for a few minutes, then asked the question.

What is so devastating for Christianity?

In a way, I didn't even want to start. I had some idea of what was coming and it troubled me.

Abraham, it's one of those things that once you see it you'll wonder how it could have gone unnoticed for so long. Virtually every Christian sect on Earth believes that Yeshuah was raised from the dead. However, their most cherished doctrine is that Yeshuah was a sacrifice for sin, and that it was his blood that made forgiveness possible. At first blush, I'm sure you agree. It sounds true from so many repetitions.

It sure does.

It's not true though, and if it were we'd be in debt forever. We would be eternally obligated with our past.

You'll need to explain that.

I sure will. Obligation is not something to build a relationship on. The Eternal One, our Father, wants us to come to Him as whole people and on even terms. That is why He has said:

Come now, and let us reason together, saith YHWH
though your sins be as scarlet, they shall be as white as snow;
though they be red like crimson, they shall be as wool.

The whole point is that the Eternal One doesn't require a bloody sacrifice for Him to forgive sin, or any sacrifice at all.

There was no innuendo in Harry's "bloody sacrifice." I marveled again at how ingenuous my friend could be.

Is that really true?

Abraham, that's really true. We can come to the Almighty any time and be forgiven. That is so perfectly clear from many biblical texts. For example:

Have mercy upon me, O Mighty One,
according to your lovingkindness, according to the multi-
tude of your tender mercies blot out my transgressions.

In that well-known Psalm 51, David was pleading with the Almighty to be delivered from his sin, his adultery with Bathsheba and the murder of her husband Uriah. David knew he needed to be forgiven. He also knew that shedding even more blood would not release him from his wretchedness:

For you delight not in sacrifice; else would I give it.
You have no pleasure in burnt-offering.
The sacrifices of the Mighty One are a broken spirit:
A broken and contrite heart, O Mighty One, you will not despise.

Yeshuah said the same thing explicitly when he instructed the Pharisees to "Go and learn what this means, 'I desire mercy, and not sacrifice.'" In that, Yeshuah was quoting the prophet Hosea:

**For I desire mercy, not sacrifice,
and acknowledgment of The Almighty One
rather than burnt offerings.**

Avi, I want to be sensitive about whatever I say against this widespread belief that there was a human sacrifice for sin. If we are honest, there is something repugnant about human sacrifice, and we all know it. So let's honestly appraise the King James translation of Revelation 1:5 where it says that, "Jesus Christ ... washed us from our sins in his own blood." A sensitive person would find such an expression truly horrifying.

Abraham, I feel emotionally bound to apologize, but I won't.

I felt for my dear friend, and came to his rescue.

Harry, I know enough about the sacrificial system in the Bible to be clear. No thing or person was ever washed in blood by the temple priests. That would have been an anathema for a Hebrew priest.

I had to wait for my own feelings to catch up. I was being drawn in although reluctantly. What Harry was saying was unavoidably arresting. I was sure Harry appreciated my tentative support, but he still did not break his silence.

You're not just saying that to spite a Christian belief, are you?

No.

I'm bothered by this, Harry, but go on.

Harry looked at me with a meekness that felt unfathomable.

I'll accept the consequences of what comes next. No one likes to have the carpet pulled out from under them, let alone be told that what they are doing is an abomination. The basic text for the Christian belief in Yeshuah as a sacrifice is found in Hebrews 9:22, which reads, "The law requires that nearly everything be cleansed with blood, and without the shedding of blood there is no forgiveness."

But Avi, whoever wrote the book of Hebrews in the Christian Scriptures didn't know what he was talking about. The Law of Moses provided for those who could not afford the cost of a blood offering. I'll read the whole text:

But if he cannot afford two turtledoves or two pigeons,

**then he shall bring as his offering for the sin that he has committed
a tenth of an ephah of fine flour for a sin offering.
He shall put no oil on it and shall put no frankincense on it,
for it is a sin offering.
And he shall bring it to the priest, and the priest shall take a handful of it
as its memorial portion and burn this on the altar,
as a food offering to YHWH;
it is a sin offering.
Thus the priest shall make atonement for him
for the sin which he has committed in any one of these things,
and he shall be forgiven.**[1]

That should be easy enough to follow, Avi. Not all offerings involved blood, and therefore the author of Hebrews 9:22 was wrong. There is forgiveness without the shedding of blood.

Those who believe that sin has to be atoned for by bloodshed, know that they need to support their belief from the law of Moses. The text most often used to support Hebrews 9:22 is Leviticus 17:11:

**For the life of the flesh is in the blood;
and I have given it to you upon the altar to make atonement for your souls:
for it is the blood that maketh atonement by reason of the life.**

However, the context gives the true meaning:

**'I will set my face against any Israelite or any foreigner residing among
them who eats blood, and I will cut them off from the people.
For the life of a creature is in the blood,
and I have given it to you to make atonement for yourselves on the altar;
it is the blood that makes atonement for one's life.
Therefore I say to the Israelites,
"None of you may eat blood,
nor may any foreigner residing among you eat blood."
'Any Israelite or any foreigner residing among you
who hunts any animal or bird that may be eaten
must drain out the blood and cover it with earth,
because the life of every creature is its blood.
That is why I have said to the Israelites,**

---

1 Leviticus 5:11-13.

"You must not eat the blood of any creature,
because the life of every creature is its blood;
anyone who eats it must be cut off."

The Hebrews were to respect the life that is in the blood. Under no circumstance were they ever to eat the blood of an animal. Anyone who ate blood was to be removed from society. This profound instruction also lay at the heart of the apostolic letter of Acts 15:

But that we write unto them, that they abstain from the pollutions of idols,
and from fornication, and from what is strangled,
and from blood.

Harry's meekness returned in full force. It showed in his face before he continued.

Herein is Christianity's endlessly multiplied anathema: they have made a ritual out of eating blood.

My friend paused. I knew very well he was referring to the Eucharist.

Paul claimed he had received the ritual of the so-called *Lord's Supper* as a private revelation. From there, his revelation found its way into the other books of the Christian Scriptures. Yet, it is unthinkable that Yeshuah could have looked his fellow Hebrews in the eye and told them to drink his blood and eat his body no matter how symbolic it was meant to be. Every one of his disciples would have immediately seen such instructions as a violation of the commandment given to Moshe (Moses), "You must not eat the blood of any creature." They would have been appalled by such instructions.

I had to agree again, despite my reluctance.

That's grim, Harry. People shouldn't be participating in Eucharist rituals even if it is only as a memorial. I'm with you. What a vile practice. I too need to accept the consequences for saying it.

Others will come around too, Abraham, and distance themselves from Christianity's most fundamental precept, that Yeshuah's death was a blood offering necessary for the forgiveness of sin. There is already a movement underway to reject this vile doctrine.

I felt my reserve beginning to leave me.

I never saw that before, Harry. If we can go by Paul's own words, then the so-called 'Lord's supper' was initiated by him and no one else.

Exactly. Paul claimed that the Eucharist came to him through one of his revelations: "For I received of the Master that which also I delivered unto you, that the Master Yeshuah in the night in which he was betrayed took bread..."

My friend looked at me with conviction.

Abraham, our own internal witness should be telling us that something is horribly wrong. What kind of people are we that we make a ritual out of drinking blood? Have we lost our senses?

Harry didn't wait for an answer.

That the 'Lord's supper' was instituted by Paul is in harmony with his explicit 'shed blood' teaching. Paul said that the Messiah died for us, and that we are justified by his blood.[2]

Avi, Paul's teaching was wrong, and conflicts with the Tanak. Paul said, "In due time, the Messiah died for the wicked." Yet, in the Hebrew Scriptures, we read:

**The fathers shall not be put to death for the children,
neither shall the children be put to death for the fathers:
every man shall be put to death for his own sin.**[3]

In another place:

**The soul that sinneth, it shall die:
the son shall not bear the iniquity of the father,
neither shall the father bear the iniquity of the son;
the righteousness of the righteous shall be upon him,
and the wickedness of the wicked shall be upon him.**[4]

How much clearer can it be, Avi? One human being cannot die for another human being. It's all too clear that Paul's teaching contradicts the Hebrew Scriptures, that Paul was not a reliable spokesman for Yeshuah.

I knew it too.

It seems to come around quite often, doesn't it Harry, that Paul was not a true apostle?

2   Romans 5:8-9.
3   Deuteronomy. 5:16
4   Ezekiel 18:20

Yes. This teaching is mostly from Paul, but he's not the only one. Other authors in the Christian Scriptures also teach that it's Yeshuah's blood that atones for sin. It's in First Peter, and I've already mentioned Hebrews and Revelation. There's no question that the Christian Scriptures repeatedly present Yeshuah as a sacrifice for sin.

Significantly, it is never taught in Matthew, Mark, and Luke except in terms of the Eucharist. Otherwise, Yeshuah himself never said that he came to atone for sin, to be a sacrifice for sin, or to shed his blood for our redemption. Yeshuah never used the word 'atonement' even once, and on the two occasions when he used 'sacrifice,' it was to declare to his listeners that they needed mercy and not sacrifice. Nor did he ever use the word 'blood' in the context of salvation.[5] The notion of a once and for all blood-sacrifice didn't come from Yeshuah's lips.

Harry made a gesture with his hand.

Avi, the Jews have always looked on the story of Isaac as a final and absolute indictment against human sacrifice. When the Eternal One prevented Abraham from sacrificing his son, it forever separated the Hebrews from the nations around them.[6]

Later, through Moses, the Eternal One declared absolutely that for the Hebrews to sacrifice their children was an abomination to Him:

**You shall not do so unto YHWH your Mighty One:
for every abomination to the Eternal One, which he hates,
have they done unto their gods;
for even their sons and their daughters do they
burn in the fire to their gods.[7]**

Surely, the Almighty and Everlasting Father would not do the very thing that He commanded His people not to do – sacrifice His own son.

There are growing numbers of people inside and outside the Church that have had enough of its lies. Many of them are now happily uprooting the 'saved by the blood' doctrine from their belief system. Yeshuah discovered that too as he grew into His relationship with the Eternal Father. It's well-stated in one of the Psalms:

5   Not one time in Matthew, Mark, Luke or John are 'blood' and 'save' ever found in the same verse. That distinction belongs to Paul in Romans 5:9.
6   Jephthah, the victorious leader in Judges 11, did not sacrifice his daughter. According to his vow, he dedicated his daughter to The Eternal One, and she remained a virgin for the rest of her life. A righteous judge, Jephthah would have known the Mosaic commandment against child sacrifice as in Leviticus 20:1-2.
7   Deuteronomy 12:31.

> **Sacrifice and offering you did not desire**
> **– but my ears you have opened –**
> **burnt offerings and sin offerings You did not require.**
> **Then I said, "Here I am, I have come – it is written about me in the scroll.**
> **I desire to do Your will, my Mighty One; Your law is within my heart."**
> **I proclaim Your saving acts in the great assembly;**
> **I do not seal my lips, Eternal One, as You know.**
> **I do not hide Your righteousness in my heart;**
> **I speak of Your faithfulness and Your saving help.**
> **I do not conceal Your love and Your faithfulness from the great assembly.**[8]

Avi, that's a passage that needs to be restated. It can nicely be reworded as: "I realize now, You don't want sacrifices. I'm hearing You on this. You don't want sin offerings. I want to do Your will though. That's what is instructed for me in Your book, and written in my heart. I am going to proclaim Your power and righteousness to the people, Your faithfulness and promise of salvation. I won't conceal Your love from the people."

Simplified: "You don't want me to be a sacrifice for sin. You want me to keep Your commandments, demonstrate Your righteousness, and make sure the people know that You love them."

That is in essence what the Messiah did when he came to proclaim the Kingdom of Heaven to the Eternal One's people. That's it in a nutshell, Avi.

My head was active, but I still had feelings.

That's marvelous. Just marvelous. The Father surely loves us and is more than willing to forgive us when we ask Him. I feel clean already! I feel free.

Abraham, your feeling is right. The Eternal One wants us to come to Him freely of our own accord. When the Eternal One brought His people out of Egypt, it was to set them free, but not to obligate them.

Why do you say that?

I said it at the beginning. If someone actually died for us, we would be under an enormous obligation to that person, especially as immortal beings who could never forget

---

8   Psalm 40:6-10. The blatant mistranslation of this passage in Hebrews 10:5 should be noted. In Hebrews, "my ears you have opened" is substituted with "a body have you prepared for me." The author of Hebrews wanted to portray Yeshuah as a physical sacrifice for sin, not as the one who knew and understood the heart of his everlasting Father. In Psalm 40, The Eternal One does not want to be sacrificed to for sin.

what that person had done. Surely, we do not want to live eternally always knowing that innocent blood had to be shed for our deliverance from sin. That's too perverse to be in our memory bank forever. It seems obvious to me. The Eternal One would not want us to feel that way toward Him, or have that kind of relationship with Him, certainly not forever.

I'm seeing it too, Harry. Our Almighty Father wants us to come to Him because of who He is, and despite what we have done. It is in His nature and ability to forgive completely. The Eternal One will forgive for His own sake, for His satisfaction and pleasure and to make Himself known.

Good for you, brother Avi. That's the final conclusion.

Harry stood up.

This is what precisely what I want to conclude with. The only requirement for forgiveness is repentance. If we are truly sorry about how we went wrong, and stop doing what we know is wrong – that's all that our loving Creator and Father requires.

Hear now, O house of Israel!
Is My way not right? Is it not your ways that are not right?
When a righteous man turns away from his righteousness, commits iniquity and dies because of it, for his iniquity which he has committed he will die.
Again, when a wicked man turns away from his wickedness which he has committed and practices justice and righteousness, he will save his life. Because he considered and turned away from all his transgressions which he had committed, he shall surely live; he shall not die.

I let a long breath leave my body.

These things are real, Harry. All that we have talked about in the last months has been real. It's all so good.

As I expected. You've always had it in yourself to respond to the truth.

Why do you say that?

Hear me, brother Avi. We have the power within ourselves to choose life or death. That's what it's all about, our free will choice.

Okay, so what's next?

I'd like to return to a scientific topic. We should talk about the theory of evolution, or rather its hypothesis.

I'd really like that.

I should give you a heads up. Our next meeting will be on the last day of this lunar cycle. I'm expecting that the New Moon day will be on the second day following the last Sabbath. Can you work with that?

Sure. Thanks for the notice, but I hope you will explain this calendar soon.

I'm planning on it.

I stood up to thank Harry and take my leave, but with a rush, something came over me and I sat down again. I knew what it was.

I'm really bothered by something, Harry. It's been nagging at me all along and I've been ignoring it.

Harry just looked at me.

Here it is. Moses wrote the Torah, or first five books of the Hebrew Scriptures called the *Pentateuch*. Therefore, it was Moses who introduced the sacrificial system to the Eternal One's people, effectively conveying the Eternal One's instructions to the Hebrews. How can we ignore that?

I looked back at Harry.

My apologies, Abraham.

Why an apology?

Sometimes I'm concerned about going too far too quickly. I don't want to say more than you can handle. I should give you more credit.

Try me, I'm not going to run away.

All right, Avi. I've dropped one shoe, I might as well drop the other.

Harry was silent for a while, composing an answer to my question.

The left shoe I dropped was that the *New Testament* is not Scripture. It's best seen as a commentary on Yeshuah the Messiah from a Gentile perspective. Let's say that by 'Scripture' we mean the real transmission of the Eternal One's mind and purpose to humankind. Then the right shoe is, that the *Old Testament* is not entirely pure Scripture. Just as with the Christian Scriptures, the authors of the Hebrew Scriptures added their own thoughts and interpretations. The human element has found its way into the Tanak too. How could it be otherwise?

I stood up again.

I want a real good answer, Harry. How can you say that?

I have anticipated your question, Abraham. I knew it would come. Humans have an unrelenting tendency to reject the truth, wherever they find it. That's especially so with institutions. Adam did it as an individual, and all the world's churches have done it as institutions. It's easier and almost essential as a collective body. No church or religious body would exist today if they hadn't altered, fabricated or perverted the truth in some way. It goes with the territory.

It's a foregone conclusion, therefore, that the Bible must have been tampered with since the time of Moshe (Moses). There's no reason to believe that the Almighty would prevent humankind from altering His words and the written records of His interaction with His people. That's why He told His people not to add or subtract from His words. It's the same when He told Adam not to eat from the tree of the knowledge of Good and Evil. The Almighty knew in advance of man's proclivity to alter His instructions, anticipating that they would. There isn't anything or any truth that humans haven't manipulated, including the Bible, and more specifically the Torah of Moshe (Moses). We would be foolish not to acknowledge that proclivity.

Here's what one Hebrew man with a long tradition of scholarship has to say:

Harry opened a book that I had noticed for the last several weeks.

> Although shocking to most modern people, especially within evangelical Christian circles, to even entertain the thought, that the entire English Bible they have today as not being the direct and absolute pure and perfect word of God as given to righteous men, is generally met with absolute disbelief and in the case of our prophets, all manner of death, the last one being a Roman Crucifixion. Although

in almost all cases most people will shut down in complete disbelief, it still won't abate the tides of verifiable historical fact.... *Unfortunate as it may be for many people, at this point for many generations on both sides of Christianity and Judaism, Scholars no longer debate whether or not the Torah {1ˢᵗ five books} has in fact been written solely from God's mouth.*

In the next paragraph, Avi, the author gives the substance of his argument:

Scholars going back to the second century CE, or for an example in medieval times, *Ibn Ezra* in the twelfth century, found troubling evidence that Moshe did not in fact write the entire Torah. *The conclusion which virtually all modern scholars are willing to accept, is that the Pentateuch-Torah was in reality a composite work, the product of many hands and over long periods of time.* (emphasis added).[9]

I'm cutting to the chase here, Abraham. Church authorities – and the Temple authorities before them – along with their scribes, translators and redactors have added large sections and practices to what we now call *the Bible*. Worse yet, they hid or even removed what they didn't like in their collective purpose, that purpose being to rule over the Almighty's people. Just 'follow the money,' Avi. Who gets the 10% tithe from the rest of the people? It's the priests, or should I say the clergy? It's in their best interest to have that tithe endorsed by Moshe and in *the Bible*. They want to be in charge and get paid.

As for removing what they didn't like, I'm of a mind with the author I quoted, Shmuel Asher, that what those authorities did their best to remove, and nearly succeeded in, was removing the true Name of our Creator and Father.

Harry hardly paused to breathe.

We know from the archeological evidence that at least some of the *Ten Commandments* did not originate with Moshe, that other ancient cultures also had portable Tabernacles, and, as shocking as it may be, they had three-chambered sacrificial temples similar to the one that Solomon built. It seems that no matter how many times the Almighty Father told His people not to be like the nations around them, the Hebrews again and again adopted the religious practices of the other nations. Incredible as it may seem, those Hebrew scribes, translators and redactors usurped the name of Moshe and added their priestly agenda to the Torah. The pattern was repeated by the Catholic

---

9   Dr. Shmuel Asher, *The Land of Meat & Honey*, Amazon CreateSpace, 2011, p 3-4.

Church, usurping the names of Matthew, John and Peter in adding their priestly agenda to the Bible.

Now here's the point so that you don't miss it: The sacrificial system and the endless slaughtering of innocent creatures did not come from our Almighty Creator and Father, nor from Moshe. The Eternal One did not tell His people to shed blood in order to appease Him or to receive forgiveness from Him, nor did the Eternal Father ordain the Eucharist. Abraham, we can know this intuitively if our minds are open and our hearts are willing to receive the truth about anything. Did you get the point?

Harry paused for the first time.

I'm not doubting you, Avi.

I took a breath too.

How can I know for sure, Harry?

I can do that easily, but please sit down again.

That made me aware that I had been standing and pacing for quite some time. My anxiety had been getting to me.

I'll do it in three ways. The first is from when the Hebrew Bible was written. Major portions of Genesis and Exodus could have been written as early as 1250 to 1100 BC, and some say as late as 950 BC. Leviticus reached its present form around 500-400 BC, although parts of it may be much older. So while the oldest parts of the Bible could have been written by Moshe originally, much of Leviticus was written by others long after Moshe was dead. Those others were the temple priests.[10]

The second way is from past witnesses, from witnesses that are still highly respected. One of Judaism's most esteemed Jewish scholars was Rabbi Moshe ben Maimon who lived in the middle ages. He was also known as Maimonides or Rambam. Maimonides suggested that the primitive sacrificial system of the Ancient Near East was incorporated into Hebrew worship as a limitation:

Sacrifice is an ancient and universal human expression of religion.

---

10   The information for this paragraph comes from the *Documentary Hypothesis*, also known as 'literary criticism' or 'higher criticism.' Whatever motivated western scholars beginning in the 18th and 19th centuries, it is amazing how much they accomplished and their work should be applauded. Like it or not, we now have a much better understanding of the Bible and its composition.

Sacrifice existed among the Hebrews long before the giving of the Torah.... When the laws of sacrifice were laid down in the Torah, the pre-existence of a system of sacrificial offering was understood, and sacrificial terminology was used without any explanation. *The Torah, rather than creating the institution of sacrifice, carefully circumscribes and limits the practice*, permitting it only in certain places, at certain times, in certain manners, by certain people, and for certain purposes. Rambam suggests that these limitations are designed to wean a primitive people away from the debased rites of their idolatrous neighbors. (*emphasis added*).[11]

The Christian theologian, Clement of Alexandria, made a similar suggestion in the second century AD. He believed it was Yeshuah, the prophet that Moshe had foretold of, that was sent to correct the people's understanding regarding sacrifice:

When meantime Moses, that faithful and wise steward, perceived that the vice of sacrificing to idols had been deeply ingrained into the people from their association with the Egyptians, and that the root of this evil could not be extracted from them, he allowed them indeed to sacrifice, but permitted it to be done only to God, that by any means he might cut off one half of the deeply ingrained evil, leaving the other half *to be corrected by another, and at a future time*; by Him, namely, concerning whom he said himself, 'A prophet shall the Lord your God raise unto you, whom ye shall hear even as myself, according to all things which he shall say to you. Whosoever shall not hear that prophet, his soul shall be cut off from his people. (*emphasis added*).[12]

I'll quote the *Clementine Homilies* again. The *Homilies* are attributed to Clement 1 of Rome (circa 80-140 AD), a student of the Apostle Simon Peter and the fourth Pope:

But that *He is not pleased with sacrifices,* is shown by this, that those who lusted after flesh were slain as soon as they tasted it, and were consigned to a tomb, so that it was called the grave of lusts.

He then who at the first was displeased with the slaughtering of animals, not wishing them to be slain, did not ordain sacrifices as desiring them; nor from the beginning did He require them...

11 From the website *Judaism 101* under 'Qorbanot: Sacrifices and Offerings.'
12 *Recognitions of Clement*, "Allowance of Sacrifice for a Time." Book 1, Chapter 36.

But how is it possible for Him to abide in darkness, and smoke, and storm (for this also is written), who created a pure heaven, and created the sun to give light to all, and assigned the invariable order of their revolutions to innumerable stars? (*emphasis added*).[13]

That leads to the third and most compelling way. Remember, I am asserting that the *Old Testament* or Tanak is also not entirely Scripture or the pure and perfect transmission of the Eternal One's mind and purpose. The most compelling reason I can make such an assertion is from the Bible's internal witness. The Tanak itself, more specifically the prophets, tell us that the Scriptures have been altered.

Just a minute. Are you telling me it's right in the Bible that what's written there has been changed from the original message? Have things been added that shouldn't be there? Is the Bible a witness against itself? I'm puzzled.

I'll give you examples, and you decide.

Okay, I'm listening.

Then try the prophet Jeremiah:

How can you say, 'We are wise, and the Torah of the Almighty is with us'? But behold, the lying pen of the scribes has made it into a lie.

Try Isaiah too:

The Earth also is defiled under the inhabitants thereof; because they have transgressed the laws, changed the Torah, broken the everlasting covenant.

Granted, the real impetus of these texts has been obscured by our modern translators. Nevertheless, it can be understood that the ancient scribes lied in their renditions of the Tanak, and that the Torah was changed by them. Our modern translators fit the pattern set by their ancient counterparts. They fudge, dodge or prevaricate with the real truth.

Abraham, it wasn't just Maimonides and Clement that saw through the deceptions. The prophet Amos asked the rhetorical question:

Did you present Me with sacrifices and grain offerings in the wilderness for forty years,

---

13 *Clementine Homilies*, 3:45.

O house of Israel?

The implication is that the Hebrew tribes did not offer sacrifices in the wilderness. The sacrifices came later as the priesthood grew in its influence. Then they added the sacrifices.

Neither did Isaiah (and other prophets) mince words about the sacrificial system. He wanted it stopped.

The multitude of your sacrifices – what are they to me? says YHWH
I have more than enough of burnt offerings, of rams and the fat of animals;
I have no pleasure in the blood of bulls and lambs and goats.
When you come to appear before me,
who has asked this of you, this trampling of my courts?

In essence, prophets like Isaiah, Jeremiah and Amos were adamant that the true worship of the Eternal One was manifested by justice and compassion, by the way the helpless and powerless were treated, and not with bloodshed and sacrificial rituals. They wanted those rituals stopped.

Bring your worthless offerings no longer.[14]

Is that a long way around giving you a proper answer, Avi?

I couldn't help myself as I felt an uncomfortable churning inside of me. I thought I had gone beyond that.

Harry, is it possible that the Torah can hold opposing views in order to provide a choice?

Harry looked at me with solicitude.

Is it?

You've jumped way ahead, brother Avi. It may seem paradoxical, but the two trees that the Almighty planted in the Garden of Eden are also planted in the Tanak. We have a choice, and that's the real issue.

Harry made a very long pause, and I made it with him.

---

14 Jeremiah 8:8, Isaiah 24:5, Amos 5:25, Isaiah 1:11-12 and Isaiah 1:13.

Abraham, we have to start viewing the Bible in a different way. We can still believe that inspiration is involved, but the human element is there too. After all, our knowledge from the Creator is a two-way process. In effect, the Almighty Father has made Himself known to imperfect beings with limited comprehension. Our Bible shows that with many examples of human ineptitude and contrasting viewpoints. Therefore, we should think of the Bible as a written record of our striving to know the mind and will of the Creator that includes our failure to comprehend what He is revealing about Himself. The authors of the Bible recorded their experience as best they could, sometimes with great clarity and vision, often with awe and uncertainty, and at other times with profound misunderstanding.

It's quite evident that the authors of the Bible sometimes got it very wrong, and yet they still wrote it down. For example, I don't think for an instant that the Almighty Father ever commanded His people to kill women and children as it was recorded on more than one occasion. Nor did the Almighty command Abraham to kill his son Isaac even though that is what Abraham must have understood.[15] No matter how we view inspiration or revelation in the process of hearing the Almighty's voice and writing it down, the human element is still there. The Bible also includes our wrong-headedness.

Again, he paused.

We need to take this into account. One of the Bible's most prevailing themes is the necessity of sacrifice and the shedding of blood. In the Tanak, it's the killing of animals. In the Christian Scriptures, it's the Eucharist or 'Lord's Supper.' In both, it's the shedding of innocent blood that's revered, if not exalted.

Harry took a deep breath.

But killing is always wrong, and no good can ever come out of it. No blood of any kind should ever be shed, especially innocent blood, so we need to ask ourselves why that feature is so prominent in the Bible. Surely, the Eternal One meant it when He said so unequivocally, "Thou shalt not kill." The only reasonable answer is that human beings have added the necessity of sacrifice to the Bible out of their own twisted desire to justify themselves and their actions. Something went wrong right from the beginning (from believing the very first lie) to make adding to the Torah and Yeshuah's teaching an inevitable consequence.

---

15 More than one commentator (both Jewish and Christian) has noted the ambiguity of Genesis 22:2. The verse could just as easily be translated as "Take Isaac up for an offering," meaning that there was to be an offering, but not that Isaac was the offering. Nevertheless, Abraham was willing to proceed with the unthinkable as a test of his obedience.

Avi, that's why the prophets came, and later Yeshuah, to speak out against an evil system that demanded bloodshed as a propitiation. Many of them paid for it – and guess how? Their innocent blood was shed by the very people who believed in the sacrificial system and that it was morally right to kill animals and other people.

We need to make a practical conclusion if we can. Actually, two conclusions. First, if we are ever going to apprehend what is true and valuable in the Bible, we will need to distinguish between what comes from the human mind and what comes from our Creator's. More simply said, distinguish what has been fabricated from what is genuine. The other conclusion? We need to give more credence to our own human sensitivity and ability to be rational beings. Neither practical conclusion can come easily because it's our own twisted reasoning and perverted sensitivity that brought about these horrible beliefs in the first place. Our minds need to be healed.

So please understand: there is truth the Bible. Our Bibles contain a record of the Eternal One's interaction with humankind, and we can still hear His voice in it. It might just be, however, that until we learn to hear His voice, the Bible will continue to lead us away from the truth and not toward the truth.

That's about it, Abraham. The shedding of innocent blood is not a cosmic truth to be retained forever and ever. It needs to be acknowledged, rooted out of our conscience, and forgotten always and forevermore. It may take more than one generation, but it can be done.

My friend faced me with piercing look of compassion.

Have we heard our Creator's voice, Avi? He has said to us, "Thou shalt not kill."

This time I sat quietly for a long time, and Harry with me.[16]

I'm intrigued by it taking more than one generation to accomplish, Harry. That's a new thought for me, that overcoming something like killing or an evil conscience may be generational. I understand what you've said. It rings true and I agree with it, but it may not be something that can be achieved in our present time.

---

16 Many translators insist that the Hebrew word for kill (**ratsah**) means murder or a criminal act. But at least one distinguished Jewish philosopher, Maimonides, held that "thou shalt not kill" is a perfectly accurate rendering of the sixth commandment, including its clear ban on capital punishment. Even if the text (Exodus 20:13) is specific for human life (no killing for any reason), many biblical texts define animals as "living beings" and my extension here is warranted on that basis. Conversely, Exodus 20:13 does not give us permission to kill animals.

Abraham, you're a brave man, so I'll add another new thought. If becoming immortal beings has anything to do with us, it might take more than one generation to achieve that as well.

My expletives were softening.

Can you elaborate?

There's a faulty interpretation that the Almighty put a flaming sword around the Tree of Life in the garden of Eden to keep mankind from eating its fruit and living forever in his fallen state. However, the flaming sword was there to protect the Tree of Life from indifference, and make it a more deliberate goal to eat from. Whatever the Tree of Life represents, it's still there, and we can find it and eat its fruit if we want to. That's all I'm going to say for now.

I'm full up already, Harry, but not too full that I can't ask an obvious question. How can we know what true in our Bibles and what's not? There needs to be an answer if from the time the Scriptures were written through to our present translations, the truth has been tampered with and even perverted.

I'll give you an easy answer. It all depends on our attitude and diligence. It may not be easy, but we can know the truth if we're willing to seek it. As the proverbs says:

> **It is the esteem of the Eternal to conceal a thing;**
> **But the esteem of kings is to search it out.**[17]

I'll only add my recurring theme to that. We need to trust ourselves too. We must be true to our own innate abilities and common sense.

Harry honored me with his look.

I marvel at our conversations. I also feel full.

Good. I'll be on my way. May the Eternal One be with you.

May the Eternal One bless you, Avi.[18]

---

17 Proverbs 25:2.
18 This salutation is found in Ruth 2:4: "And, behold, Boaz came from Bethlehem, and said to the reapers, YHWH be with you. And they answered him, YHWH bless you."

9. HUMANS DID NOT EVOLVE

Shalom, Harry.

Shalom, brother Avi.

Harry, I'm so grateful for what the Eternal One is doing with me. I have been thanking Him all week. It's hard for me to explain how sure and refreshed I feel about what He is doing.

I'm sure too, Abraham, that we're not alone in feeling this way. May the Eternal One continue in the mighty work that He is beginning in our time.

Harry, I'll start our talk on human evolution. It's really a done deal ever since we talked about the age of the Earth. With only about six thousand years of real time, evolution becomes impossible. Humankind with all the life forms came into being fully formed right from the beginning. Human beings did not evolve: end of story.

That's truth in all its simplicity, Avi. What I want to focus on, however, is the manner in which human evolution has been foisted on our consciousness. The idea that humans evolved from lower life forms is so entrenched in the public mind that we need to know how it got there. We should understand how we have been deceived.

Now that you mention the six thousand years, we should talk about that again. Actually, I have been waiting for an opportunity to reiterate my confidence in Bishop Ussher's work. It has become apparent, even in the secular world, that James Ussher was truly an outstanding scholar. What is often not accepted is Ussher's steadfast faith in the Bible and his literal interpretation of Genesis. Admittedly, that belief is repugnant and unacceptable to many modern academics, but it has not kept them from acknowledging Bishop Ussher as one of the great intellects of his time. It is worth repeating that Bishop

Ussher was a very credible man, and he continues to be respected by others even today.[1]

There's a good reason for why we can still have confidence in Bishop Ussher's time-line. He used the ages of the patriarchs as they are recorded in the book of Genesis to construct his historical chronology and the year of Creation. The Hebrew Scriptures provide an almost unbroken male lineage from Adam to Solomon, complete with the ages of the individuals involved. To those years, Usher added the reigns of Israel's kings, which he correlated with the date of Nebuchadnezzar's death in 562 BC. Given that the ages and reigns are so precisely recorded in the Scriptures, Bishop Ussher arrived at 4004 BC as the year of Creation.

What is significant about the Scriptural concept of time is that it is based on the life span of individuals and specific events in the lives of those individuals. Modern dating methods are based on tree-rings, radiocarbon dating and astronomical events such as eclipses and supernovas. However, these methods are highly subjective and often ambiguous. It has even been suggested, quite plausibly, that past celestial events may have altered the arrangement and appearance of the heavenly bodies, making them unsuitable for dating historical events. The Bible consistently uses factual human years for record-ing time. All else failing, actual life-times and real human events are still the most reliable means for the measurement of time.[2]

That is not to say, Avi, that Ussher's date of 4004 BC is sacrosanct.[3] He did, however, give us a reasonable and pragmatic date for the time of Creation. Many other qualified scholars have given us similar and even identical dates. The Scriptures allow us to date the beginning of time in terms of human lifespans, and that is why Ussher's chronology is plausible and has withstood the test of time. Humankind had its beginning only a few thousand years ago, no matter what the exact date is.

Thank you, Harry. So how was the world deceived into believing that humankind evolved over a period of hundreds of thousands and even millions of years?

Abraham, if ever there was a tale of deception, human evolution surely ranks as one of the most ingenious. So-called scientists have arranged fossils to suit their hypothesis,

---

1   Even the historian Arnold J. Toynbee conceded that Ussher's speculative and much-lampooned date of 4004 BC "approximately marks the first appearance of representatives of the species of human society called civilization" (*The Atlantic Monthly*, June 1942... as quoted in Jenkins, 1969, p 25).

2   As it has already been alluded to, the nature of time is highly subjective. In a coming chapter, it will be shown that the years and the months were of different lengths than they are now. It is significant that the Scriptures measure time in terms of human life spans rather than measure human life spans in terms of time. There is a subtle difference. It can equally well be said, "Time was made for man, not man for time."

3   Bishop Ussher deduced that the first day of Creation began at nightfall preceding Sunday, October 23, 4004 BC, in the *proleptic* Julian calendar, near the autumnal equinox.

produced imaginary diagrams to illustrate evolution, used psychological methods of persuasion, and added unbridled speculation to their bag of tricks. It's no secret, however, that their deceptions have also been fully unveiled and made public. Not all scientists are so foolish and deceptive.

From the beginning, there was no real evidence of human evolution in the fossil record. Some creative minds did the next best thing. They invented evidence. A first attempt was the Piltdown Man discovered in England in 1912. Forty years later, the deliberate hoax was exposed. The fossil collection had been brought from Africa along with some elephant bones, and buried in the Piltdown cave. The tools found with the fossils had been shaped by a steel knife and artificially rust colored. The skull belonged to a five hundred year old man, and the jawbone to a recently deceased ape with its teeth carefully arranged and joints filled in to appear human. All the pieces were stained with potassium dichromate to make them look very old. In the zeal to find fossil evidence for human evolution, even the best known experts were fooled by the Piltdown Man.

In 1922, a fossil molar was found in and labeled as the Nebraska Man. A well-known paleontologist took it to be human, and based on the tooth, pictures of a head and body were reconstructed. That was followed by a famously published picture of the Nebraska Man with his wife in a wild setting. The tooth was found to be from an extinct American pig in 1927. It is likely that more astute scientists prevented the tooth from being used as evidence in the Scopes Monkey trial.

One of the most recent frauds was in 1999 when *National Geographic* illustrated a dinosaur with birdlike plumage. It soon turned out to be the fantasy of a Chinese farmer who had rearranged pieces of real fossils from different species. *National Geographic* published an apology, but still earned a stern rebuke by an ornithologist from the Smithsonian in Washington, who wrote, "*National Geographic* has reached an all-time low for engaging in sensationalistic, unsubstantiated, tabloid journalism."[4] That witless illustration has been dubbed "the Piltdown Chicken."

Harry looked at me with his discerning gaze.

Avi, the evidence for human evolution is wishful thinking and nothing more. Even without any deliberate attempt to deceive, the desire to produce evidence is overwhelming. Take the much touted Lucy fossil, for example, which its discoverer pronounced was "the most important find made by anyone in the history of the entire human race." Re-evaluation has shown that Lucy could not have walked upright and is anatomically identical to modern tree-dwelling apes. Similarly, Neanderthals were once considered

---

4   Olsen, S.L.,*Open Letter to: Dr Peter Raven, Secretary, Committee for Research and Exploration, National Geographic Society*. The Open Letter is available on the web.

a brutish human-like subspecies, but a new consensus has emerged that Neanderthals were fully intelligent, and fully functional human beings.[5]

It is truly amazing how much the acceptance of human evolution has to do with creative imagination. Artistic renderings of pre-humans have become ubiquitous. There are depictions of apelike humans in countless books, magazines, museum displays and television programs. Movies like *Quest for Fire* depict apelike humans in a social structure complete with language, laughter and romance. It's astounding how an artistic paleontologist can take a small piece of skull, reconstruct an entire cranium, layer it with artificial flesh, implant humanlike eyes, and photograph his creation for publication. All that without a single convincing fossil that such creatures ever existed!

There is always a blatant, even if undeclared, insinuation in the gospel of human evolution, which is that people believe in it. Conversely, people who don't believe in evolution are not very intelligent.

I genuinely believe that's changing. After many decades of searching, those same intelligent people have not been able to supply any real evidence supporting their beliefs in human evolution. They are not looking very intelligent at all. It's even come to the point that many, many people are beginning to laugh at evolutionists and can no longer take them seriously.

There is a story that is probably true about an Anglican bishop's wife. On hearing about evolution, she replied, "I do hope that what Mr. Darwin is saying is not true; and if it is, I hope it does not become generally known." Today, the reverse is true. Evolutionists are worried, and their complete failure to prove evolution is slowly finding its way into the public consciousness. Many of them are now hoping that their own findings and conclusions do not become generally known.

Harry, I've done enough reading on my own to know that what you are saying is true. There are probably no more than a handful of fossil skulls that are used to support human evolution. Somewhere I read that all the fossils evincing human evolution together would hardly fill a bathtub. In fact, the fossil record is against the theory of evolution.

Harry nodded his appreciation and continued.

---

5   "There are a large number of cultural habits that distance Homo sapiens from animals. No other organisms, either living or fossil, made tools to make other complex tools, buried their dead, had controlled use of fire, practiced religious ceremonies, used complex syntax in their spoken grammar, and played musical instruments, yet we know from their fossils that Neanderthal engaged in all." See Impact Article #223, May, 2000, *Neanderthals Are Still Human!* by anthropologist Dave Phillips.

Let's first recall what evolution has proposed about the development of human intelligence. From reconstructed skulls, it has been proposed that humans once had a brain capacity of 600 cc (cubic centimeters) 3.5 million years ago. By three million years ago, the human brain capacity had increased to 850 cc, and two million years ago to 1150 cc. Today, the human brain has a capacity of 1400 cubic centimeters. Evolution claims that human intelligence increased commensurate with brain size.

To summarize a complex story, at one time *hominids* decided to come down from the treetops and live on the ground. When faced with the danger of large land animals with superior strength and speed, pre-humans had to develop superior skills, alertness and a larger brain. As these survival skills continued to improve from generation to generation, brains got larger and larger, and human intelligence gradually evolved to its present capacity.

Supposedly, human beings have progressed through a number of stages to their current level of intelligence. Again, in simple terms, there have been three major evolutionary phases: hunter gathering, farming and technology. In another version, the three stages are the Stone Age, the Bronze Age, and the Iron Age. These stages encompassed fifty thousand years of human evolution. Evolutionists see our present intelligence and advanced technology as an evolutionary development, evolving progressively over a long period. They believe that evolution has brought us to our current level of brain size and intelligence.

Abraham, my friend, I'm going somewhere with this timeline and human intelligence.

We have on the Earth one great monumental witness against the theory of human evolution. That monument dispels any notion about our being at the height of learning, science and technology, demonstrating that in the distant past humans were at least equally intelligent and inventive. Indeed, archeological findings tell us that humans may have had even larger brains than we have now, ranging from 1700 to 2200 cubic centimeters. It's well known that Neanderthals had brains much larger than modern humans, and Cro-Magnon brains were even larger. There is ample evidence that the ancients accomplished feats of unsurpassed wonder and amazement, many of which cannot be reproduced or explained by modern ingenuity. The one monumental witness that I am referring to is the Great Pyramid at Giza. The Great Pyramid is a lasting testimony to the wisdom, knowledge and ability of the human beings who preceded us by thousands of years. The pyramid at Giza stands in lasting defiance to the idea that humans have evolved intellectually.

Avi, I can't think of another building or man-made structure that has been more scrutinized than the Great Pyramid. It has been explored, measured and written about from

Greek times to the present for over 2500 years. Ancient inscriptions have been found in Egypt, and quite possibly the Great Pyramid is mentioned in the Bible.[6] All attempts to explain the construction and purpose of the Great Pyramid have seemingly failed, and the speculations range from the "divinely built" to alien visitations. The classical explanation that the Great Pyramid was built by the pharaohs of the fourth dynasty is far from certain and lacking hard evidence. To this day, despite all the attention given to the Great Pyramid, it remains shrouded in mystery.

Yet all of mankind stands in awe of the Great Pyramid's construction. Its physical structure reveals an advanced knowledge of mathematics and astronomy, the use of advanced measuring devices, awesome engineering, and mind boggling construction. On that last point, 2.6 million blocks of stone weighing from twenty to two hundred tons were fitted to a tolerance of one fiftieth of an inch. Supposedly, the blocks were cut, dressed, delivered, and cemented in place at the rate of one block every three minutes for twenty years. Other mysteries have been revealed by the Great Pyramid. The builders knew the circumference of the Earth including its curvature and mass, the pyramid's location at the gravitational centre of the continents, and its exact position in terms of latitude and longitude. Amazingly, the Pyramid was built on top of a colossal inverted mountain of granite to hold the Pyramid's super-massive weight. The more that is discovered about the Great Pyramid, the more we are inspired with awe.

Avi, we could go on and on about the Great Pyramid's awe-inspiring construction, but the one thing we can conclude with certainty is that its builders were at a level of unparalleled ability. They possessed certain fields of knowledge that we no longer have today. It is that conclusion that points us in the direction of understanding the origin and meaning of the Great Pyramid at Giza.

The Hebrew Scriptures tell us that humans very quickly learned how to live in the physical world. They immediately acquired expertise in agriculture, animal husbandry, metallurgy, art and music, and building cities. The books of Enoch and Jasher suggest proficiency in medicine, birth control and possibly genetic manipulation. Artifacts have been found that imply the use of light bulbs, batteries, microwaves and aircraft, as impossible as that may sound. Legends also abound about the lost civilizations of Atlantis and Lemur. Like the Great Pyramid, the past is shrouded in mystery, but still points to a time of unprecedented learning and highly advanced engineering. Some of this may be speculative, but there is too much of it to ignore. We have to conclude that human beings were very, very clever in the distant past, near the beginning of human history. It's quite believable that they were not only equally intelligent, but also superior to us in some ways.

---

6   Jeremiah 32:20, "You have shown signs and wonders in the land of Egypt, and to this day in Israel and among all mankind, and have made a name for yourself, as at this day."

Just as Paracelsus said in the sixteenth century:

> Truly, it has been said that there is nothing new under the sun, for *knowledge is revealed and is submerged again, even as a nation rises and falls*. Here is a system, tested throughout the ages, but **lost again and again by ignorance or prejudice**, in the same way that great nations have risen and fallen and been lost to history beneath the desert sands and in the ocean depths. (*emphasis added*).

What I am telling you today is not without precedent. It's supported by legend. Josephus wrote about it two thousand years ago, and many modern scholars are making a similar conclusion. The most likely explanation for the Pyramid at Giza is that it was built before the Great Flood, and survived the Flood along with many other structures. The Pyramid at Giza may even have been built for that very purpose. As Josephus wrote about the builders of the Great Pyramid and the Sphinx:

> All these proved to be of good dispositions. They also inhabited the same country without dissensions, and in a happy condition, without any misfortunes falling upon them, 'til they died. They also were the inventors of that peculiar sort of wisdom which is concerned with the heavenly bodies, and their order. *And that their inventions might not be lost before they were sufficiently known, upon Adam's prediction that the world was to be destroyed at one time by the force of fire, and at another time by the violence and quantity of water, they made two pillars, the one of brick, the other of stone*: they inscribed their discoveries on them both, that in case the pillar of brick should be destroyed by the flood, the pillar of stone might remain, *and exhibit those discoveries to mankind*; and also inform them that there was another pillar of brick erected by them. Now this remains in the land of Siriad [Egypt] to this day. (*emphasis added*).[7][8]

Josephus was referring to the children of Seth, the third son of Adam. It was Josephus' belief that Seth's children built the Sphinx and the Great Pyramid before the Great Flood. Tradition has it that Enoch, Seth's grandson, designed the Great Pyramid, and for this reason it is often called the "Pillar of Enoch." Josephus was also referring to the very long lives of Seth and his children and that they were of "good disposition." Noah had

---

7   Josephus Flavius, *Antiquities of the Jews*, Book I, Chapter 2:9-10.

8   There are historical accounts of two Sphinxes, one made of stone and the other of brick. It's the one carved out of stone that remains. The other was destroyed by the forces of nature. Al-I'Drisi (AD 1099-1166) who wrote about it in *Kitab al-Mamalik wa al-Mansalik* and *Al-Kitab al-Jujari*.

preached for 120 years before the flood came while Enoch was still living along with his son Methuselah. Seth, who lived to be 912 years old, died shortly before Noah was born. Adam had died about a hundred years earlier, but was alive during the time of Enoch and Methuselah. According to Josephus, Seth's children enjoyed their long lives together in the same region, happy and free of misfortune, during which time they acquired much knowledge and wisdom.[9] [10]

Am I overloading you, Avi?

You're doing fine. I'm following both points: the amazing technical abilities of the Great Pyramid's builders, and that it was built before the Great Flood. That last part intrigues me a lot.

Good. I'll expand on that.

For a long time it was thought that the biblical flood wiped out all traces of the antediluvian world, the civilizations before Noah, but that perception is changing rapidly. It is now being proposed that the remains of the Stone Age, or the Neolithic Age, are actually from before the Flood. All the stone megastructures are remarkably similar and can be found worldwide. Examples other than the pyramids at Giza are Stonehenge[11], the giant stone statues of Easter Island, and the megalithic ruins of the ancient city of Tiahuanaco in Bolivia. Megalithic stone structures can be found in other areas of the Middle East, in Northern and Western Europe, Mexico, South America, and in other places in the world. Neolithic mining operations are also now thought to be antediluvian. The oldest metallurgical mine in the world was discovered at Medzamor in Armenia. At this mine, craftsmen worked with copper, bronze, lead, zinc, iron, gold, tin, antimony and manganese. It has become accepted by some researchers that mankind entered the metal age prior to the flood, and that the biblical flood brought the Neolithic Age to a close.

I want to emphasize again the sensational technical achievements of the civilizations that preceded the Great Flood. A new explanation has emerged for how the Great Pyramid was built. The latest experimental evidence demonstrates that its huge stone blocks were cast instead of cut from a quarry. The pyramid builders mixed crushed limestone with a caustic soda and other ingredients to make a rock slurry. This limestone

---

9   Recall that Enoch did not die when he was 365 years old. The Almighty 'took him' somewhere else to save him from an untimely death. Perhaps He took Enoch to Egypt, or perhaps to South America where the stone monuments of Cuzco and Tiahuanaco have an unsettling resemblance to the Great Pyramid.

10 Humans were healthier in the past too. The reason will become apparent by the end of this book.

11 Radiocarbon dating suggests that the first stones were erected in 2400-2200 BC, whilst another theory suggests that bluestones may have been erected at the site as early as 3000 BC. The usual date for the Flood is 2349 BC.

concrete was carried to the pyramid in baskets and put into moulds, where it solidified. The moulds were portable and moved block by block in constructing the Great Pyramid. One can only conclude that the pyramid builders understood the technology of polymers in a way never equaled again until the most recent advances in that science.[12]

I'm very convinced, Avi, that the Great Pyramid at Giza demonstrates a highly advanced culture from around 3000 BC. The Great Pyramid, along with many other ancient monuments, shows that humans had acquired a level of knowledge that was lost and even surpassing what we know today. Those monuments are a reminder of great technological achievement in a worldwide network that predated the biblical flood.

The point I'm making is that the Great Pyramid is a testimony against the theory of evolution, at least intellectual evolution. There is no ever-upward straight line of human evolution encompassing tens of thousands of years. We know of at least one time of phenomenal scientific understanding within the first two thousand years of human history. Humans could only have been created as fully intelligent beings in order to build a monument as mind-boggling and lasting as the Great Pyramid.

Abraham, no creature evolved from a lower life form to design and build the Great Pyramid of Giza! Human beings were created fully intelligent.

I looked at Harry, and saw profound feeling well up onto his face.

What are you feeling, Harry?

I'm moved by your keen receptiveness, and am immensely grateful for your companionship.

That led to one of our ever-recurring moments of silence, those moments when the profoundness of our discussion became fixed. What we were understanding was very real.

I was referring to something, Avi, when I said, "No creature evolved from a lower life form." I have a quotation from a respected evolutionary scientist of the late twentieth century, Stephen Jay Gould. He listed two striking characteristics of the fossil record:

(1) Stasis: Most species exhibit no directional change during their tenure on Earth. They appear in the fossil record looking much the same as when they disappear.

---

12 See *Why the Pharaohs built The Pyramids with fake stones* by Joseph Davidovits.

(2) Sudden appearance: In any local area, a species does not rise gradually by the steady transformation of its ancestors; it appears all at once and "fully formed."[13]

Gould introduced the theory of *punctuated equilibrium*. He had noticed that the various species in the fossil record appeared suddenly and complete – that there were no transitional forms. Such a conclusion coming from a renowned evolutionary scientist is not only astonishing, but also in harmony with the biblical account of how humans came about: they were created "fully formed."

Gould was not alone. One of his contemporaries agreed, again in a way that cannot be ignored:

> ...I fully agree with your comments on the lack of direct illustration of evolutionary transitions in my book. If I knew of any, fossil or living, I would certainly have included them.... *Gould and the American Museum people are hard to contradict when they say there are no transitional fossils....* I will lay it on the line – there is not one such fossil for which one could make a watertight argument. (*emphasis added*)[14]

Avi, I've already made the point previously, and I could quote more respected and credible scientists. The fossil record does not show that human beings evolved. Quite the opposite: the fossil record proves that humans did not evolve. This has been conclusively demonstrated and acknowledged by many paleontologists for almost fifty years.

So there we have it, Abraham. The Bible, the Great Pyramid at Giza, and the fossil record are all in harmony. Humans came into being completely formed and fully intelligent. No more needs to be said.

I'm really grateful, Harry. I believe the biblical account and the fossil record too. The way you brought the history of the Great Pyramid to life is a big bonus. Humans were smart from the beginning.

---

13 Stephen Jay Gould (1941-2002) was an American paleontologist and evolutionary biologist who taught at Harvard University and worked at the American Museum of Natural History. He was one of the most influential and widely read writers of popular science of his generation. The quote comes from an essay by Bert Thompson, *Biological Evolution*, available on the web. See page 20.

14 Again, the quote appears in Bert Thompson's *Biological Evolution*. Thompson is quoting from a letter by Colin Patterson, a senior paleontologist of the British Museum of Natural History and "one of our generation's foremost authorities on evolution." See page 21 of this outstanding essay by Dr. Bert Thompson.

I waited, hoping my friend would expand on my last point. He didn't disappoint, and picked up on it immediately.

You know, every once in a while I come across the book *Hamlet's Mill*. It tries to harmonize ancient myths with science. The book's author disagrees with seeing history, or evolution, as a long sequence of unfolding events:

> And yet, were history really understood in this admittedly flat sense of things happening one after another to the same stock of people, we should be better off than we are now, when we almost dare not admit the assumption from which this book starts, that *our ancestors of the high and far-off times were endowed with minds wholly comparable to ours*, and were capable of rational processes – always given the means at hand. It is enough to say that this flies in the face of a custom which has become already a second nature.

> Our period may some day be called the Darwinian period, just as we talk of the Newtonian period of two centuries ago. *The simple idea of evolution, which it is no longer thought necessary to examine, spreads like a tent over all those ages that lead from primitivism into civilization.* Gradually, we are told, step by step, men produced the arts and crafts, this and that, until they emerged into the light of history.

> Those soporific words "gradually" and "step by step," repeated incessantly, are aimed at covering an ignorance which is both vast and surprising. One should like to inquire: which steps. But then one is lulled, overwhelmed and stupefied by the gradualness of it all, which is at best a platitude, only good for pacifying the mind, *since no one is willing to imagine that civilization appeared in a thunderclap...*

> *The lazy word "evolution" had blinded us to the real complexities of the past.* (emphasis added).[15]

That's from a very unusual book, but not one without some wisdom.

I took a deep breath.

How should I deal with the hypothesis of evolution when it comes up, as it so

---

15 Giorgio de Santillana, *Hamlet's Mill*, p 68-69.

frequently does?

It's easy, Avi. Just keep in mind that the words evolution and intelligence are not synonymous. Many, many intelligent people don't believe in evolution, including thousands of intelligent scientists. Evolution's popularity doesn't make it true either, nor do statements like "evolution is a proven fact," or "evolution is supported by overwhelming evidence." Such claims are little more than empty words from people who want to believe that evolution is true. You really don't need to respond to the belief in evolution every time it comes up.

We need to choose our battleground carefully, and evolution isn't it. In any event, the theory of evolution has already been soundly defeated even though its defeat is not well known.

I nodded my head and understood.

Evolution is a fairy tale for grownups. Isn't it, Harry?[16]

It's been said often enough. Too often for many scientists.

We've come a long way in our talks Harry. I don't know what you have in mind for next week, but I'd like to review our very first discussion. I've assimilated that the Earth is not a planet. That wasn't even difficult. You must, however, have some understanding of what the Earth is, as opposed to what it is not. Can we revisit this subject?

I'd be glad to. After all, my desire is that we go well beyond dispelling wrong beliefs. I'm trusting that we will end up with a much deeper understanding of who we are now and what we will be in the future. I'm already looking forward to the conclusion of our talks.

Good, but what did you have planned for next Sabbath?

The promised topic. I was going to explain how the months and weeks are set by the moon. Today is the last Sabbath of the month. This month will have thirty days instead

---

16　The quote, "Evolutionism is a fairy tale for grown-ups. This theory has helped nothing in the progress of science. It is useless." has been attributed (perhaps wrongly) to the French scientist Louis Bounoure. However, another famous French scientist, Paul Lemoine, has written, "Evolution is a kind of dogma which its own priests no longer believe, but which they uphold for the people. It is necessary to have the courage to state this if only so that men of a future generation may orient their research into a different direction." Such statements are often an embarrassment to scientific colleagues, and some would like to explain them away or pretend they were never made. One explanation is that the French are jealous because Darwin was not one of their own. (See E.T. Babinski's editorial *Cretinism or Evilution? No. 3.*)

of twenty-nine, making tomorrow a sort of non-day. I'll use tomorrow to prepare for our next meeting. So come two days from now on the New Moon day for both the morning and afternoon. How does that sound?

Good. It will be a double header.

May the Eternal One be with you, Harry.

May the Eternal One be with you, Abraham.

10. THE EARTH IS NOT A PLANET II

I had had six weeks to think about the Earth not moving. I had spent much time outdoors during the day and after dark. I watched as the sun traversed the summer sky. I saw the moon rise from below the Earth's horizon. In a few hours, I observed the motion of the stars. During those weeks, I let it sink into my being that everything was moving relative to my position on the Earth. Ever so slowly, I began to feel from within me that the Earth is fixed and immobile. The motion I observed was real motion and not an illusion.

The experience was compelling. My consciousness drifted from being in a place to being in a whole. At the same time, I felt vulnerable, and my thoughts drifted into a prayer like mode. In my heart of hearts, I acknowledged The Creator of the universe, and my dependence on Him.

Shabbat Shalom, Harry.

Harry looked up from what he had been reading. There was gratitude in his expression, gratitude for my coming. There was a pot of tea sitting on a small table next to him, and a few books. Before pouring me a cup, he stood up to greet me.

Shabbat shalom to you too, Abraham. As my believing grandmother used to say, "The morning has gold in its mouth." Better yet, as a poet insisted, it is The Creator who has "commanded the morning."[1]

That's exactly what I was thinking this week, Harry. There is **being** and **consciousness** within the created order. The universe can't just be a mass of atoms, or physical matter. There must be something else besides forces like gravity and electromagnetism.

I laughed out loud at myself.

---

1   Job 38:12.

I don't know where that came from. I'm not much of a scientist, and not nearly as well read as yourself. I'm a little embarrassed.

You needn't be. Wisdom has a way of making itself known. The Father is giving you understanding.

Do you really think so?

Absolutely. Remember, there is a way of knowing something beyond scientific knowledge. Call it revelation or intuition or something else, but at some time, we need to be told who and what we are. In that regard, the Hebrew Scriptures tell us that the Earth is fixed, immobile, and central to the created order. As one biblical scholar put it, "The Bible teaches that the Earth is Geocentric physically, galactically and spiritually."[2]

I'm all ears, Harry.

Here's an interesting paradox, Avi. Unbelievers have often attacked the Bible for teaching that the sun revolves around the Earth. For four hundred years now, the Earth-centeredness of the Scriptures has been used to make the Bible look foolish and science to look wise. The Bible is said to be a primitive and outdated book because it teaches that the sun is moving, not the Earth.

In the current scientific milieu, many Christians are adamant that the Scriptures do not teach that the sun is moving relative to the Earth. They claim the Scriptures are phenomenological, that the sun only appears to be moving from our human perspective. Instead, they say, the Scriptures are not scientific, and more like allegory. As Galileo said, "the Holy Spirit's intention is to teach us how to go to Heaven, and not how the heavens go."[3] (Little do they understand that Galileo was wrong on both counts). The current scientific view has a very powerful hold on many otherwise believing people. Inadvertently, many Christians are rejecting the Bible's teaching and defending popular science. The Scriptures are an embarrassment for them because they contradict the ideas of popular scientific thought.

So isn't that a paradox? Unbelievers are correct about what the Scriptures teach, while many believers deny the Scriptures. Surely, it is as the Messiah said, "The sons of this world are for their own generation wiser than the sons of the light."

Avi, this is only one good example of where we need to let the Scriptures say what they say, that the literal meaning is the real meaning. The literalness of the Scriptures is

2   Dr Thomas M. Strouse, *He Maketh His Sun to Rise*, p 13.

3   From the *Letter to Madame Christine of Lorraine* written by Galileo in 1615.

apparent right from the start in one of the most powerful sentences ever written:

In the beginning, The Almighty One created the heavens and the Earth.

Apparently, there is no word in Hebrew that is equivalent to the English word for universe. Genesis 1:1 does not say, "The Almighty One created *everything.*" The verse divides Creation into two components; the heavens is one component, and the Earth is the other. As the *Wycliffe Bible Encyclopedia* says:

> The word heaven, or the heavens, is used in the Scriptures in a number of different senses. In the most general of these it includes all that is distinguished from the Earth. When employed this way, the words heaven and Earth exclude one another; but when taken together, the two embrace all the universe of [the Almighty].[4]

In Genesis, the Earth is depicted as a very special place. The sun, moon and stars do not appear until the fourth day of Creation, and were made for the sake of the Earth, as lights and to keep time. The Earth is not in the firmament or expanse of Genesis chapter one. The Earth is surrounded by the firmament, but not part of it. To quote from Wycliffe again, the term heaven "is used to embrace all that is visible in the expanse of the universe above man... the term heaven includes the vast realm in which are the sun, the moon, the planets, and the stars." Again, the Earth is a distinct component in what the Creator brought forth.

Avi, what I am going to tell you next may sound strange to your ears, but it is standard biblical interpretation. I'm sure it will take no time at all to become comfortable with it.

Harry looked at me with confidence and affection, and continued.

Genesis 1:6 says that the Mighty One made the expanse to separate the waters under the expanse or firmament from the waters above the firmament. In other words, there is a layer of water beyond the stars enveloping the entire created order. The Earth's surface is three-quarters water with more water in the atmosphere. Beyond the atmosphere is the firmament or what we call space, containing the sun, the moon and the stars. Beyond the stars is the rest of the water, probably in a crystalline state. The Scriptures teach that the created universe is a closed system surrounded by a layer of water. This is what is meant by, "Let there be an expanse between the waters to separate water from water." The firmament containing the sun, moon and stars is what separates the waters below the firmament from the waters above the firmament.

---

4   Moody Bible Institute of Chicago, 1975. See **Heaven**.

I have another illustration for you, Abraham. My nephew, Oliver Knapp, has drawn them for me. He's quite a skilled graphic artist. Here's what the heavens and the Earth look like from the opening verses in Genesis:

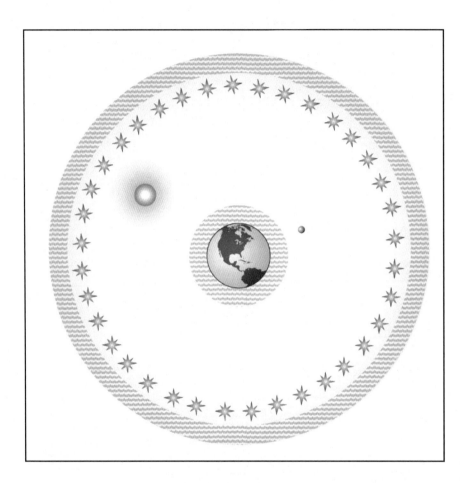

What do think about this, Avi? Does it sound strange?

In a way, it does, but I would never dismiss an idea just because it comes from the Bible. That's just too easy even though it's often done. The question I would ask is, how does it stand up to scientific scrutiny?

Harry looked at me with gratitude.

It took me a little while to adjust, Avi. It was one of those times I forced myself to consider what the Scriptures were saying. Once I gave it a chance, it began to make sense. It's why I mentioned the Hans-Thirring experiments with a non-moving body inside a rotating sphere. Thirring described it as "the field inside a uniformly rotating, infinitesimally thin, hollow sphere of uniform density."[5] That is very similar to the biblical universe which is spherical, rotating, and bounded by a layer of hyper-crystalline water.[6] Science actually supports the idea of a spherical rotating universe with the Earth at rest in its centre.

I also mentioned the Celestial Sphere. In science it's an imaginary sphere with the Earth at its centre, and with all the objects of the sky imprinted on its inside surface. The Celestial Sphere doesn't account for distance because observationally we can't tell how far away the stars are. We only see stars of varying brightness against a dark background, and we see them rotating around us in unison every twenty-four hours. Even though the Celestial Sphere is a very useful tool in astronomy and navigation, scientists insist that it's an imaginary sphere. However, in the biblical model it's very real with the Earth at the centre of a rotating sphere.

Abraham, in the biblical model there are three heavens. In Genesis One, there are only two. The Hebrew word, *hashshamayim*, is one of several Hebrew words that is always dual, and demands the meaning of two. So in Genesis 1, the first heaven is the Earth's atmosphere, where life is sustainable; and the second heaven is the expanse or firmament containing the moon, sun, planets, comets and stars. There is no third heaven in Genesis One, but other verses imply that the third heaven was created at the same time.[7] The third heaven is called the highest heaven or the heaven of heavens. Psalm 148:4 tells us that the third heaven is also inside the watery boundary of the universe. The highest heaven is where the Almighty dwells with His heavenly host albeit invisible to the human eye. There are traditions about seven heavens, but only three heavens are identified in the Scriptures.

Avi, I have an idea that may help complete the picture.

Harry looked at me carefully in an awkward and self-conscious way.

Do you mind if I speculate a little? It's my own idea.

---

5   *The Effect of Rotating Distant Masses in Einstein's Theory of Gravitation,* by Hans Thirring (Translated from the *Physicalische Zeitschrift*, 1918.)

6   In the throne room of heaven is a "sea of glass like crystal" or "a sea of glass mingled with fire" (Rev 4:6, 15:2). The fire could be the light of the stars just under the third heaven. See below.

7   See Job 38:7, Nehemia 9:6, and Colossians 1:16.

Please do, Harry. What you are saying makes sense to me.

Thank you. My idea about the third heaven helps me to visualize the created order. It's like this.

Several texts say that the Highest Heaven is in the North, and one says that it is above the stars,[8] but how can heaven always be in the North? My idea comes from Ezekiel's wheel within a wheel, with a small wheel inside a large wheel. The Highest Heaven is the smaller wheel rotating between the crystalline boundary of the universe and the layer of stars just beneath it. Think of it as a cogged wheel meshing with the cogs of the rotating crystalline sphere. As the crystalline sphere rotates – and with it the entire second heaven including the sun, moon and stars – the third heaven rotates in the opposite direction. Maybe, as the cosmos rotates westward, the third heaven rotates eastward which allows the third heaven to always be in the North. My idea is supported by Job 14:22, in which "Eloah walks in the circuit of the heavens." The entire cosmos or second heaven has a rotational motion which allows the third heaven to remain in place in the North.

---

8   Isaiah 14:13, Psalm 75:6 and Job 26:7.

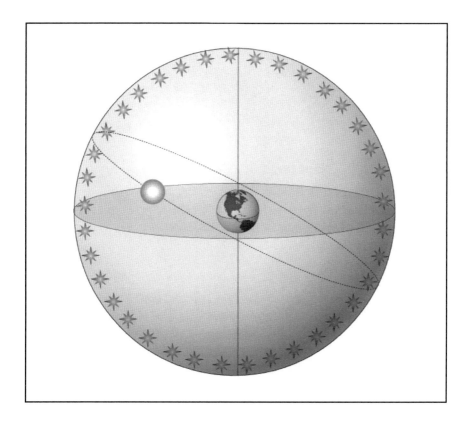

To complete the picture, the second heaven or cosmos including the third heaven is rotating around the Earth and the first heaven. In other words, the Earth with its atmosphere is fixed at the centre of the universe, and is motionless. The only motion in the universe relative to the Earth is the rotation of the second heaven or cosmos. Looking down from the third heaven, the Earth is fixed and motionless.[9] It is said to be The Creator's footstool. It's hard to imagine a footstool that's in constant motion. Keep in mind that the third heaven is inside the created universe, even if my idea of a wheel within a wheel is a bit speculative. The highest heaven is not just a spiritual realm, or something that is above and beyond the created universe. The abode of the Almighty is a real place, and He dwells to the north on the axis of the rotating cosmos. That completes the biblical picture of Creation.

I bless the Father, Harry. The Earth is truly a very special place!

---

9   Psalm 93:1 is the classic proof text, "The world is firmly established; it cannot be moved."

Yes, it is. Isaiah 45:18 says the Earth was formed to be inhabited. That puts paid to the foolishness of other created beings inhabiting other places in the cosmos. The universe was designed to have life at its centre and nowhere else. That's the place we now inhabit.

I stood up and paced about. That seemed to be the signal for when one of us needed a break. Harry settled quietly back into his chair. After a while, I came back with a thought.

It seems to me that when Joshua commanded the sun and the moon to stand still, it is one of the best proofs that the sun is normally moving. After all, everyone agrees that the moon is moving, so if the sun and the moon both stop moving in the same context, then the sun must be moving just as the moon is moving. It can't be said that the moon actually stopped, while the sun only appeared to stop.

That's right, Avi. The text actually says, "the sun stood still, and the moon stopped." In the same passage, David describes the sun's motion as a circuit in heaven repeated day after day from one end of heaven to the other. Also, in Ecclesiastes, the sun rises and sets, the winds blow in circular courses, and the rivers flow without ceasing. Everything has motion except for the Earth, which remains forever, or "stands secure." In the Scriptures, the Earth is normally fixed in its position.[10]

Harry stood up too.

Not surprisingly, there are arguments against the Earth being at the centre of a revolving sphere or universe. I will mention only two. The first argument is very interesting, and has to do with the speed of rotation. Supposedly, if the entire universe is rotating, then everything farther out than Jupiter must be going at speeds faster than the speed of light, and anything at the outer edge of the cosmos at speeds impossible to imagine. Presumably then, at those speeds the cosmos would simply fly apart.

However, contrast the biblical universe with the 'scientific' one. In the Scriptures, the entire created order is a closed system, where the cosmos is surrounded or enclosed by a layer of hyper-crystalline water. In the Big Bang model, the universe also has a boundary, but it is expanding nevertheless, and its boundary moving outward and supposedly to infinity. Currently, it is believed that the universe has a diameter of 156 billion light-years, and that the outer stars are moving away at nearly the speed of light. In such a universe, it's reasonable to assume that the universe is not rotating every twenty-four hours. If it was, it would fly apart at a rate even faster than the rate of its expansion. In contrast, in a closed system bounded by an outer shell of crystalline water, it is the rotation of the universe that

---

10 See Joshua 10:12-13, Psalm 19:4-6 and Ecclesiastes 1:5-8. See also Isaiah 38:8 and II Kings 20:9-11 where the sun's movement is reversed.

keeps it from collapsing in on itself. Such a system must rotate at a certain speed, and by design that speed is every twenty-four hours. In scientific terms, it's the centrifugal and centripetal forces that keep the Earth in place and the universe from collapsing.

Moreover, it is the entire universe that is rotating, and not each individual object in the system. In other words, the crystal boundary, the stars, the sun and the moon, all rotate in unison.[11] No one body in the universe is moving at the speed of light relative to any other body in the universe. Such an argument only shows a lack of understanding in the fundamental difference between the biblical universe and the scientific one. In the biblical model, the universe is a closed system while in the current scientific model, the universe is open and expanding.

A second argument against the geocentricity of the Scriptures is that "all the scientists can't be wrong," or "surely NASA knows the Earth is moving." Well Avi, the truth is that all scientists can be wrong. In fact, the whole world can be wrong. It's just as the Christian Scriptures say, that because humankind refused to honor the Creator, He sent them a strong delusion so that they would believe a lie instead of the truth.[12] I am told that only 18% of Americans believe the sun revolves around the Earth. Supposedly, 82% believe the opposite, that the Earth revolves around the sun. For the theory of Evolution, the statistics are more favorable. About 45% of Americans believe that humankind was created less than ten thousand years ago, and only 55% of Americans believe that the Almighty had nothing to do with the origin of life.[13] So yes, not all scientists are wrong, but the world is still a very deluded place, and scientists can be deceived as much as the rest of us.

What the scientists at NASA "know" is more subtle. They are much too clever to let what they think they know interfere with their work. The NASA website says, "The planetary community's chief source for such information is the Astronomical Almanac, which is prepared jointly by the U. S. Naval Observatory and the Royal Greenwich Observatory."[14] That can only mean that NASA uses fixed-Earth formulas the majority of the time because the information from the two observatories are fixed-Earth observations. Plotting the motions of the stars and planets by their appearance is a practice that began with the Babylonians and continues in modern times. The position of a planet is plotted in relation to the Earth's horizon and the time of day when it is observed. No assumption is made about the Earth's motion when plotting the position and motion of the stars and planets. The supposed rotation of the Earth and the Earth's supposed orbital motion are not taken into account. The tables of the Astronomical Almanac are based

---

11 Actually, the sun rotates more slowly than the stars which is why we see the sun traverse the nightly sky every twelve to thirteen months.
12 A combination of Romans 1:18-26 and 2 Thessalonians 2:10-11. MUST READ PASSAGES!
13 Gallup polls: 1982-2004
14 http://eclipse.gsfc.nasa.gov/TYPE/preface.html (August 2010)

on fixed-Earth assumptions. NASA scientists probably all do believe that the Earth turns on its axis, but that is not the basis for their astronomical work. Those who want to say that NASA "knows" the Earth is moving do not understand how NASA scientists do their work.

Harry came and sat down. I could tell he wanted to say more, but I wasn't in a hurry because I wanted to let what he had said sink in. I was getting the impression that we were not just discussing ideas or being intellectual. There was substance in what Harry was saying, something that my inner being was attaching to. I was deeply immersed in my thoughts when Harry began to speak again.

Avi, I find it disconcerting to think that the Earth is a small and moving body in the vastness of space. The idea that everything is moving, including the Earth, is unnerving. When I allow myself to think that the Earth is orbiting the sun, with the sun rotating inside a galaxy, with the galaxy receding into space, and space expanding at an enormous speed... I feel disconnected from reality. Such things are surely just ideas that have nothing to do with how things really are. I feel that if I allow such ideas to fill my mind and being, the truth gets crowded out. In doing that, I lose my connection with what is real.

What Harry was saying was so similar to what I had just been thinking that I responded easily.

That's just what I was thinking, Harry. All those theories about the universe are still just theories and ideas. All those visual images about sun and planets in motion are still just visual images. They don't match up with what I see and experience. In my perception, everything is moving except the Earth. That's what I felt the other night when I looked up at the stars.

When I looked over at my friend, he had only a slightly pensive look on his face. I wondered why he didn't just laugh at the absurdity of the scientific theories about Creation, but he never did. It was not his way to laugh at ideas any more than to laugh at people. Harry's indifference to ideas and theories was so impersonal, and beneath that was his ever-present compassion. He picked up a little book and answered quietly.

I have this book written about the Milky Way. Right in the first paragraph, on only the third line the author says, "But this rising and setting is an illusion. Indeed, your view of the sky is deceptive and reveals very little of the truth."[15] It's a wonder how this man can be so sure that what he sees with his very own eyes is just an illusion, that he cannot trust

15   *The Milky Way, Galaxy Number One* by Franklyn M. Branley, Thomas K. Crowell Co, New York, 1969.

in his own senses. He can tell himself that what he sees is a lie. How sad.

How can that be, Harry? Isn't science driven by observation, experiment, and verifiable facts?

Not theoretical science. Here's a quotation from a paper I have in my files:

> The inventor of the electric world we live in, Nikola Tesla, was spot-on when he remarked that modern non-applied science has become nothing more than manipulative indulgence in fancy "thought experiments" and abstract, fuzzy math, which have no relation to reality. Instead of theories being made to fit reality, what we have is the opposite: reality being adjusted or in fact completely overthrown.[16]

Abraham, I see no reason why we should accept all the scientific theories and ideas about the universe. Many of them can never be proven. The far distant stars cannot be explored in the same way that the Earth was once explored, nor can they be explored in a laboratory. Nor can we do experiments involving billions of years in time and space. No one can objectively verify that the universe is expanding. There is so little that connects the scientific theories about the universe with experience. In effect, the only way we can accept these theories is by denying our senses, rejecting our experience, and throwing away our common sense. So let's just close our eyes and ignore our daily encounter with sunrise and sunset.

In the end, it's much easier to believe what the Scriptures say about Creation. Genesis One tells us the Earth is surrounded by the first heaven, which is the atmosphere. Next comes the second heaven containing the sun, moon and stars. Finally, there is a layer of water enclosing the entire universe. In other words, there are a series of spheres: the Earth, the atmosphere, the firmament, and a physical boundary of crystalline water. The biblical model is simple and straightforward by comparison.

Nor is it difficult to comprehend that The Creator Himself has a dwelling place inside the created order. Of course, He cannot be contained by His own Creation, but many scriptures tell us that He has His habitation in the heavens.[17] So in some way He is inside the create order and not just everywhere. The author of Revelation had a similar idea:

And I heard a great voice out of heaven saying,
Behold, the tabernacle of the Almighty is with men,

---

16 *The Rotating Earth.. Theory, Fact or Fiction?* Web based, author unknown. Recommended reading for beginners. This paper covers all the main characters and events in the history of the geocentric debate.
17 Genesis 24:3, 1 Kings 8:30, 2 Chronicles 6:21, Psalm 123:1 and Isaiah 40:22 for example.

**and he will dwell with them, and they shall be his people,
and the Almighty Himself shall be with them, and be their Mighty One.**[18]

Harry paused and sat quietly before resuming.

The Scriptures also say there are limitations to how much we can understand. The stars cannot be counted, and yet the Father calls them all by name.[19] It's quite possible that some the stars are images reflected off the layer of hyper-crystalline water surrounding the universe. Job 37:18 describes the sky as a molten or cast metal mirror. From time to time, astronomers have also considered that some of the visible stars may be reflected images, so our limitation comes from something other than not being able to see all the stars. Similarly, we are told in Jeremiah that the heavens cannot be measured or the foundations of the Earth searched out.[20] There are practical reasons and unknown factors that limit man's ability to probe the Earth and especially the cosmos.

Moses Maimonides, the great Jewish scholar of the twelfth century, wrote:

> But of the things in the heavens man knows nothing except a few mathematical calculations, and you see how far these go. I say in the words of the poet, "The heavens are the Lord's, but the earth He hath given to the sons of man" (Ps. cxv. 16); that is to say, God alone has a perfect and true knowledge of the heavens, their nature, their essence, their form, their motions, and their causes; but He gave man power to know the things which are under the heavens: here is man's world, here is his home, into which he has been placed, and of which he is himself a portion. This is in reality the truth. For the facts which we require in proving the existence of heavenly beings are withheld from us: the heavens are too far from us, and too exalted in place and rank. *Man's faculties are too deficient to comprehend even the general proof the heavens contain for the existence of Him who sets them in motion. It is in fact ignorance or a kind of madness to weary our minds with finding out things which are beyond our reach, without having the means of approaching them.* We must content ourselves with that which is within our reach, and that which

---

18 Revelation 21:3
19 Genesis 15:5, Jeremiah 33:22 and Psalm 147:4.
20 Scientists have probed less than seven miles (12 km) into the Earth, and less than twelve billion miles into space. The Kola Superdeep Borehole is still the deepest borehole ever drilled, reaching 12,262 meters (40,230 ft) in 1989. The Voyager 1 spacecraft launched by NASA in 1977 is now 11.4 billion miles from the Earth. Such probes have penetrated only a small fraction of the known depth of the Earth and estimated size of the universe.

cannot be approached by logical inference let us leave to [God]. (*emphasis added*).

Maimonides' words remain true. Modern cosmology is still based on mathematical calculations and Earth-bound physics. The biblical Job was once asked, "Do you know the ordinances of the heavens? Can you establish their rule upon the Earth?"[21] The same challenge remains for every present-day scientist: Do you know the physical laws of deep space, and do they apply here on the Earth? The answer – cosmologists can't discover the "the ordinances of the heavens." Few scientists, however, would like to admit that their knowledge is limited to their earthly environment, or that the physics of deep space is unknowable.

Avi, I hesitate about getting philosophical, but what we call science today is attempting to do the impossible. Scientists want to discover a "theory about everything," but if such a theory exists, its laws must include the thoughts and actions of the very scientists who are trying to discover the theory. Likewise, any theory produced by a human mind can never completely explain the human mind that produced the theory. It's truly absurd, much like the farmer trying to lift the bale of hay on which he is standing. Eventually the farmer may see the problem, but the scientist who keeps trying to do the impossible hasn't realized that he is making himself the centre of everything. Is that too philosophical, Avi?

I shook my head rather vigorously.

Avi, most scientists won't even consider what the Hebrew Scriptures say about cosmology. They can't even imagine that the Bible might have something to offer in their search to understand the universe. So much so, that for them, rejecting biblical insight is tantamount to intellectual liberation. For them, rejecting the Scriptures will make them more objective and impartial as scientists. It makes them feel liberated.[22] No wonder we read in Psalm 2:

Why do the nations rage, and the peoples meditate a vain thing?
The kings of the earth set themselves, and the rulers take counsel together,
Against YHWH, and against His anointed, saying,
'Let us break their bonds asunder, and cast away their cords from us.'
He that sits in the heavens will laugh: the
Master will have them in derision.

---

21 Job 38:33
22 As Philip E. Johnson put it in ***Reason in the Balance***: "Naturalism and its evolutionary satellite declare that the "death [intellectual discrediting] of God" is the essential metaphysical prelude to a true understanding of "how things really are" (p 109).

All at once, the ground seemed to rear under my chair. I wanted to hold onto something, but everything was tottering. Even my mind was being wrenched back and forth. I wanted to panic, but instead closed my eyes and allowed the reeling to continue. I felt the premonition at the core of my being.

Then I heard Harry's voice and saw him looking at me in his normal way.

Eventually we will need to talk about something I mentioned earlier, that the Almighty will shake the heavens and the Earth again.

Another wave of reeling came over me, but I kept calm. I knew I had experienced what Harry was referring to even before he said it.

However, let's stick with our topic for now, Abraham. The biblical view of the created universe is geocentric or Earth-centered. That's still true no matter how much some Bible believers argue against it. What's really astonishing, however, is that science is confirming that the universe is geocentric – no matter how much some scientists are arguing against it. The truth is hard to accept in the world of science as much as in the world of religion.

Here's something from a paper I wrote a few years ago:

> Observational scientists have been acknowledging geocentricity for several decades. In his 1937 book, *The Observational Approach to Cosmology*, the now famous Edwin Hubble wrote, *"Such a condition would imply that we occupy a unique position in the universe, analogous, in a sense, to the ancient conception of a central Earth."*[23] In a 1995 article in *Scientific American*, one of the world's leading theorists in cosmology, George Ellis, declared, *"I can construct you a spherically symmetrical universe with Earth at its center, and you cannot disprove it based on observations."*[24] Even the ultra-renowned physicist Stephen Hawking has said, "all this evidence that the universe looks the same whichever direction we look might seem to suggest there is something special about our place in the universe... [that] *we must be at the center of the universe.*"[25] By the end of the twentieth century, it was not only geocentricists who were aware of the Earth's apparent centrality, orthodox scientists were also acknowledging that the universe did appear to be Earth-centered.

23 Gibbs, W. Wayt, 1995. "Profile: George F.R. Ellis; Thinking Globally, Acting Universally," *Scientific American* 273 (4):28-29.
24 *Scientific American* 273 (4):28-29
25 Hawking, Stephen W, *A Brief History of Time*, Bantam Books, 1988, p 42.

The observational evidence had become overwhelming. One simple observation is that the number of stars and galaxies increases fairly equally in all directions. That is, if you count all the stars in one direction, and compare it with the count in the opposite direction, the number is always about the same. Similarly, radio sources are isotropic or have the same value when measured in every direction. After Hubble discovered the red-shifts, they were whimsically called "the fingers of God," because, as measurements of distance, they show long lines, all pointing inwardly toward the Earth, and from every direction. The mass (matter) of the universe also has a pattern with the Earth seemingly at the densest part of the universe. That is, the universe becomes less and less dense as one moves away from the Earth. Quasars, a specific kind of galaxy, form concentric shells around the Earth, or a series of shells all centered on the Earth. The most compelling evidence was discovered in 1965 in a study of the microwave background radiation. A 1976 article in Scientific American, acknowledged, *"This observation seems to suggest that the universe is remarkably symmetrical and, what is even more extraordinary, that we happen to be at its center."* What's more, the universe itself seems to be rotating around a central axis according to the satellite experiment, COBE, launched in 1989. Such observational evidence can be found in standard scientific text books, and while they are open to interpretation, the apparent centrality of the Earth has been widely acknowledged. (*emphasis added*).[26]

I know that's a lot of details and needs some careful reading, but these are the kind of things that astronomers are saying quite openly. Not all scientists have their academic blinders on, and many are intellectually honest. They understand what all the new telescopic and satellite information is revealing about our universe.

No matter in which direction we look, the Earth seems to be equidistant from everything else, meaning that the Earth seems to be at the centre of everything. In a way, that appearance isn't surprising. The Copernican Principle indirectly states that any location in the universe should appear to be at the centre of the universe, but the theory is now in doubt, and very sophisticated experiments are being devised to test the Copernican Principle. At least some scientists are willing to consider that the Copernican model might be wrong. Many scientific premises have been overturned in the past, and so too may the Copernican model of the fourteenth century.

---

26 "The Earth is NOT a Planet" 2011.

That's quite technical, I know. The scientific language and technical details can't compare with the simplicity of Genesis chapter one, but the similarity is still there and obvious. Both descriptions put the Earth at the centre of the universe. What's more, the Scriptures and science both have the Earth at the centre of a revolving universe although the speed of rotation is very different. Finally, the universe is composed of a series of concentric spheres. In the Scriptures, the spheres are called heavens. In science, the concentric spheres are bordered by layers of quasars. The language may be very different, but the biblical and scientific descriptions of the universe are fundamentally similar.

I'll repeat myself. With all the new and very powerful telescopes of the twentieth century, astronomers have made a surprising discovery. The universe looks to be the same in every direction, and the Earth appears to be at the centre of the universe. In just one example, the galaxies of stars are in elongated clusters that point back to the Earth. These long filaments of galaxies stretch out and away in every direction. Again, scientists have dubbed them the "Fingers of God" because they point to the Earth as a very special place. That's the picture we have of the Earth's place in the universe from our modern telescopes.[27]

Which brings us back to what the Bible says about the Earth. If you remember, in the act of Creation, the Almighty stretched the universe out and away from the Earth in every direction. He worked on the Earth first, and then stretched out the firmament to reveal the sun and the stars. Now, nearly four hundred years after Galileo, our astronomers are inadvertently telling us the same thing. The biblical picture was right all along!

Avi, I'm not trying to prove that everything the Bible says is true. Obviously, you know by now that I don't believe that, but to categorically dismiss the Bible as a source of truth is prejudicial and closed-minded. The Hebrew Scriptures – and the Christian Scriptures – have much to tell us about ourselves and the reality we live in. Fundamental to that is the Earth's place in the universe. Try as they might, many scientists are proving what they desperately don't want to believe, that we human beings are the very purpose that the universe was created for in the first place.

I'll finish on this note. We can talk about the Scriptures as revelation, and some of it surely must be. It's just as possible that the ancients understood the nature of the universe intuitively, and were more directly perceptive of the world around them. It seems they

---

27 The description "Fingers of God" results from an interpretation of the observed red-shift in galaxies. Involved in the same interpretation is an alternative definition of gravity, that gravity is 'pushing' rather than 'pulling.' In other words, gravity is pushing away from the Earth instead of pulling towards the Earth. That is what one would expect in a rotating universe; it's the rotation of the universe that keeps it from collapsing. The mass of the universe is being 'pushed' outward. See "The Observational Impetus For "Le Sage" Gravity" by Halton C. Arp.

had no impetus to deny what their senses were telling them, or conclude that the motion they observed in the heavens wasn't real motion. What they wrote as 'scripture' was born of experience from what they saw with their own eyes day after day. As the Psalmist said:

> **The heavens are telling of the glory of El;**
> **And their expanse is declaring the work of His hands.**
> **Day to day pours forth speech,**
> **And night to night reveals knowledge.**
> **There is no speech, nor are there words;**
> **Their voice is not heard.**[28]

Avi, I contend that what the ancients observed and experienced is what they wrote as Scripture. That doesn't mean they didn't have insight that can only come from above. That part bothers secular scientists and keeps them from using the Bible as a resource. Nevertheless, some of them are coming around to the true nature of the universe by being honest about what their telescopes are telling them. We are, after all, rational beings and cannot depart from the truth indefinitely. Inevitably, we have to return to what is reasonable and in harmony with our experience, not to mention common sense.

Harry breathed in deeply and absorbed his surroundings. He plainly enjoyed his yard and being outdoors.

All right, Avi. Let's go back to having a conversation. I've lectured enough. I want to know what you're thinking too.

I had been collecting my thoughts even as I listened to Harry's 'lecture.'

I caught something you said earlier. You made a remark about Galileo's saying that "the Holy Spirit's intention is to teach us how to go to Heaven, and not how the heavens go." You remarked that he was wrong on both counts. I'm curious about what you meant.

When I looked over at Harry, I thought that his heart was about to burst. His face was full of wonder, surprise, gratitude and affection. Harry was doing the opposite of what I had just done. He was allowing me see the intensity of his feelings. Here was a man who could easily bare his soul.

I appreciate being listened to, Abraham. I don't have all the answers and still need to be corrected myself, but if we can just listen to each other, we'll make progress in the right direction. There's always some truth in any dialogue. I'm so grateful for our time together.

---

28 Psalm 19:1-3.

Just then, there was a loud chattering between two ground squirrels nearby. Harry's eyes twinkled as if to ask, "Is that us?"

To answer your question, the so-called Holy Spirit is not telling us how to go to Heaven. No one is going to Heaven, and certainly not to Hell. Our religious leaders, who by endless repetition have taught us to read their foolishness into the Scriptures, have imposed that fiction on us. Our conception of heaven and hell doesn't come from the 'Holy Spirit' or the Bible.

The other matter is also not true because the Spirit of the Almighty is telling us how the heavens go, and so does the Bible. Galileo's statement was a beginning in the separation of science and religion. In effect, Galileo was saying that the Bible cannot make statements that are scientific, and that science can make statements that are not spiritual. Not everyone agrees. Historically speaking, the separation of science and religion took more than a few centuries following Galileo. Even today, there's a significant minority of scientists and lay-scholars who still believe that the Scriptures are telling us "how the heavens go."

Let's go for a walk, Avi.

I was glad for the opportunity, still feeling that I needed to clear my head. I wanted to feel the Earth under my feet again. It made me feel secure.

Only one side of Harry's lot was on a busy street. The rest of his property was quiet and lined with old trees. With no walkway and no traffic, we could enjoy strolling on the streets. The walk affected Harry's mood too. For an elderly man, his pace was healthy and almost playful. He enjoyed being in motion.

Abraham, we have spent two mornings on the Earth not being a planet or orbiting the sun. What conclusions have you made?

I have made two conclusions, Harry. The first is that human beings can be deceived en masse. More to the point, humankind can and does believe in many lies. I understand why you emphasize the Earth not being a planet. It's such a good example. It's safe to say most people won't even consider it, that the Earth isn't a planet, but that's deception, isn't it? Human beings don't know when they are deceived.

I thought about your reference to Romans 1:18-26 and 2 Thessalonians 2:10-11. It does seem as if unbelievers can't even choose their own delusion, and that the Almighty sends them an appropriate lie, but that's Paul again and needs to be taken with a grain of salt. A lie can't come from the Creator because He is not a liar. Only truth and goodness can come from Him. Humans surely create and choose their own lies. We can't blame the Almighty for our own delusions.

Perhaps this is the place to say that the Almighty Father didn't put the contradictions and opposing views in the Bible. They weren't put there by His intention. Humans added much and probably took away too. I know that makes it difficult for us to know what's what in the Bible, but with practice we can know the difference if we're willing try.

I noticed a certain fatherliness on Harry's face.

My other conclusion? The truth is in some way always connected with our everyday experience. That the sun rises and sets daily is a witness to the truth. What we see is real. On the other hand, the notion of stars many billions of light years distant and moving away from us at nearly the speed of light has nothing to do with experience. That notion appeals to the imagination and sounds like fiction; so too is the idea that the Earth is spinning and whizzing through space and changing its location minute by minute. We don't experience that or have any sensation of it. The biblical description of the universe is much easier to believe than the so-called scientific description because of its direct connection with our experience.

Harry, it occurred to me a few days ago that if navigators can plot their position at sea by the stars, then the stars must also tell us the time. Therefore, I went on the internet, and sure enough, there is a twenty-four hour clock on the Earth's horizon with three stars always pointing in a straight line.[29] As the sky turns, those stars tell the time. All the A.M. hours are on the Western horizon and all the P.M. hours on the Eastern horizon. Pretty neat, and it works through all the seasons. However, it would not work on Mars, for example, where the configuration of the stars changes throughout the year. That celestial clock is unique to the Earth and the Earth's position at the centre of a rotating universe. Amazing.

Harry gave me a pat on the back with a look as close to amusement as he could possibly muster.

Avi, where did you get all that?

I think about our discussions during the week, Harry, and things come to me.

You know, what's good about this is that we don't have to be super intelligent to know what's true. It can take hard work, and definitely a desire to learn, but anyone with average

---

29   The Pole Star, the Great Bear and Cassiopeia.

intelligence can acquire real knowledge. As the Psalmist David said, "I have more understanding than all my teachers, for thy testimonies are my meditation."[30] David didn't have a degree in science, but he knew that the sun moves in a circuit.[31] We shouldn't allow ourselves to be intimidated by highly educated jargon. Talk is cheap, no matter how intelligent it sounds. We can go a long way with some common sense and a bit of Scripture here and there.

I want to add a caveat, though. Common sense is an acquired ability to some extent, and we aren't just born with it. It takes time and practice. Otherwise, we just fall back on what we think we know. That's why we're talking about all the traditions that we take for granted. We accept them because we haven't honed our ability to use common sense.

I'm proud of you, Avi, although not surprised.

I nodded my thanks to Harry. He had listened so carefully and with such keen attention. Harry was a teacher all right, but a learner at heart.

Actually, it's been quite easy. Once I allowed myself to think outside the box, I learned quickly. If I wasn't so willing, I could never have broken with Copernicus and four hundred years of history. If anything, pride could hold me back, but I have no stake in the matter. My reputation and livelihood aren't an issue. I wish I could say the same for all professional scientists and theologians. There's too much at stake for them.

There was another of those long pauses. Perhaps strangely, I wanted to dwell on my own thoughts. They were still new to me and refreshing.

Harry waited before he spoke.

We can't underestimate what Copernicus did for humankind's future. Historians have often said that no idea ever changed human thinking more radically than the one Copernicus proposed around 1500 A.D.[32] Besides undermining the Scriptures, it took humankind out of our favored position in the universe, and laid the groundwork for the theory of evolution. It took all of four hundred years, but finally the doctrine of

---

30 Psalm 119:99

31 Psalm 19:4-6

32 "Among all the discoveries and convictions not a single one has resulted in a deeper influence on the human spirit than the doctrine of Copernicus... Humanity has perhaps never been asked to do more, for consider all that went up in smoke as a result of this change becoming consciously realized: a second paradise, a world of innocence, poetry and piety, the witness of the senses, the conviction of a poetic and religious faith..." (J. W. von Goethe. *Geschichte der Farbenlehre, Dritte Abteilung, Zwischenbetrachtung*, Walter van der Kamp translation in his paper *The Achilles' Heel of the Creationists' Position*, p 10.)

Copernicus became fixed in the human mind. Now it's nearly impossible to go back except for some very brave men and women who, like you, are willing to think outside the box. That's why I'm so proud of you, Avi.

We walked on, and I waited for Harry to complete his summation.

Geocentricity confirms that there is something fundamentally true about the Bible. In good measure, geocentricity is all about throwing off the shackles of heliocentricity and declaring that the Scriptures are indeed trustworthy. That includes the many statements in the Bible about the Earth being fixed and at the centre of the created universe.[33] Finally, geocentricity completely exposes and destroys the theory of evolution since the Earth is by design a very special place. An Earth at the centre of a rotating universe is undeniably unique. That's why the biblical truth of Genesis 1:1 is so resounding.

In the beginning, the Mighty One created the heavens and the Earth.

I absorbed the reverence of the moment, and then spoke up.

Harry, is this going to change anything? What if a small minority believe the truth about the created universe.

That's a good question, Avi, and something I'm hoping we can share a vision about. It's my prayer that, as the Almighty's people, we can unshackle ourselves from the things that are not true. A greater unity is sure to follow. May the Creator and our Father hear the cry of our bondage.

I wasn't being skeptical when I asked the question, Harry. I'm with you on this. We need to be set free from our intellectual and spiritual taskmasters. That won't begin to happen, however, until we comprehend the depth of our imprisonment by both science and religion. At least I'm catching on.

Yes, you are, and I'm so pleased.

Thank you, Harry. In my conclusions, it can't be overemphasized that we are a deceived people. I mean those of us who believe in the Almighty, the Messiah and the Scriptures. I mean those of us who have a genuine piety, biblical sense of morality and

33 Technically, the Earth may not be at the exact centre of the created universe. If the Earth is slightly off-centre, it can explain the parallax of some stars and other observed phenomena. *Parallax* is the apparent shift in the position of some stars during the course of a year. As the universe rotates, a small number of stars seem to be annually nearer and then farther away. Note: the measured parallax is very, very small, and far from able to give us any certain knowledge about the size of the universe.

do many good things. It's like the prophet Jeremiah said, "The heart is deceitful above all things, and desperately sick; who can understand it?" We have taken to heart all the lies that our fathers and forefathers have told us – lies that are second nature to us now, and we think they're real. We're in a hopeless situation, Harry, until we become aware of it.

As soon as I said it, I had to close my mouth. I couldn't say any more.

Harry was quiet too, until he said:

How dearly the Almighty Father would like to bring His people back to Himself before it's too late.

We walked on for a short distance until we came back to Harry's property. What had been said weighed heavily on me. I knew it was true. I had long ago felt the futility of believing what I had been taught from my youth on. I had given up trying to make sense of the confusion. Now I was willing to face up to the situation.

I looked at Harry again, trying to fathom his demeanor. Despite my friend's interminable sorrow, his outgoing good-will seemed boundless. His sense of well-being included me, or whomever else he was with. Harry didn't have a negative bone in his body. Even when he talked about the things that are not true, he was still my friend.

You're a good friend, Harry.

Thank you, Abraham. We need to encourage each other as much as we can.

As soon as we were back, Harry handed me a sheet of paper.

We are not alone, Avi. A surprising number of secular scientists have embraced geocentricity, and a less surprising number of biblical scientists. Their reasoning is often quite different, but they share a similar premise about the nature of the universe. Here are a few paragraphs along that line. One of them I've already quoted. Take it with you or read it now while I make lunch. It will take me about a half-hour.

I was glad for the time alone. I moved my chair closer to Harry's small pond and sat down. Not wanting more information, I pocketed Harry's paper.[34]

---

34 "Again, the twentieth century has witnessed a surprising proliferation of basically geocentric models of the cosmos... Very importantly, the majority of these are "secular," having been developed by scientists with no explicit interest in, or appeal to, divine revelation. Examples here include the work of P. Gerber, H. Thirring, G. Brown, G. Birkhoff, P. Moon and D. Spencer, J. Nightingale, J. Barbour and B. Bertotti, G. F. Ellis, D. Lynden-Bell, and others. The common component in each of these models is Mach's Principle, the

11. SATURDAY IS NOT THE SABBATH

My friend returned right on schedule.

I'm sure you'll enjoy my lunch. It's curried vegetable soup with fresh bread. The vegetables come from my garden and I bake the bread myself.

Blessed is the Most High for all that He provides.

Enjoy, Avi. I don't know about you, but I'm hungry.

All was within easy reach on the small table between us. I was thankful too, and

---

idea that the universe may be a bounded sphere revolving around the Earth or a point quite near the Earth. After agreeing on this, each embarks in its own direction. Some are based on Einstein's Theory of General Relativity, others upon classical Newtonian mechanics, others still upon newer physical models. After discussing a number of these, Christian astronomer G. Bouw concludes:

All of these physicists (and there is not a geocentric Christian in the bunch) conclude that there is no detectable, experimental difference between having the Earth spin diurnally on an axis as well as orbit the sun once a year, or having the universe rotate about the Earth once a day and possessing a wobble centered on the sun which carries the planets and stars about the Earth once a year. In none of these models would the universe fly apart, nor would a stationary satellite fall to the earth. In every one of these models the astronauts on the moon would still see all sides of the Earth in the course of 24 hours, the Foucault pendulum would still swing exactly the same way as we see it in museums, and the Earth's equator would still bulge. In other words, each of these effects is due to either the centrifugal force, Coriolis force, or some combination of the two, and can be totally explained in any geocentric model...

Encouraged by these developments, biblically oriented scientists and philosophers have stepped forward as well. Modern biblical geocentrists include the father of the movement, W. van der Kamp (1913-1998), the heir to his mantle, Dr. Gerardus Bouw, and a growing cadre of thoughtful colleagues including Dr. Russell Arndts, Dr. Robert Bennett, R. G. Elmendorf, Dr. J. Hansen, Dr. M. Selbrede, P. Stott, and Dr. Robert Sungenis. Most of these men have daringly devoted a significant portion of their career to rescuing modern physics and cosmology from their thralldom to relativity, hoping to restore them once again to what they see as their true and proper foundation: the geocentric cosmology of the Bible."

Quoted from, *The Case for Cosmic Geocentricity*, at clr4u.org (Come Let Us Reason).

we ate slowly with only a smattering of conversation. Once the coffee was poured, Harry began to speak again.

I've faced many changes in my life by putting actions to my words. Not too long ago, I became a committed vegan or began to walk on the path of *veganism*.[1] Much earlier, I began to keep the Sabbath days according to the moon. I firmly believe there's no truth without action.

Changes come in stages. Given my Christian background, I kept Sunday religiously from childhood. Then about twenty-five years ago, I switched to the seventh-day Sabbath associated with Judaism. Now for the past five years, I've made another change by keeping the Sabbath according to the moon's phases. I'm happy with the outcome no matter how long it took.

Until you came along, Harry, I'd never heard of such a thing.

That's not surprising, Avi, although a lunar calendar is still being used in many parts of the world for traditional holidays. As a way of keeping the biblical Sabbaths, however, it's a fairly recent development. I don't think it's been even twenty years since the movement began.

How large is the movement, Harry?

I hesitate to guess, but certainly in the tens of thousands of followers. In terms of the world population, it's a very small minority. However, it is a growing movement.

How did it get started?

I don't know, Avi. An early keeper told me that it began in Australia and then faded out. There's also a claim that someone dreamed it up while in prison. Like all such movements, this one didn't come without controversy and rejection. A common accusation is that keeping the Sabbath by the moon's phases constitutes worshipping the moon, but of course it doesn't.

How did you get started?

When I first heard about it, I thought it was hair-brained, but the subject kept coming up, so I decided to give it serious attention and do the research. Once I did, it took me only a few days to realize it was right.

---

1   *Veganism* is the practice not eating animals or animal products. It's also a conviction that rejects the treatment of all sentient (living) beings as commodities. A follower of veganism is known as a *vegan*.

Why?

Mainly because of the history. All the ancient cultures kept their months by the moon. The very word 'month' comes from the moon. We also know those ancient peoples divided their months into four equal weeks according to the moon's four phases. Each month, therefore, had four weeks in a cycle that was reset by the moon's reappearance.

I've already mentioned how accomplished the Babylonian astronomers were. From the clay tablets they left behind, we know they kept a lunisolar calendar of twelve lunar months, each beginning with a new crescent moon. That historical fact fits with the accusation that the Jews got their lunisolar calendar from the Babylonians during their captivity in the sixth century BC, but the Sumerians used the identical calendar in the fourth millennium BC, including periodically adding a thirteenth month when their annual crops were not ready for harvesting. The Jews didn't get their lunisolar calendar from the Babylonians.

The use of a lunisolar calendar is a universal phenomena. All the ancient peoples used some version of a lunar calendar, and vestiges of it can still be found throughout the modern world in virtually every country. The common thread in all lunisolar calendars is in their application to agriculture, and secondarily in the regulation of communal events. Planting and harvesting was regulated by the moon and so were the periodic festivals. For the ancients, human activity blended with celestial events. Their calendar was the calendar of Creation. For them there was a purpose in the way the heavens were designed. It's just as the Creator said:

And The Mighty One said,
Let there be lights in the firmament of heaven to divide the day from the night; and let them be for signs, and for seasons, and for days and years.[2]

I'm still answering your question, Avi. Why did I adopt the lunar calendar? There are no biblical instructions about the lunar calendar *per se*, but its use is everywhere if you know where to look. The Hebrew word for season (as in the verse above) is *moed,* or the plural *moedim.* The root meaning is an appointed time or festival. The verse is more properly translated as:

... and they shall serve as signs, and for festivals, and for days and years.

With the same application of the Hebrew root, Psalm 104:9 reads as:

---

2   Genesis 1:14.

Elohim appointed the moon for festivals.

Jewish historians and biblical scholars agree that the moon determined the three annual festivals of ancient Israel. That much is clear within the Hebrew Scriptures. What is not entirely self-evident is that the moon also determined the weekly Sabbaths. With careful scrutiny, however, it can be shown that all the numerically identifiable Sabbaths in the Scriptures fall on the eighth, fifteenth, twenty-second or twenty-ninth day of the month. Particularly evident in the Tanak are the Sabbaths falling on the fifteenth day when the moon is full. Two of the three annual festivals begin on the fifteenth day of the month. We can also identify Sabbaths in the Christian Scriptures that follow the same pattern. In fact, Yeshuah kept the Sabbaths according to the moon, which was quite normal in his time.

There's also an abundance of external evidence.[3] Philo, the famous Jewish philosopher of the first century AD, certainly believed that the weeks were according to

---

3   "The New Moon is still, and the Sabbath originally was, dependent upon the lunar cycle.... Originally, the New Moon was celebrated in the same way as the Sabbath; gradually it became less important while the Sabbath became more and more a day of religion and humanity, of religious meditation and instruction, of peace and delight of the soul" (*Universal Jewish Encyclopedia*, "Holidays," p 410).

"With the development of the importance of the Sabbath as a day of consecration and the emphasis laid upon the significant number seven, the week became more and more divorced from its lunar connection" (*Universal Jewish Encyclopedia*, Vol. X, "Week," p 482.).

"The week of seven days was connected with the lunar month, of which it is, approximately, a fourth. The quadripartite division of the month was evidently in use among the Hebrews and other ancient peoples; but it is not clear whether it originated among the former. It is unnecessary to assume, however, that it was derived from the Babylonians, for it is equally possible that observations of the four phases of the moon led the Hebrew nomads spontaneously and independently to devise the system of dividing the interval between the successive new moons into four groups of seven days each. There is ground, on the other hand, for the assumption that both among the Babylonians and among the Hebrews the first day of the first week of the month was always reckoned as coincident with the first day of the month." See the website: jewishencyclopedia.com, under *Week*).

"Among all early nations the lunar months were the readiest large divisions of time... (and was divided in 4 weeks), corresponding (to) the phases or the quarters of the moon. In order to connect the reckoning by weeks with the lunar month, we find that all ancient nations observed some peculiar solemnities to mark the day of the New Moon." *The Popular and Critical Bible Encyclopedia*, 1904 edit., Vol. 3, p 1497.

"The first 28 days of every month were divided [by the Assyrians] into four weeks of seven days each; the seventh, fourteenth, twenty-first, twenty-eighth days respectively being Sabbaths, and that there was a general prohibition of work on these days." Williams, Henry Smith (1863-1943), *A History of Science: in Five Volumes*, Volume I, p 24.

From excavated tally sticks, researchers have deduced that people were counting the days in relation to the Moon's phases as early as the Paleolithic age. In the scientific parlance, that's the Stone Age, beginning about 750,00 to 500,000 years BC and lasting until the end of the last ice age about 8500 BC.

the moon.[4] There are also frequent instances in the Dead Sea Scrolls where the weeks are in harmony with the moon's phases. Historians who study ancient calendars see the same framework, over and over, with weekly Sabbaths falling on the seventh, fourteenth, twenty-first and twenty-eighth day of the month. The Hebrews were apparently unique in their veneration of the New Moon day, and having their months begin one day earlier.

Harry looked at me quizzically.

How am I doing?

Tell me how this works in practice, please.

Okay. The key is in determining when the months begin. Historically, from as far back as records were kept, it has always been by the sighting of the new moon's first visible crescent. This is so well documented by innumerable examples throughout the entire ancient world that it's beyond dispute. The Jewish records are likewise unequivocal. At least two reliable witnesses had to report their sighting of the first visible crescent to the officials of the Sanhedrin for the beginning of the month to be established. The first crescent had to be visibly present in order for the months to begin. I emphasize 'visibly'.

Many practitioners sight the moon's first visible crescent for themselves. Personally, I wait for the announcement that comes from Jerusalem via an email. In any event, the day following the evening of the moon's first visible crescent is a New Moon day and constitutes the first day of the month. The next day is a work day, the first of six consecutive work days. The eighth day would be a weekly Sabbath, again followed by six work days. The next Sabbath is on the fifteenth day of the month, and so forth until the twenty-ninth. Then another visible crescent will occur on the twenty-ninth or thirtieth and the cycle begins again.

That's interesting. Why do you go by Jerusalem time?

Call me sentimental if you want to, Avi, but according to Hebrew thinking, Jerusalem is at the centre of the Earth, not London. That's why we read in the Scriptures:

And many peoples shall come and say, "Come,
let us go up to the mountain of YHWH, to the house of the Elohim of

---

4   "Again, the periodical changes of the moon, take place according to the number seven, that star having the greatest sympathy with the things on earth. And the changes which the moon works in the air, it perfects chiefly in accordance with its own configurations on each seventh day. At all events, all mortal things, as I have said before, drawing their more divine nature from the heaven, are moved in a manner which tends to their preservation in accordance with this number seven." See: *Allegorical Interpretation*, I IV (8).

Ya'aqob, and let Him teach us His ways, and let us walk in His paths,
for out of Zion comes the Torah,
and the word of YHWH from Yerushalayim."

Those words come from the prophet Yeshayahu (Isaiah) as he looked into the future. This prophecy is still unfulfilled, but it's my belief that someone has to call the shots, and also a new international dateline will need to be established. In the meantime, I like the idea of using Jerusalem time for determining the beginning of the month. Right now there is a group of Karaite Jews headed up by Nehemia Gordon in Jerusalem who methodically report the New Moon's appearance from month to month.[5] That works well for me and many others, too.

In practice, I keep the Sabbath rest from sunrise until sunset. The twenty-four hour Sabbath from sunset to sunset is traditional and many texts in the Hebrew scriptures are against it. So instead of working like we normally do during the daylight hours, I rest. For me, that means not doing any regular work, as little buying or selling as possible, limiting my creative work such as writing, and avoiding activities that are purely for entertainment. Ideally, Sabbaths should include human interaction or fellowship, particularly in the home with other family members. Essentially, however, I keep the day by resting. The benefit of keeping a rest day cannot be over emphasized. Only those who regularly have a complete stop from all manner of work can appreciate how valuable the weekly Sabbath is.

I noticed the earnest look in Harry's face.

That has nothing at all to do with our Gregorian calendar. Does it, Harry?

Very little. According to the lunar calendar, the Sabbaths float through the Gregorian months. With each New Moon day, the Sabbath jumps ahead either one or two days. The true Sabbath can be on any day of the week including Friday, Saturday and Sunday.

I stood up and walked a bit. I was excited about our topic and had come prepared.

I can summarize the conventional position, Harry. The Sabbath day of the *Old Covenant* was changed with the Messiah's resurrection. Then the day of Yeshuah's resurrection, believed to be on a Sunday, became the new Sabbath day. There is a difference, however. Christian orthodoxy claims that Sunday is not a Sabbath at all, but the celebration of a new reality. Supposedly, it's as Paul said, "The old has passed away; behold, the

---

5   Go to: karaite-korner.org. Please note that Nehemia does not endorse a 'lunar' Sabbath. He honors the traditional seventh-day, Jewish Sabbath. Nevertheless, the Jerusalem Karaites do an invaluable service and are much appreciated.

new has come."

The change from Saturday to Sunday is all about church authority and tradition. It was during of the Council of Trent that the Church's authority above and beyond the Scriptures was formalized.

I unfolded a paper I had brought.

In 1562 the Archbishop of Reggio wrote:

> The authority of the Church is illustrated most clearly by the scriptures, for on one hand she recommends them, declares them to be divine, and offers them to us to be read, and on the other hand, the legal precepts in the scriptures taught by the Lord have ceased by virtue of the same authority. *The Sabbath, the most glorious day in the law, has been changed into the Lord's day.* These and other similar matters have not ceased by virtue of Christ's teaching (for He says that He has come to fulfill the law, not to destroy it), but *they have been changed by the authority of the Church.* (emphasis added).[6]

That's the conventional position, Harry. Sunday keeping replaced the Sabbath fairly early in church history. Then it became entrenched on the basis of the Church's authority.

You're right, Avi. That leads to an interesting historical point. The Council of Trent was held in response to Protestant charges against the Catholic Church. The most serious threat to the Catholic Church was the Protestant declaration of *Sola Scriptura* – that the Scriptures alone would be the final authority on all matters of faith. On that point, the Catholics were the most vulnerable, and Sabbath keeping became the main issue. After much debate, an insightful Reggio perceived that the Protestants were not being consistent with *Sola Scriptura*. It was perfectly obvious – the Scriptures taught a seventh-day Sabbath – but the Protestants were keeping Sunday based on Church tradition. That observation by Reggio deflected the most critical of all the charges the Protestants aimed at the Catholic Church.

Thanks, Harry. I also know that it was Constantine the Great who made Sunday observance a law throughout the Roman Empire. Until that time, most Christians were keeping a seventh-day Sabbath. Later, in another council, the Church commanded that Christians everywhere should work on the Sabbath instead of resting,[7] and those

---

6   Gaspare de Posso Archbishop of Reggio, Council of Trent.

7   Council of Laodicea, Canon 29: "Christians must not judaize by resting on the Sabbath, but must work

who kept the seventh day were anathematized. By the way, Harry, there's a long string of Sabbath keeping Christians from the first century to the present day.[8] In fact, many Protestants are still keeping the seventh day as a Sabbath.

So much for church history, Harry, and the disagreement over the Sabbath day. Now most Christians keep Sunday, the Jewish people keep Saturday, and the Muslims keep Friday. Maybe I'm starting to sound like you, but they're all wrong and their disagreement is artificial. All of them are by tradition. Right, Harry?

My friend gave me a blank stare, so I continued.

All of us, virtually the whole world, abide by the Gregorian calendar in one way or another. We go by a calendar that hangs on our walls for the days, months and years. If we want to know what day it is today or arrange an appointment a year from now, we simply check the calendar. That includes, of course, the day we will be keeping as a Sabbath.

Something told me to stop talking. I wasn't Harry and didn't want to be.

What you said is correct, Avi, but it's not only our religious authorities who have tampered with the calendar – not just Pope Gregory XIII. The secular world has taken a whack at it too. In the first century BC, Julius Caesar wanted to replace a multitude of inaccurate and diverse calendars with a single official one. A Greek astronomer and mathematician named Sosigenes convinced Caesar to separate the calendar from the moon's regular cycle. Thereafter the calendar was based on the sun's annual rotation from equinox to equinox, and the months were no longer set by the moon. The Julian calendar went into effect in 45 BC.

Nineteen hundred years later, our scientific leaders decided that the Earth's supposed annual rotation was not accurate enough to provide a uniform standard of time. Consequently in 1967, the second (1/60 of a minute) was redefined by the oscillations of an atom of cesium. Cesium clocks are so accurate that they quickly became the international standard for measuring time. This ingenious modern invention replaced the previous definition of the second based on the solar year.

I guess we can say that we have been liberated from the cycles of the moon and the sun since they have become irrelevant for calendars and the measurement of time. Am I being sarcastic, Abraham?

on that day, rather honoring the Lord's Day; and, if they can, resting then as Christians. But if any shall be found to be judaizers, let them be anathema from Christ."

8   Including the Anabaptists and Mennonites. See **Andreas Fisher and the Sabbatarian Anabaptists** by Daniel Liechty.

Not really.

Avi, few of us ever stop to think about how artificial the modern Gregorian calendar is. So let's think about it. The day in the Gregorian calendar begins at midnight in the dark with no visible marker. There is no way to visually tell the difference between 11 PM, 12 AM and 1 AM. Biblically and by experience, the day begins in the morning at sunrise. Daylight is what signals the coming of a new day. Those who want to dispute that the day begins in the morning, in favour of the traditional 'sunset to sunset' definition, should consider the biblical definition:

And Elohim called the light Day, and the darkness he called Night.

Then think about the month. In the Gregorian calendar, each month has a different number of days, and each day a different number attached to it. There are no markers to indicate when a month begins or the length of the month. This becomes all the more obvious when you consider the biblical and once universal practice of beginning the month with the reappearance of the new moon every 29.5 days on average.

Finally, think about the year in the Gregorian calendar.[9] Like the day, the Gregorian year begins in the dark with no visible indicator. Actually, the winter solstice – when the sun is at its lowest on the horizon – is on December 22, or eight days earlier. That makes January 1 an arbitrary date with no visible marker, and another event that takes place in darkness at midnight. By convention, the twenty-four hour clock starts a few meters from a brass line in Greenwich, England and ends on a very squiggled International Date Line in the middle of the Pacific Ocean. A leap day is added every fourth February,[10] and a leap second each year at the end of June or December.[11] It's all autocratic, no matter how well it works.

Avi, there is a movement that began in 1930 to introduce a new world calendar. It's a perpetual calendar because it remains the same every year. The world calendar has twelve months divided into four equal quarters. The quarters each have exactly ninety-one days or thirteen weeks. Each quarter begins with a month of thirty-one days followed by two months of thirty days each. Each quarter begins with a Sunday as the first. Two 'world

---

9   The Gregorian calendar is also called the *Western calendar* or the *Christian calendar*, and is the world's most widely accepted civil calendar. The main difference with the Julian calendar is in its addition of ten days to correct for seasonal drift. More specifically, the correction was to align Easter with March 21, the day established by the Council of Nicea in 325 AD.

10   Every year divisible by four is a leap year. However, every year divisible by 100 is not a leap year. However again, every year divisible by 400 is a leap year.

11   Currently there are proposals to abandon leap seconds in favor of 'leap hours' and that civil time be astronomically linked to the sun. Conversely, *Geocentric Coordinate Time* calculates the positions of the moon, the planets and all artificial satellites in relation to the centre of the Earth.

days' are added, one as a year-end worldwide holiday, and the other periodically as a leap day. These days are not numbered. They are designated as 'W' days and correspond with December 31 and June 31, respectively.

Here's the rub, Abraham. The 'W' days would disrupt the weekly cycle of the Gregorian calendar. All the weeks would still have seven days, but the additional 'W' day at the end of the second and fourth quarter would disrupt the sequence. Therefore, the proposed world calendar has been vigorously opposed by Jews, Christians and Muslims alike. It would confuse their annual worship days, and especially confuse their seventh-day Sabbaths, whether Saturday, Sunday or Friday. The recurring and unbroken sequence of the seven-day cycle would be quickly lost if the world calendar was ever accepted. The weekly cycle is utterly fundamental to all three of the Abrahamic faiths.

Harry stood up, took a few steps, and stood there with his eyes to the ground.

I'm getting ahead of myself, but here's the issue. Whether they say it or not, every Jewish person, Christian or Muslim believes that the weekly cycle of seven days has been continuous from the time of Adam until the present. That means for at least six thousand years the weekly cycle has never been broken, forgotten or altered. It means that by simple mathematics human beings have preserved – perfectly preserved – the weekly cycle through more than 313,000 repetitions.

My friend picked up a sheaf of papers and leafed through them.

Here's a quotation to that effect:

> In spite of all of our dickerings with the calendar, it is patent that the human race never lost the septenary [seven-day] sequence of week days and that the Sabbath of these latter times comes down to us from Adam, through the ages, without a single lapse.[12]

I don't know what you think, Avi, but that strikes me as rather unbelievable. We know historically that some countries once had seven-day weeks that did not coincide with the Sabbaths of the western world. Samoa, for example, in 1802. There's also the Philippines in 1845 and Russia in 1867. In those years, each country had to add or drop days to harmonize their weeks and Sabbaths with the rest of the world. It's certain that the seven-day week has been maintained in the western world since 1852 when Pope Gregory XIII introduced the modern calendar, but before that it's anyone's guess how many days have been lost or added during the previous 5,856 years or more than three hundred thousand

---

12 Attributed to a Dr. Totten of New Haven, Connecticut, Professor of Astronomy, Yale University.

weekly cycles. No one kept track. Statements like the one I just read, "without a single lapse," have little credibility. Who can believe such an unprovable claim?

Harry sat down again with a gloomy look.

What do you think, Avi?

I shrugged my shoulders.

I can't believe it either.

I allowed myself a gloomy feeling too, and then continued.

I know the defence, Harry. It comes down to that the Almighty has Himself preserved the seven-day cycle, or that the Messiah was keeping the correct Sabbath in the first century AD. No one can validate either claim, that's for sure. From what you've been telling me, the Messiah was keeping the Sabbaths according to the moon's phases.[13]

When I looked at Harry, I saw relief flicker in his eyes.

Thanks, Avi. It's true.

Again, there was a pause before he continued. The topic seemed to weigh heavily on my friend and he seemed reluctant to continue.

It's worth repeating: the perpetual seven-day week is fundamentally sacred to all three Abrahamic religions. Consequently, there is a multitude of arguments against the lunisolar calendar and its lunar weeks. The troubling issue is not in how well it works or doesn't work. The real irritant of a lunisolar calendar is in its challenge to the traditional seven-day week. Admittedly, it's also a challenge to the world's economic system, but the crucial vexation of the lunisolar calendar is in its rejection of the world's weekly Sabbath. That's why it's causing so much consternation and motivating so many critics.

Abraham, very few religious people will even consider the lunar week as an alternative to the perpetual cycle of seven-day weeks. Their minds are closed. It's a done deal. Period.

This is a sorry business, Harry.

---

13 Yeshuah kept the same Sabbath as the rest of the Jews in his time. That would have been the Sabbaths that Philo described – lunar Sabbaths. There's no hint of any conflict over the Sabbaths between Yeshuah and the religious leaders of the 1st century AD. They all kept the same Sabbath. The Essenes, however, kept a different calendar, and one that did conflict with the Jews.

It certainly is. The inability to change has consequences. We can't keep doing the same things over and over while hoping for a different result. At some time, the piper will have to be paid.

In other words, Harry, we can't keep living a lie. The outcome is too worrisome to even contemplate.

Harry gave me his somber look.

You're catching on very well, Avi. You're beginning to understand that our conventions and traditions will determine our future if we stay with them. Those traditions are not benign. In the next few weeks, our discussions will lead us in that direction. We need to change our way. Urgently.

Harry leaned his chin into his hand momentarily, and proceeded.

The point I am making is that much of our modern calendar is arbitrary or made up, while the biblical calendar is unaffected and natural. The year begins in spring, the month with the moon, and the day in the morning. Each of those beginnings comes with unmistakable signs. The year begins with the vernal equinox, the month with the moon's first visible crescent, and the day with sunrise. The beginnings are all experiential and the same for everyone.[14]

I like that, Harry. You keep things real and true to our experience.

Thank you. We should be aware of how much we are affected by abstract thinking, scientific theory and religious doctrine. They all tend to take us away from what is real and true.

Amen. I'm convinced!

Avi, if we want to be authentic people, then we need to have authentic beliefs. To that end, the Sabbaths that the Eternal One instituted are nowhere to be found on the

---

14 There is a long standing tradition that the day begins at sunset, and that tradition is read into many biblical texts. This is one more tradition that needs to be dispelled. Genesis 1:4,5 & 8 define 'day' as the period of light bounded by two periods of twilight, dusk and dawn. The period of darkness is called 'night.' By those boundaries of twilight, The Eternal One separated the light from the darkness. This definition is sustained in the Christian Scriptures. Yeshuah asked, "Are there not twelve hours in a day?" And on the road to Emmaus, the disciples said, "Abide with us; for it is toward evening, and the day is now far spent." According to the Scriptures, the day does NOT not begin at sunset.

Gregorian calendar.[15] All of its years, months and days are subjective and arbitrary.

What is real as a calendar?

The real calendar is the calendar we find in the heavens. It's the sun, moon and stars that tell us when the days, months and years begin and end like no other clock or calendar ever can. It's the true universal time. Greenwich Mean Time is not.

Avi, there is a natural rhythm to life, a rhythm that was established at Creation. Its source is in the sun, moon and stars, and all life forms are bound by it. In science, we call it bio-rhythm. Modern controlled scientific experiments have probed the detailed nature of this bio-rhythm. Oysters and tides, potatoes and oxygen levels, mice and daylight have specific rhythms even when relocated or totally isolated. Practically all living creatures have a cycle related to, but not synonymous with, the sun's twenty-four hour rotation. Every organism responds with natural rhythms directly in response to some all-pervasive environment. As one professor of astronomical anthropology put it, there is "something outside ourselves, an entity so strange and novel that today we must strain our senses even to recognize it."[16] That professor falls just short of acknowledging a bio-rhythm that the Almighty Himself established at Creation.

Humankind, however, seems to have a propensity to establish artificial rhythms even though the natural ones are undeniably evident. Apparently, human beings would rather do things by their own ingenuity than be in harmony with what the Almighty has ordained from the beginning. At the heart of that propensity is a rebellion against the Creator and Designer of all life. It is a rebellion that is uniquely manifested in humankind's desire to change or modify the natural calendar. That is surely alluded to by the prophet Daniel:

> **And he [mankind] shall speak words against the Most High,**
> **and shall wear out the saints of the Most High,**
> **and he shall think to change the times and the law.**[17]

The 'times' referred to in this verse are specifically the times of the annual festivals that the Eternal One gave to His people through Moshe, but it can easily also mean the weekly Sabbaths that Israel was commanded to keep. In "thinking to change the times," humankind has been largely successful. People almost everywhere now keep an artificial

---

15 The Gregorian calendar, also known as the Western calendar, was a revision of the Julian calendar, and introduced by Pope Gregory XIII on February 24, 1582. All modern chronology hinges on that important date, even though the date itself has no intrinsic significance.

16 *Empires of Time: Calendars, Clocks, and Cultures* by Anthony F. Aveni, I.B. Tauris Publishers,, p 37.

17 Daniel 7:25

Sabbath, the Sabbath of the Gregorian calendar.

Avi, there is an ongoing and vigorous effort to deny the origin of the seven-day week. There are any number of people, groups and religious bodies that are either closing their minds or vigorously denying the reality of the lunar calendar. Most of the other topics we've talked about are being treated with indifference, but this one has provoked a lot of indignation and outrage.

One accusation is quite common. It's the accusation that people who keep a Sabbath day according to the moon are actually worshipping the sun, moon and stars. Deuteronomy 4:19 is frequently quoted by the accusers:

> **And beware lest you lift up your eyes to the heavens,**
> **and when you see the sun, moon, and stars, even all the host of the**
> **heavens, you be drawn away and worship them and serve them,**
> **things which YHWH your Almighty One**
> **has allotted to all nations under the whole heaven.**

Happily, the last part of the verse contradicts our accusers. It says that the sun, moon and stars were created for all the nations under the whole heaven. All of humankind has been provided with a clock and calendar that was imbedded in the heavens at Creation. How sad that the obvious is being ignored or argued against.

I don't know anything about that, Harry. This is all new to me.

It's new for almost everyone. I'm not aware of anyone keeping the Sabbath days according to the moon longer than two decades ago. It seems to be a truth that was lost for a very long time, and is only now being rediscovered. That newness may explain why the resistance is so spirited.

Does it really matter on which day we keep a regular Sabbath?

Only in this way. As real people we want to be in be in harmony with real things, with what our Creator established in the beginning. The Sabbath day is our most explicit way to acknowledge the Creator of everything. That's the meaning of the text:

> **And on the seventh day Elohim finished His work which He had made;**
> **and He rested on the seventh day from all His work which He had made.**
> **And Elohim blessed the seventh day, and hallowed it;**
> **because that in it he rested**
> **from all his work which Elohim had created and made.**

The commandment is repeated in Ex. 20:1-17:

Remember the Sabbath day, to keep it set apart.
Six days shall you labor, and do all your work;
but the seventh day is a Sabbath unto YHWH your Mighty One:
in it you shall not do any work, you, nor your son, nor your daughter,
your man-servant, nor your maid-servant, nor your cattle,
nor the stranger that is within your gates:
for in six days YHWH made heaven and earth, the sea, and all that is in
them,
and rested the seventh day:
wherefore YHWH blessed the Sabbath day, and hallowed it.

Moreover, Sabbath keeping is predicted in the world to come:

For as the new heavens and the new earth,
which I will make, shall remain before Me, says YHWH,
so shall your seed and your name remain.
And it shall come to pass, that from one new moon to another,
and from one Sabbath to another,
shall all flesh come to worship before Me,
says YHWH. [18]

Ezekiel said it too about the future:

Thus says the Master YHWH:
The gate of the inner court that looks toward the east
shall be shut the six working days;
but on the Sabbath day it shall be opened,
and on the day of the new moon it shall be opened.
And the people of the land shall worship at the door of that gate
before YHWH
on the Sabbaths and on the new moons. [19]

Isaiah repeatedly made it clear:

If you turn away your foot from the Sabbath,
from doing your pleasure on My set apart day;
and call the Sabbath a delight,

18 Isaiah 66:22-23
19 Ezekiel 46:1,3

and the set-apart day of YHWH honorable;
and shalt honor it, not doing your own ways,
nor finding your own pleasure, nor speaking your own words:
then shall you delight yourself in YHWH;
and I will make you to ride upon the high places of the earth;
and I will feed you with the heritage of Jacob your father:
for the mouth of YHWH has spoken it.[20]

Finally:

I am YHWH your Mighty One:
walk in My statutes, and keep My ordinances, and do them;
and revere my Sabbaths;
and they shall be a sign between Me and you,
that you may know that I am YHWH your Mighty One.[21]

I'm throwing a lot of Scriptures at you with some hesitation, Abraham, but keeping the Sabbath day is one of the most well enunciated commandments in the Hebrew Scriptures. The commandment presents for us a way to recognize ourselves as created beings, and a way to identify ourselves with the Creator Himself. It's the foremost way by which He can be known.

I gave Harry a hard look.

We would never know that if we listened to Paul or the Church, would we?

No, we wouldn't, and I wouldn't want to understate the value of the Sabbath, but my point continues to be that the biblical Sabbath is a real event and not an arbitrary day. We know the Sabbath by the light of the sun and stars and the light's reflection on the moon. This is the Sabbath of the Scriptures, ancient history and modern experience. It's the way the world was made.

Harry took a long breath and exhaled audibly.

There's a major consideration I left out earlier. It has to do with the year's beginning and how it relates to eschatology. It's very revealing, but first I'd like to explain the motions of the sun, moon and stars. After all, the Almighty put the sun, moon and stars in their places so that we can tell time, anticipate the seasons and keep the annual festivals. We can only do that from our perspective here on the Earth. Those heavenly time pieces

---

20 Isaiah 58:13-14
21 Ezekiel 20:19-20

won't work from anywhere else in the universe. Only here.

Are you okay with that?

Sure.

The biblical unit of time called 'day' is straightforward, although there are subtleties. The simple definition is from sunrise to sunset, from the visible appearance of the sun to its visible disappearance. However, the sun's light is still present during the times of dawn and dusk. The night begins and ends, technically speaking, with the appearance and disappearance of the stars. Twilight is the time when neither the sun nor the stars are visibly present.[22]

The term 'month' actually comes from the moon. One 'moonth' is the time it takes for the Earth, moon and sun to realign themselves, and for the moon to go through its four phases. A lunar month is 29.5 days long. Simple arithmetic shows that twelve months of 29.5 days is about eleven days short of a 365-day year. Hence, an intercalary month must be added every second or third year, making a year either twelve or thirteen months long. The intercalation of an extra month is fundamental to the Hebrew or biblical calendar.[23]

From long ago it was understood that there is a nineteen-year lunisolar cycle called the *Metonic cycle*. Every 19 years the lunar cycle and the solar cycle match up, making the month-end and the year-end the same. This is quite precise, to within about two hours. There are exactly seven intercalary months in each nineteen-year cycle, or 235 months of 29.5 days each in every *Metonic* cycle.[24] [25]

By the way, the moon really does orbit the Earth each day. Our convention is that the Earth is turning on its axis each day and it takes 29.5 days for the Earth and the moon to

22 Philo called the times of dawn and dusk 'boundaries.' "God... did not only separate light and darkness, but did also place boundaries in the middle of the space between the two, by which he separated the extremities of each" (*On the Creation*, IX-32).

23 An intercalated calendar is a *lunisolar calendar* where the moon's cycle is harmonized with the solar year. The Islamic calendar is a strict *lunar calendar*, following the lunar cycle without regarding the solar year. Consequently, in the calendar of Islam, the months are out of phase with the seasons. The Koran insists that there are only twelve months in a year (9:36).

24 The 19-year cycle is called the *Metonic cycle* after the Greek astronomer, Meton of Athens. However, the cycle was known much earlier. The Babylonians were using a 19-year cycle in their calendar by the 8th century BC. The Sumerian cultures practiced some form of intercalation by circa 2100 BC, suggesting they too were aware of the 19-year cycle. Moses lived around 1500 BC.

25 NASA publishes lunar tables giving the date and time of all phases of the Moon for the six thousand year period, 2000 BC to 4000 AD. The tables are provided primarily for historical research. The tables assume that nothing has changed or will change in the course of 6000 years. The assumption is that the universe is serene and its motions unchangeable.

return to the same relative positions. In actuality, the path of the moon's orbit is not on the same plane as the Earth's equator. If it was on the same plane, we would experience a solar eclipse and a lunar eclipse very month. Geocentrically, with the moon orbiting the Earth each day, it takes 29.5 days for the Earth, sun and moon to return to the same relative positions. That relative position is marked by what we call the New Moon.[26]

The third basic unit of time, after the day and the month, is the year. The solar year or *tropical year* is measured by the sun's motion, but let's first understand that the sun has two motions, a daily motion and a yearly motion. The daily motion is in the sun's twenty-four hour circuit, the motion we see each day as the sun rises and sets. The other motion of the sun is helical or spiral. With each daily circuit, the sun moves from above the Earth's equator to below the Earth's equator and back again in the course of a year.[27] In other words, it's not the Earth's tilt that causes the seasons, it the sun's annual motion relative to the Earth's equator. Saying that the Earth is tilted on its axis is an arbitrary statement in favor of those who believe that the Earth is orbiting the sun. The length of one year is the time it takes for the sun to complete one helical cycle, and is measured from one vernal equinox to another. That length is 365 days, 5 hours, 49 minutes and 19 seconds.

Avi, this is where it's going to get interesting and challenging. Imagine the Earth's equator extended outward and imprinted on its starry background. In its annual helical motion, the sun will cross that equator twice, once in spring and once in autumn. Those precise moments in time are known as the *vernal equinox* in the Northern Hemisphere and the *autumnal equinox* in the Southern Hemisphere. The point at which the sun crosses the Earth's extended equator is determined by its position relative to the stars. Every year the sun returns to the same position against its background of stars. The moon, on the other hand, returns to the same position relative to the stars at the end of each nineteen-year cycle.

Are you following me so far, Abraham?

I am. I can visualize the sun and the moon traversing the sky against their background of stars, but, aren't the stars moving too?

---

26 There can only be a solar eclipse during a new moon (essentially when the moon is invisible), and there can only be a lunar eclipse during a full moon (when the moon is visible).

27 Picture it this way. At the height of summer, the sun is orbiting the Earth on the plane of the Earth's Equator, and appears directly overhead at noon. As the summer progresses into the Northern Hemisphere, the sun will eventually orbit the Earth on the plane of the Arctic Circle, making a perfect circle just above the horizon. At the end of the summer in the Northern Hemisphere the sun will reverse northward spiral, return to its position on the equatorial plane, and spiral into the Southern Hemisphere. There, as the sun orbits the Earth on the plane of the Antarctic Circle, it will again make a perfect circle just above the horizon. In this way, you can visualize the upward and downward motion of the sun's helical path around the Earth.

Yes, exactly! The stars are moving too. All the heavenly bodies make a daily rotation around the Earth, including the stars. However, the stars, the sun and the moon are making their daily rotations at different rates, and that's why the sun and the moon appear to be moving relative to the stars. Good for you, Avi.

Are we still talking about the weekly Sabbath, Harry?

Yes, we are. What I'm explaining is that the real calendar and real time are in the motion of the sun, moon and stars just as it is declared in Genesis 1:14:

> **And The Almighty One said,**
> **Let there be lights in the firmament of heaven**
> **to divide the day from the night;**
> **and let them be for signs, and for seasons,**
> **and for days and years.**

I'm glad you asked that question. As I said at the beginning of this talk, our modern method of time keeping has become very artificial and quite disconnected from the physical realities of the Creation. We need to get reconnected with the true Sabbath, the day that marks time in the way that our Creator intended.

Good, Harry, and thanks again. Please go on.

Sure. We need to keep our bearings and know where we are headed. Getting the big picture is not always easy, and can seem quite complicated. In our next few sessions, we are going to see that the passage of time can't be defined or encapsulated by our man-made calendar. Just remember, Joshua made the sun to stand still for several hours and extended the length of that day.

I took the initiative to get up and pour each of us another cup of coffee. I was getting very interested, but my mood was becoming somber. I sat down again without saying anything, and waited for my friend to continue.

Avi, the length of a year is different when measured by the stars instead of by the sun. According to the stars, the year is about one day longer. In their daily rotation, the stars take about four minutes per day longer than the sun. Conversely, the sun's daily rotation is four minutes slower than the stars, making the sun appear to be advancing through the starry sky in an east to west direction. As the year progresses and the stars rotate, the sun advances through each of the twelve constellations in the Zodiac.[28]

---

28 These motions are usually not seen because the stars are invisible when the Sun is in the sky. However, if one looks regularly at the sky before dawn, the annual motion is quit obvious. The first stars to rise are not

Now here is the really big picture. The entire heavenly sphere has another rotation called *precession,* and it takes twenty-six thousand years to complete. The common explanation for precession is that the Earth is wobbling on its axis in a way similar to a spinning top. The geocentric explanation, however, is that the universe itself has a wobble centered on the Earth, or more likely on the sun.[29] Either way we are talking about a wobble. This circular wobble of the universe makes different parts of the sky visible during its twenty-six thousand year cycle, and about every 2167 years ,the vernal equinox will appear in a new constellation. This motion is known as the *precession of the equinoxes.*[30]

This is what we should understand about *precession*. Over long periods, a calendar based on the stars will drift out of sync with the seasons at the rate of about one day every seventy-two years. To give that a context, the vernal equinox is in its third constellation since Creation. It was in Taurus at the time of Adam, Aries at the time of Abraham and Moses, and Pisces in the time of Yeshuah. Beginning around 2160 AD, the vernal equinox will be in Aquarius. At this time in history the sun appears, to an observer on the Earth, to be located between Pisces and Aquarius on the first day of spring. In conclusion, the vernal equinox does not follow the motion of the stars.

Listen up, Avi. Other factors influence when spring begins. In practice, the vernal equinox is only precise at the very centre of the Earth in a direct line with the sun's position on the equator, but in actuality, on the surface of the Earth, spring begins at different times in different places. Rainfall patterns, ocean currents, latitude and altitude, sun spots and other long cycles also factor into the beginning of spring. Now that brings us to the heart of the Hebrew calendar. The Eternal One told Moses that the Israelites were to begin their year in the month of *Aviv*.

I couldn't help interrupting.

Is that a pun? Avi with *Aviv*?

Harry looked at me blankly, and I thought to myself, "One day, I'll get him to laugh." My friend's look changed to one of inscrutable acceptance before he went on.

---

always the same, and within a week or two an upward shift is noticeable. For example, Orion can't be seen in the dawn sky in July in the Northern Hemisphere. But in August it can.

29 It is unlikely that the Earth is at the exact centre of the universe. If some other point (such as the sun) is at the centre of the universe, it would explain the phenomena of *parallax*. Parallax is the very small shift in location that some stars exhibit during the course of a year. In a way Copernicus was right about the sun being at the centre of the universe. In modern cosmology, however, the universe is curved and has no centre.

30 The equinoxes move from west to east, opposite to the motion of the sun.

Aviv is a term referring to when green ears of barley have reached full size. Aviv can also mean spring as in *Tel Aviv*, a major city in Israel. Tel Aviv is 'hill of spring' in Hebrew.

Harry went glum for a few seconds.

It doesn't mean 'tell Avi.'

I smiled inwardly at a small victory.

Abraham, I'm sure the ancient Hebrews were fully aware of the vernal equinox and the rising of the constellation Aries for the year's beginning. The ancients were much more in tune with the celestial sphere and its impetus than we are. For them, the heavens propelled the seasons and told a great story. As the Psalmist said:

The heavens declare the honor of The Mighty One,
and the firmament proclaims His handiwork.

Tragically, we have lost touch with the meaning and function of the rotating sphere called the 'heavens'. It seems that our astrologers pay more attention to the heavens than our astronomers. They at least believe that the position and movement of celestial bodies influences human affairs and world events.[31] Our astronomers spend more time with computer monitors and digitized information than actually looking at the stars. Nor do astronomers consider that the heavens have meaning and purpose.

Nevertheless, our sense of time and order comes from the sun, the moon and the stars. It's from those heavenly bodies that we perceive the divisions in time: our days, weeks, months and years. This may not be easily perceived going by the Gregorian calendar, but with practice it becomes obvious. The divisions of time are all natural and established by the Almighty when He created the heavens and the Earth.

The day is obvious: from sunrise to sunset. The month too: from new moon to new moon. The week and the year are a little less precise; the weeks are indicated by the moon's four phases, and the year by the equinoxes. For all the harmony in the heavenly calendar, the Hebrews added another dimension. They included the natural rhythm within the Earth's own biosphere. By that, I mean the rhythm that is inherent and natural to all plant and animal life. The Hebrew calendar was not entirely solar-lunar.

Herein lies a great mystery with a revealing explanation. The mystery is: Why did

---

31 This author believes that the celestial bodies likely do influence human affairs and world events. Hence, the Almighty's people were warned against allowing the sun, the moon and the stars to guide them. They were to be a segregated people and their future determined by the Eternal One - not by the celestial bodies.

Moshe tell the Israelites to begin the year in the month of barley ripening in accordance with the Earth's own bio-rhythm? Why did he not tell them to go by the spring equinox or by the sun's annual appearance on the celestial equator? All over the ancient world, stone monuments and observatories were constructed to know with certainty when the year began, and yet, the Hebrews in Moshe's time did not go by the spring equinox. Why?

Harry waited a bit. I was sure he wasn't trying to be dramatic, but it had the effect nevertheless. Then he resumed from where he had left off.

The Hebrews had a feel for the Earth's bio-rhythm. At least Moshe did when he commanded the Israelites to keep the month of Aviv. Keeping *aviv* was understood to mean when life began to renew itself from its dormancy in winter. It meant observing the signs of new life: the return of the swallows, the blossoming of almond trees, and the age of the new lambs for example. Paramount was observing the barley crop. Barley was *aviv* when the grains had matured enough to be eaten parched although not yet ready for harvest. More than anything else, *aviv* signaled the beginning of the year for the Hebrews.

The biblical year begins with the first New Moon after the barley in Israel reaches the stage of ripeness called *Aviv*. Most often, this ripeness would be in the twelfth month, but about every three years, it would be in the thirteenth month. The biblical year does not begin with the vernal equinox, making the Israelites quite distinct from the nations around them, and from the Julian solar calendar that came five centuries later. Observing the month of Aviv insured that the Hebrew calendar would always be in sync with the seasons. It was the seasons themselves, specifically Spring, that set the Hebrew calendar, not the vernal equinox.[32]

I was getting anxious.

Harry, I don't know if I can go on the way I have been. Something has to change. I have to do something.

In my tone, I was distraught.

It's right that you feel that way, Avi. It doesn't matter what we know or how much we know. Somewhere we have to make a commitment and act. Otherwise it's all for naught.

---

32   The traditional Jewish calendar was calculated very precisely over a thousand years ago, based on a lunation period of 29 days, 12 hours, 44 minutes and 3 1/3 seconds, differing from modern calculation by only one day in 15,000 years. The traditional Jewish calendar, however, begins the year with the vernal equinox and not aviv. It's often called the 'calculated' calendar because it projects the New Moons hundreds of years into the future. No direct observation of the moon is required.

Is the Sabbath the issue?

At one time, I would have said yes unequivocally. I still put the Sabbath high on the list of what we should do. It's so fundamental, and it's assuredly significant that the true Sabbath is being rediscovered in our time. There's a whole range of people and groups that are making observing the New Moon a very important part of their lives. Most note-worthy are the modern day Karaites, who meticulously observe the New Moon's appearance in Jerusalem, and also when the barley ripens in Israel. Thanks to them and many others, keeping the true Sabbath has been made possible once again.[33] I'm very grateful.

Are you prevaricating, Harry?

I believe there's something even more fundamental than the Sabbath, Abraham, but before you ask me, let me assure you that I am leading up to it. I don't want to say what it is yet.

All right. I trust you, but I'll ask you a leading question. What does aviv have to do with eschatology? Is there a connection between when the barley ripens and some future event?

My friend looked at me with astonishment and gratitude.

I'll answer you this way, Abraham. The universe is not as serene as we would like to think. There have been cataclysmic events in the heavens in the past that have utterly shaken humankind's equanimity. We can still be quite glib about the future. NASA has projected the moon's phases to the year 4000 AD. Somehow, they were confident that everything will continue as it has for another three thousand years, but the cycles and units of time have been disrupted in the past, and they could be disrupted again. By that, I mean the years, month, weeks and days.

There's an old Jewish tradition that ties Sabbath keeping with the welfare of the uni-verse. The tradition says that if the Almighty's people fail to keep the Sabbaths, the uni-verse will collapse in on itself. That tradition suggests that we humans have an awesome responsibility. We're involved in some way with the future, and Sabbath keeping is assur-edly included.

---

33 The Karaites are non-traditional Jews with an ancient history. For the purpose of keeping the biblical calendar, they have a very helpful website at karaite-kroner.org. The Karaites, however, do not associate the New Moon with seven-day weeks. In that regard, they are not yet free from their Jewish traditions. They observe the New Moon as the beginning of each month, but keep their Sabbaths according to the Gregorian calendar.

I looked over at my friend.

We're coming to some kind of conclusion, aren't we? Something quite startling.

Harry looked back at me and nodded his head too.

Yes, Avi. In just a few more weeks.

I tried to stay calm, but felt like doubling over with anxiety and despair. Perhaps Harry sensed it.

It's troubling, Avi. As human beings, we have become estranged from so much. We don't know ourselves as created beings. We don't know our place in the universe. We don't know how to live. On top of that, we have allowed our minds to be filled with absurdities. No wonder we're so troubled.

I feel it, Harry. Where do we turn, or should I ask, to whom? Our spiritual leaders aren't giving us the answers we need, and certainly not our secular leaders. I think I can say that carte blanche for all our so-called leaders. I can't help feeling that we've become hopelessly lost.

You're already on the right track, Avi. Especially when you express that you need to do something. Never mind the so-called leaders. Our truest response is one person at a time, each one of us by our own accord.

I breathed it in.

We're real beings, aren't we?

Yes, Avi.

I breathed in again.

This has been a good session, Harry. It's leaving me with a sense of well-being. So where do we go from here?

I'm thinking, Avi, that we should have an unprepared day. Let's get together next Sabbath without an agenda. Maybe we can call it an intermezzo because we are drawing nearer to a conclusion in our talks. We'll just talk about whatever comes up.

That's good, Harry. I've learned so much so quickly. I'd be glad for a pause.

May the Eternal One be with you, Avi.

And He with you, Harry.

MESOLOGUE

Shalom, my friend.

Shabbat shalom, Abraham.

I'm happy, Harry, with no pun intended. I've learned so much in less than two months. I never would have guessed, but it's been so gratifying

For me, too. I puzzle and marvel. I can't understand what's happened between us, but have stopped trying to figure it out. This is a unique experience for me, and I'm simply amazed.

I know what you mean, Harry. From the very beginning, I sensed an opportunity, and was ready to learn. I didn't guess at how much though.

Abraham, as much as I don't consider myself a teacher, you've been a first rate student. I marvel at your lack of resistance to my series of "nots."

I puzzle too, Harry. I'm not sure why I did it, but I let my guard down. You could just as easily have bamboozled me with foolishness, but am confident you haven't. It's all too good not to be true!

You're not bothered by all my "nots"?

Not at all, but I can see how they might be perceived as negative. It goes against our nature to be criticized or told that what we believe is wrong. We'd rather hear good news than bad, and be pumped up with confidence.

You've hit the nail on the head there, Avi. It's like the prophet said:

They say to the seers, "See no more visions!"

and to the prophets, "Give us no more visions of what is right! Tell us pleasant things, prophesy illusions."

It's clear to me, Avi, that knowing the truth comes with a price. We have to face up to some bitter realities if we want to know what's really true. As incomprehensible as it may be, many people would rather hear lies, and many would rather teach lies.

It hasn't always been easy, and I've had some uncomfortable nights, Harry. What's helped me most is knowing that there is only One being that I can pray to, and that's the Eternal One, the Mighty One of Abraham, Isaac and Jacob. Even when that doesn't go well, I can still say, "I know You are there, and that You hear me."

I don't think you learned that from me, Avi. That's something that you figured out for yourself.

Maybe, but when I pray to the Eternal One, I'm certain that I'm praying to the same Being that Yeshuah prayed to. Yeshuah surely had a relationship with his Father, and found his strength in Him. It's the same thing for me.

That's wonderful. We can't truly pray to a Trinity, the saints, Mary, Allah, or some Divine Spirit. We can't even pray to Yeshuah, although many think they should. In the end, it's whoever calls on the Name of the Eternal One that will be saved. He is the only way to wholeness. Good for you.

Thank you, Harry. This is the example that Yeshuah set for us. I'm sure that he had the most intimate relationship with the Eternal One that any man ever had. Now when I'm reading the first few books of the Christian Scriptures, I'm seeing just such a man. He is the one that overcame every possible obstacle to worshipping the one true Almighty Father, and Him only to the exclusion of everything else.

I turned to look at my friend, and saw that I had his complete attention.

There's a progression in those books. We don't know much about how he grew from a child into adulthood, but we are told that he did grow in wisdom and stature, and in favor with both the Almighty and his people.[1] When he began his ministry as an adult,

---

1   Actually, we know much more about the Messiah's so-called 'missing years' than is generally allowed, and about who he was as a real historical person. The Christian Scriptures imply that Yeshuah had travelled outside his homeland. The case has often been made that Yeshuah went to England with his great uncle, Joseph of Arimathea. Traditions abound that he went to India or at least as far as Persia (Parthia), and even to South America. This would explain why Yeshuah seemed so little known in his homeland when he began his ministry.

his focus was on announcing the coming Kingdom of Heaven and performing many miracles in accordance with his message. After a time it must have become obvious to him that the Kingdom of Heaven was not going to come in his time, and that he was going to be killed just as the messengers before him had been killed. I don't think Yeshuah knew that from the outset, but his purpose as the Messiah was fully clear to him in his resurrected body when he explained everything to his disciples on the road to Emmaus. We can easily see that progression in the books of the Good News.

I paused and reflected on what I had just said. I sensed Harry's glance my way, and continued.

I was reading the Gethsemane story this morning. Yeshuah's pathos is so evident. Here was a man to whom the Almighty had given great vision, power and authority, and it was all coming to an end. He was going to be arrested, imprisoned and put to death at the hands of men, by human authority and understanding. It was not easy for him to accept, and he had to pray three times before yielding to it and becoming powerless.

We sat there for what seemed a long time before I concluded.

I can understand that there is a time to be powerless, and a time to act. Yeshuah could have called legions of angels to rescue him, but for him it was the time not to act. The end result was that, instead of him trying to save own his mortal life, the Eternal One raised him from the dead and gave him an eternal life.

I looked over at Harry, and it was my turn to feel very meek.

You are so right, Abraham. There is a time to stop and be powerless.

There was no change in our mood, and I waited for Harry to continue.

I keep remembering two Scripture verses that I once memorized. That was in a high school bible class in which I was expected to memorize a hundred verses in the course of the year. Later, I memorized about fifteen hundred verses and could recite them all, but I can only recall two of them.. The first was in II Chronicles 7:14:

If My people, who are called by My name, shall humble themselves, and pray, and seek My face, and turn from their wicked ways; then will I hear from heaven, and will forgive their sin, and will heal their land.

And the second in Joshua 1:8:

**This book of the law shall not depart out of thy mouth,
but thou shalt meditate thereon day and night,
that thou mayest observe to do according to all that is written therein:
for then thou shalt make thy way prosperous,
and then thou shalt have good success.**[2]

It's these two verses that have stuck in my mind more than any other, and over time I have realized that the whole truth is in those two verses.

What that means, Avi, is that first we have to stop acting. We need to stop doing the things we've always done no matter how good our intentions, and stop believing the things we've always believed no matter how sincere we've been. We need to stop, humble ourselves and turn from "our wicked ways" even though we haven't perceived them as wicked.

Next, we have to start acting in accordance with the commandments given by our Almighty Father through Moshe, to meditate on those commandments and to do them. By those actions, we will prosper and be successful.

That's it, Avi, and that's exactly what we see in the life of the Messiah. He came down so hard against the traditions of his time, especially against the leaders who set aside the commandments for the sake of their traditions. Then, by all accounts, he fulfilled his Father's commandments to the point of perfection. Even more, there was "no deceit found in his mouth." He did not repeat the same lies that were bandied about in his generation.

Was Yeshuah successful? We know that he will be. As one prophet said:

**He shall see his seed, he shall prolong his days,
and the pleasure of YHWH shall prosper in his hand.
He shall see of the travail of his soul, and shall be satisfied.**

In the world to come, Yeshuah will have many brothers and sisters who are immortal beings like himself, and the Eternal One will prosper him as the Messiah. Yeshuah will see in his brethren the reward of his earthly travail, and he will be completely satisfied.[3]

---

2   Christians following Paul have universally misunderstood the word for 'Law.' The Law of Moses is better understood as his Teaching or Instruction. The Hebrew word is 'Torah.' English translations also use 'Right Rulings,' and simply 'His Word.' The Law should be understood as the wisdom that comes from the Creator, and as the only way of life leading to real prosperity and success. The Torah is profoundly more than a detailed system of Do's and Don'ts.

3   Isaiah 53:10-11. See also the great messianic Psalm 22: "Even he that cannot keep his soul alive, a seed

Harry changed the mood abruptly.

Let's go for a walk, Avi.

I noticed again my friend's readiness to be active. Despite his age and love of learning, Harry enjoyed being physically occupied. We walked for quite some time before he spoke up.

Let's talk about the third blatant lie that I've found in the Bible. The first is when the evil one explicitly contradicted the Creator's very words by saying, "You shall not die." The second was when the religious leaders said, "You, being a man, make yourself out to be the Almighty One." Those two lies are so blatant because they explicitly contradicted the truth. Yeshuah even told the religious leaders of his day that they were all liars.

The third biblical lie is found in Acts, chapter seven. There, a certain group of *Freedmen* accused Stephen of speaking against the Torah, and that Yeshuah had changed the customs that Mosheh handed down.[4] The text, however, specifically says that the Freedmen set up "false witnesses." From that, we know the opposite – that Stephen did not speak against the Torah, and that Yeshuah did not change Mosheh's customs.[5] We know that for certain. Yeshuah had explicitly said, "Don't think that I came to destroy the Law or the Prophets."

We walked on for a time in a comfortable quietness. The town Harry lived in was small and historic with tree-lined streets and a park-like common area. Those areas extended along a sizable river after which the town had been named. We were headed toward the river. After a while, I picked up the thread of our conversation.

I can easily agree that the laws of Moshe are as relevant now as when they were given to him by the Eternal One. It leads me to believe that how we live is much more important than what we believe.

Avi, that's true. For that very reason, the Almighty's people have prevailed to a certain extent. Our good behavior has tended to nullify the effects of our false beliefs. In spite of ourselves, we are inclined to be a people with morals. We can still act like saints much of the time. That's no excuse, however, and we will be judged someday for the words that

shall serve him. It shall be told of the Master unto the next generation. They shall come and shall declare his righteousness unto a people that shall be born, that he hath done it."

4   The Freedmen were probably hellenized Jews who did not believe in Yeshuah, but were zealous for their Mosaic traditions.

5   It is truly surprising how often commentators will insist that there is a certain amount of truth in what Stephen was accused of, and how often these verses are read as if they really are true.

come out of our mouths. We can't keep lying to each other and to the world.

That's true, Harry. There are so many really fine believing people is this world who are quite innocent and well intentioned. That certainly conveys a message to unbelievers.

No doubt about it, Abraham. Our behavior is a very powerful message.

That also means that we shouldn't judge each other too harshly, or judge each other at all. That would negate the message.

Yes.

That brought a lull into our conversation. Something wasn't being said.

Harry, you're avoiding something. I suspect you find it very painful when the Almighty's people are so naively innocent. I'm sure you don't like biting down on your tongue.

You're right. It can be really cruel for anyone to impose their naivety on other people. It's disrespectful too. Those who do that need to be forgiven.

I can see where this is going. These innocent believers can't be corrected.

It appears to be so most of the time.

Who are we talking about, Harry?

If I have to put a label on them, I'd say most Christians.

Are they being hypocritical?

No, many of them genuinely believe what they are saying, and live accordingly. Yes, there is a legion of hypocrites out there, but that's not the people I'm referring to. I'm talking about those who never question their beliefs, refuse to, and confidently go on spouting nonsense. That sort of innocence is painful.

What's the answer to that situation, Harry?

I don't know, Avi, short of a miracle. These same people feel that they are being led by the Holy Spirit, not knowing that it's by their own spirit. In effect, they've become their own standard, and judge everything else by it. It's not a pretty picture.

Couldn't something shake them out of it, Harry?

It could, but that's a problem too. They would view being shaken as a test of faith. They could just as easily label it as the work of Satan or the Anti-Christ.

This is a serious problem!

Yes, it is.

Again, Harry, what needs to be done?

Every individual will have to give a proper response someday. Nevertheless, the Almighty used Pharaoh and his army to drive His people out of Egypt. Israel's coming out of bondage was not entirely voluntary. Ultimately, our Almighty Father will not give His honor away, and He will deliver His people Himself, whatever it takes.

I thought for a while.

I'm not sure I like that.

Nor should you, Avi. The door is open and there's nothing hindering us from return-ing to our heavenly Father. Yeshuah did, and we can too – voluntarily and with purpose. It's our choice whether we want to be driven out or not.

There's wisdom in that, Harry. There sure is.

We walked on for quite some time before Harry resumed our conversation.

Eventually, we'll need to deal with this matter, and now it has come sooner than I expected. It's all about that awful word that no one likes – the word 'repentance.' It's a word that we need to get comfortable with.

How so?

Repentance is usually understood to mean the turning away from wrong deeds, but it really means a return to right deeds, or the return to a place from which we have fallen away. Repentance essentially means to turn around and go back. There should be some remorse, but that's not the impetus. The real motive is a heartfelt return to the original instructions of our Almighty Father.

What does that mean?

It means, Avi, to keep His commandments.

I was compelled to silence as we kept walking.

I have a good idea what's going on in your mind, Avi. I've been through it too, and it took me a long time to get over.

From that comment, I expected my friend to continue. After a few minutes, it became apparent to me that he was not going to elaborate. We continued walking, and then, the unexpected happened. Suddenly, I became very angry. It came to me seemingly out of nowhere, and I didn't know why, but my anger was seething, and I wanted to lash out at Harry. I looked at my friend without being able to mask my feelings.

My astonishment was compounded when Harry returned my look. His interminable patience was gone, and unmistakably I saw resentment in his eyes. It was directed at me!

All I could do was continue walking. This wasn't my friend Happy Harry that I was walking next to. I tried to remember if he had ever resented me in the past. There had once been an occasion, but that was different. This time I was sure that I hadn't done anything to earn his displeasure. This was his problem, and I was sure of it.

We walked for a long time with me trying to sort out my anger and Harry's resentment. His continued silence didn't help, and my anger didn't go away. Finally, I acted on it.

You're just going to have to open your mouth and explain yourself. You can't just tell me that you know what's going on in my mind.

I couldn't have been more stern. I was speaking as if to a child, and I knew it.

I don't know what your problem is, Harry, but don't take it out on me! Besides, this isn't like you at all.

Much to his credit, Harry didn't return my anger, but I could tell that he still didn't want to talk. His resentment continued.

Tell me what's wrong, Harry. Please.

We walked on and my friend remained silent. I was thinking, "This man is acting

THE BOOK OF NOTS IN SCIENCE & RELIGION

like a spoiled child who only wants it his way." My anger had dissipated, but not his resentment. I was about to give him a playful poke in the ribs when he finally spoke up.

What you're thinking is that once there was a dispensation of law, but now there's a dispensation of grace. You're thinking that once the Almighty was dealing with Israel, but now He's dealing with the Church. You're thinking that the law is too difficult and impossible to keep, and you can only be righteous through faith.

Still, Harry said it in a way that seemed close to seething. I felt for him.

You're correct, my friend. Those thoughts go through my mind as clear as a bell. I've heard it so many times that it's become second nature. Paul once scribbled, "We are not under the law, but under grace," and Martin Luther sloganeered, "Justification by faith alone."[6] That doctrine has been central to Christianity for five hundred years now.[7] It's deeply ingrained in my thoughts.

I was about to continue when a little voice of caution whispered in my ear. I knew I needed to be careful. I put my hand on Harry's shoulder.

I truly believe that Yeshuah was the Messiah, or at the very least a true representation of the Messiah. The parallels of what was written about him in the Christian Scriptures and the Hebrew Scriptures is unmistakable. Yeshuah was the Messiah in his teaching, his works and his character. The parallel with Isaiah 53 is uncanny. No one could have just made it up.

I looked intently at my friend.

Please don't misunderstand me, Harry. I think believing that Yeshuah was the Messiah is huge. Hardly anything can compare with believing that humankind's savior has already been present on this Earth. It's so utterly life-changing!

But Harry, believing in Yeshuah is not going to make us righteous. That is what Luther

---

6   Luther actually added the 'alone' to his declaration "Justification by faith alone" to make his point. For him it meant that justification could only come by faith, and by faith alone.

7   Not all the reformers agreed. Menno Simons, and Anabaptists generally, did not accept Martin Luther's doctrine of justification by faith alone. They saw that doctrine as an impediment to the true doctrine of a "living" faith which results in works, and detected a tendency toward antinomianism in the Reformed doctrine of justification by faith. Even now, critics of Anabaptists and Menno Simons point to this distinction with suspicion, suggesting that it leaves people to devise a righteousness of their own based on Law. However, Menno Simons believed that works do justify and were proof of a truly converted life.

meant, that we can have the Messiah's righteousness by believing in Yeshuah. Nor are we going to be saved by simply believing in Yeshuah. That's what Paul meant by saying all we need to do is believe Yeshuah was the Messiah and that he was raised from the dead. Those are wonderful beliefs, but of and by themselves, those beliefs are not going to make us righteous. That's a fiction no matter who said it.

I wasn't going to wait for Harry's confirmation.

An honest and thoughtful person will see right away that no one can be righteous by simply believing in something. It would be foolish for someone to say, "I believe, so now I'm righteous." Paul was wrong when he said, "A man is justified by faith apart from works." How blatantly foolish.

As soon as the words came out of my mouth, I felt cut short. I didn't want to sound authoritarian by stating the obvious so bluntly. I looked over at Harry, feeling apologetic.

I'm deeply sorry, Avi.

Why? Did I say too much?

Not at all. I'm the one at fault. I was passing judgement on you, and I had no reason to do that. I am very sorry.

Please explain it to me, Harry.

On a number of occasions I've made the same statement, that we need to keep the commandments. Without exception, I've got nothing back but a wall of rebuttal. Those who I said it to were indignant and wouldn't budge an inch. Somehow, I automatically expected the same from you. I shouldn't have, but I did. I'm sorry.

Oh, Harry. That's okay. I just couldn't understand your strange behavior. I was shocked by it.

That was unbelief on my part. We have been doing so well all along. I shouldn't have expected anything different.

Is it possible that you take those rebuttals personally? Are you being overly sensitive?

Harry gave me a piercing look. I was glad he was back to himself. I never minded Harry's straightforward manner.

Yes, and it's something I need to deal with. I've pointed out that there is obvious anti-Semitism in the so-called *New Testament*. It goes even deeper. Rejecting the commandments is a rejection of all the Almighty's people, and not just the Jews. That's why I take it personally even though I shouldn't.

You see, Avi, I believe that we who have tried to live righteous lives and have believed in Yeshuah as the Messiah are all from the seed of Abraham, and I don't mean spiritually speaking only. I mean literally and genetically too. We are Abraham's offspring physically and spiritually.

I find it very offensive, Avi, when people like Paul tell me the Law of Moses was only temporary or that the law was "nailed to the cross." Such people are inordinately foolish, and are bulldozing over the Almighty's people without an ounce of compunction, their naivety notwithstanding. It seems very wicked when you're on the receiving end.

I felt my eyes bulging. I thought I was being too forceful.

I'm not trying to be vindictive, Avi. It needs to be said. Those who speak against the Law of Moses are going against what is intrinsic to the Eternal One's people. As Isaiah said,

To the law and to the testimony:
if they speak not according to this Word,
it is because there is no light in them.

That is the resounding reality of the Eternal One's people, and Yeshuah the Messiah confirmed it unequivocally. No one could have said better:

Do not think that I have come to abolish the Law or the Prophets;
I have not come to abolish them but to fulfill them.
For truly, I say to you, until heaven and earth pass away,
not an iota, not a dot, will pass from the Law until all is accomplished.
Therefore whoever relaxes one of the least of these commandments
and teaches others to do the same
will be called least in the Kingdom of Heaven,
but whoever does them and teaches them
will be called great in the Kingdom of Heaven.

When Harry finished and our eyes met, I saw in him what most identified him as a person. I saw his wholeness and depth of being. Harry's insight and wisdom came from his appreciation of the Almighty's commandments. From there he understood the Messiah and the Messiah's life. They were the same for Harry – the Torah and the

Messiah – and he held fast to them for the sake of his being.

We were walking in a semi-wooded area alongside a public park. When I saw a park bench off to one side, it was my cue.

I want to sit down for a while, Harry. I want to think.

We sat down without another word at a comfortable distance from each other. I wanted to be quiet, but had no desire to be introspective. I was grateful for my friend's companionship even as we sat in silence for a long time. Easily an hour must have passed.

I'll say it again, Harry. I'm happy. It's not just because I've learned so much with pleasure, but now that we're talking about keeping the commandments, I am realizing why I feel happy. It's because the truth has become much more tangible. Having faith is good and so is knowledge, but nothing better than having a track to run on. It's our doing that makes us truthful. To paraphrase your verse from Joshua: We need to do according to all that is written. For then we will make our way prosperous, and then we will have good success.

I saw the gratitude in Harry's face.

Abraham, the main argument against the commandments is that they are very hard and impossible to keep. That is utterly untrue. Moshe plainly told the Almighty's people:

**For this commandment that I command you today is not too hard for you, neither is it far off.
It is not in heaven, that you should say,
'Who will ascend to heaven for us and bring it to us,
that we may hear it and do it?'
But the word is very near you.
It is in your mouth and in your heart,
so that you can do it.**

We walked on. My mind was gelling.

I'm going to make an assumption, Harry. You have acquired much knowledge and wisdom over the years. I think there's a connection between your obedience and your wisdom. Without keeping the commandments, you never would have grown the way you have.

That fits with an experience I had in the past. I once knew some people who were avid commandment keepers. It puzzled me at the time, but it was obvious they knew a lot more than I did, in scriptural knowledge especially. They impressed me as being quite courageous as well.

I've thought about it over the years with mixed feelings. At one time, it became clear to me that keeping the commandments established by the Almighty at the beginning is the only real answer. Those rules are the answer to the question of how we should live. It seemed obvious to me at the time and very attractive, but I balked at it. I didn't want to go that way.

I knew where my thoughts were leading.

Harry, I'm going to commit to keeping the laws that were given to us by the Eternal One through Moses. I fully believe that there is life and wisdom and hope in them. There are some questions in my mind, but I'm not going to waver on it any more. I'm not going to get caught between two opinions. I'm going to be obedient.

You don't need to respond to that, Harry. This is me talking. This is my decision.

We walked a bit before he spoke.

You don't need me to support your commitment either. I can see that in you. However, what you just did is repent, even if you didn't think of it in that way. You just now returned to the Mighty One of Israel. May the Eternal One be with you, Abraham.

I'm speaking intuitively, but what should prevent me from being baptized? That's surely directly linked to repentance!

Nothing, Avi.

I thought of it because we'll be at the river in a few minutes, and it's very secluded there. I want to be baptized.

I can help you with that, but I won't baptize you myself. I'll just be there as a witness. I will help you into the water where you can say a prayer and immerse yourself. Just be free about what you're doing and speak your mind without restraint.

When we came to the river, everything came together easily. I discreetly removed my outer clothing leaving on my boxer shorts and light undershirt. Harry took off his socks and shoes and rolled up his pant legs. We helped each other into the water over some slippery rocks. The shoreline dropped off quickly until Harry's rolled up pants started to get wet. We just stood there for a brief moment. It was exceptionally quiet where we were, and the late morning sun was shining brightly. It all seemed so simple.

Forgive me, everlasting Father for not always walking in your ways. Forgive all your people for our disobedience. I want that your people will return to you, Abba Father. Hear our prayer of repentance. Hear my prayer.

I took a step forward and stooped down until I was completely immersed. Without hesitating, I stood up and Harry helped me recover my balance.

I'm so thankful, Abba, for your faithfulness, and your forgiveness. May your kingdom come, and your will be done on Earth as it is in Heaven. Help me in my new life.

Harry added more.

I call upon Heaven and Earth as a witness to this act of repentance. May the name of the Eternal One be praised forever. So may it be.

As we stepped out of the water, I thanked Harry for his help with a grateful arm on his shoulder. I went behind a bush to ring out my undergarments, but kept them on under my dry clothes. It was warm enough that being slightly damp didn't matter, and I wasn't about to carry my underwear around in public.

Let's start back, Abraham. You're probably getting hungry and I have some quotations that I want to share with you. We'll go around the town, so it will take us another hour.

The walk back was unusually pleasant. My sense of well-being grew as we walked, and I was sure Harry was feeling the same. Neither of us had expected the day to unfold as it had, and our 'bump on the road' misunderstanding had transformed into something very uplifting. It was a good walk back.

Harry's late lunch was generous. He brought out 'pigs in a blanket' made with fried mushrooms, a side dish of cooked spinach, pickled olives, cut raw vegetables and a bowl of fruit. I was quite sure there was no pork involved. We ate with whole hearts, still enjoying each other's company.

Then out came a bottle of well-aged port. We touched glasses.

Abraham, this has been a happy day for me too, but not entirely unexpected. Actually, I prepared something very appropriate. I can see how real this experience has been for you, and want to confirm that you're headed down the right path. It's an ancient path that many have walked on before you.

There is a record of how the first believers in Yeshuah walked. The first quote I have is by a man named Epiphanius, who wrote the following in 374 AD:

> But these sectarians... did not call themselves Christians... but 'Nazarenes'.... However they are simply complete Jews. They use not only the New Testament but the Old Testament as well, as the Jews do... They have no different ideas, but confess everything exactly as the Law proclaims it and in the Jewish fashion... except for their belief in Messiah, if you please!
>
> *For they acknowledge both the resurrection of the dead and the divine creation of all things, and declare that God is one, and that his son is Yeshuah the Messiah.*
>
> They are trained to a nicety in Hebrew. For among them the entire Law, the Prophets, and the... Writings... are read in Hebrew, as they surely are by the Jews. They are different from the Jews, and different from Christians, only in the following. They disagree with Jews because they have come to faith in Messiah; but since they are still fettered by the Law... circumcision, the Sabbath, and the rest... they are not in accord with Christians.
>
> As to Christ, I cannot say whether they too are captives of the wickedness of [heretics], and regard him as a mere man - or whether, as the truth is, they affirm his birth from Mary by the Holy Spirit. (*emphasis added*).[8]

The second quotation comes from Eusebius a few decades earlier than Epiphanius:

> The ancients quite properly called these men Ebionites, because they held poor and mean opinions concerning Christ. For *they considered Christ a plain and common man, who was justified only because of his superior virtue, and who was the fruit of the intercourse of a man with Mary...*
>
> There were others, however, besides them, that were of the same

---

8   *Against Nazarenes*, Panarion 29, edited. Available on-line.

name, but avoided the strange and absurd beliefs of the former, and did not deny that the Lord was born of a virgin and of the Holy Spirit. But nevertheless, inasmuch as they also refused to acknowledge that he pre-existed, being God, Word, and Wisdom, they turned aside into the impiety of the former, especially when they, like them, endeavored to observe strictly the bodily worship of the law.

These men, moreover, thought that it was necessary to reject all the epistles of the apostle [Paul], whom they called an apostate from the law; and they used only the so-called Gospel according to the Hebrews and made small account of the rest.

The Sabbath and the rest of the discipline of the Jews they observed just like them, but at the same time, like us, they celebrated the Lord's days as a memorial of the resurrection of the Saviour.

Wherefore, in consequence of such a course they received the name of Ebionites, which signified the poverty of their understanding. For this is the name by which a poor man is called among the Hebrews. (*emphasis added*).[9]

I've printed out the quotations for you, Avi. May I suggest that you read them carefully several times? You will quickly see how close the Nazarenes and the Ebionites were to many of the things we have talked about in the last few weeks. I believe that you will find it very encouraging. You are in good company from long ago. I like what the *New Testament* author wrote. To paraphrase slightly:

You were straying like a sheep,
but have now returned to the true Shepherd
and Guardian of your soul.

Thank you, Harry. This has been so valuable and humbling. I'm very grateful to the One who has done it with me, but I have the impression that something more needs to be talked about. Surely, our obedience activates a promise.

Yes, we've been alluding to it all along. By all accounts, history as we know it is coming to a climactic end. We need to talk about eschatology or the end times.

9 Eusebius, *Ecclesiastical History,* Book 3, 27. It is more often thought that the Ebionites came by their name from the saying, "Blessed are the poor in spirit: for theirs is the kingdom in heaven." Both Eusebius and Epiphanius disagreed with the Ebionites and considered them heretics even though they preserved a fairly accurate assessment of their beliefs and practices.

I'm as much interested in eschatology as anyone else.

Then we'll start next Sabbath.

We stood there quietly for quite some time, exchanged eye contact, shook hands and briefly embraced.

Shalom, my friend Abraham.

Shalom, my friend Harry.

12. WE ARE NOT GENTILES

May He be with you, Harry.

May the Eternal One be with you, Abraham.

Avi, we're going to have an exhilarating session today! Those of us who are familiar with the prophets know that they tell a story that is more profound than anyone could ever imagine. They tell us the true story of salvation and the complete history of human-kind in advance.

Is it really that simple?

Yes it is. Without a doubt.

Then I'm all ears, Harry. I want to know what salvation is really about.

It was now mid-summer, and the days had gone from warm to comfortably hot. Shade from a mature tree, an early light breeze, and the trickling sound of Harry's artificial waterfall all reinforced the pleasure of being outdoors. Harry had brought out crusted buns and marmalade with the tea pot. The morning could hardly have been better.

For most people, eschatology is all about the immortal soul. Ultimately, that soul must spend eternity in either Heaven or in Hell. That may be overly simplistic, and I apologize if it sounds crass or even vulgar, but it is what many people say they believe in as their future and eternal state.

Once again, the reality is very different. The Eternal One has chosen a specific man and a specific people for His own purpose to love forever. He will save these people on the day of trouble. In much the same way, the Eternal One also chose Yeshuah to be the savior of the whole world. However, eschatology is primarily about the salvation of those specific people that the Eternal One has chosen for Himself, and it doesn't have anything to do with Heaven and Hell.

Avi, there is a day of trouble or calamity coming. It is mentioned frequently in the Scriptures as the Day of the Eternal One. It's more popularly called the Day of Yahweh, and in the English translations as the Day of the Lord. It is also-called the Day of Wrath. It is on that Day that "whoever calls on the Name of the Eternal One will be saved." Salvation isn't about being saved from a metaphysical hell, but rather from the wrath of the Almighty that will come upon the Earth. The wrath will be worldwide in a time of almost indescribable catastrophe.

I saw the fleeting look of grief in Harry's eyes.

But that's for next Sabbath, Avi. Today we need to start at the beginning, and the beginning is with your namesake. He has rightly been called "the father of all who believe," and he is the real beginning of "The greatest story ever told," as in another saying. It's that story that I want to retell today.

Abraham obeyed when the Eternal One commanded him to leave his native land and go to Canaan. With the command came the promise to make Abraham a great nation. The same promise was extended to Abraham's son Isaac, to his grandson Jacob, and to his twelve great-grandsons through Jacob. More than four centuries later, the Eternal One delivered Abraham's seed from their bondage in Egypt, and brought his children's children into the land of Canaan.[1]

Avi, we can't get too involved with the question of how many people actually left Egypt with its logistics and problems of translation, but it's hardly likely that 2.5 million Israelites left. Some reasonable estimates have been as low as seven thousand individuals. Forty years later, only forty thousand armed men crossed the Jordan River, considerably fewer than the six hundred thousand armed men that supposedly left Egypt in the Genesis account. That does not, however, gainsay the Eternal One's promise to multiply Abraham's seed as the stars of the heavens and the sand of the sea. That promise is still central to "the greatest story ever told."[2]

---

1   Now YHWH said to Abram, "Go forth from your country, and from your relatives and from your father's house, to the land which I will show you; and I will make you a great nation, and I will bless you, and make your name great; and so you shall be a blessing. I will bless those who bless you, and the one who curses you I will curse. In you all the families of the earth will be blessed." So Abram went forth as YHWH had spoken to him (Genesis 12:1-4).

2   I will multiply your seed as the stars of the heavens, and as the sand which is upon the seashore.... And in your seed shall all the nations of the Earth be blessed because you obeyed my voice (Genesis 22:16-18).

As the story progresses, twelve families or tribes entered the land of Canaan after their forty years in the wilderness. Each tribe was named after one of the sons of Jacob, whose name has been changed to Israel. They were Reuben, Simeon, Levi, Judah, Zebulun, Issachar, Dan, Gad, Asher, Naphtali, Joseph and Benjamin. Joseph was the father of two tribes, Manasseh and Ephraim, making the total number thirteen. Once in Canaan, Joshua divided the land among twelve tribes, excluding the tribe of Levi. As priests for the entire nation, the Levites were to receive a tithe from all the other tribes. The tribe of Judah was also unique. All the future kings of Israel, as a nation, were to come from the tribe of Judah.[3] Israel was to be a nation of priests and kings.

Harry gave me another of his discerning looks.

Are you wondering where this is going, or what this has to do with the belief in Heaven and Hell?

I know what you're leading up to, Harry, that salvation will come upon the Earth, and to the people who inhabit it.

Exactly. I'm giving you the bare-bones version of what is written in the Law and the Prophets. Moses made predictions about the nation of Israel, and the prophets saw how many of his predictions were fulfilled in their time. Much of this story is also found in the records of secular history.[4]

We should read the passage, Abraham. Moses knew it from the beginning of Israel's history.

There was pathos in my friend's voice:

When all these blessings and curses I have set before you come on you

---

3 Judah's kingship was a promise given to David. "When your days are over and you rest with your ancestors, I will raise up your offspring to succeed you, your own flesh and blood, and I will establish his kingdom. He is the one who will build a house for my Name, and I will establish the throne of his kingdom forever. I will be his father, and he will be my son. When he does wrong, I will punish him with a rod wielded by men, with floggings inflicted by human hands. But my love will never be taken away from him, as I took it away from Saul, whom I removed from before you. Your house and your kingdom will endure forever before me; your throne will be established forever (2 Samuel 7:12-16)."
4 This author highly recommends the books written by Steven M. Collins. His, *The "Lost" Ten Tribes of Israel...Found!,* is one of the best on the history of ancient Israel; and his, *Parthia: The Forgotten Ancient Superpower And Its Role In Biblical History,* is superb. These are 'must read' books in my opinion.

Authors such as Collins are fulfilling a prediction made by Sir Isaac Newton (1643-1727 AD). "About the time of the end, a body of men will be raised up who will turn their attention to the prophecies, and insist upon their literal interpretation, in the midst of much clamor and opposition."

and you take them to heart
wherever YHWH your Mighty One disperses you among the nations,
and when you and your children return to YHWH your Mighty One
and obey Him with all your heart and with all your soul
according to everything I command you today,
then YHWH your Mighty One will restore your fortunes
and have compassion on you
and gather you again from all the nations where He scattered you.

Even if you have been banished to the most distant land under the
heavens, from there YHWH your Mighty One will gather you and bring
you back.
He will bring you to the land that belonged to your ancestors,
and you will take possession of it.
He will make you more prosperous and numerous than your ancestors.
YHWH your Mighty One will circumcise your hearts
and the hearts of your descendants,
so that you may love him with all your heart
and with all your soul, and live....

You will again obey YHWH and follow all His commands I am giving you
today. Then YHWH your Mighty One will make you most prosperous
in all the work of your hands and in the fruit of your womb,
the young of your livestock and the crops of your land.
YHWH will again delight in you and make you prosperous,
just as he delighted in your ancestors,
if you obey YHWH your Mighty One
and keep His commands and decrees
that are written in this Book of the Law
and turn to YHWH your Mighty One
with all your heart and with all your soul.[5]

Harry put down his Scripture text with a profound reverence.

Moses soon realized that the people he had led out of Egypt would not be staying in Canaan. He perceived that they were to be scattered among the gentile nations, and banished to very ends of the Earth. But he knew too that one day they would be returned

---

5   Deuteronomy 30:1-10.

to Canaan and become a people again. This is just what Yeshuah said in his prophecy concerning the latter days:

Immediately after the distress of those days
'the sun will be darkened, and the moon will not give its light;
the stars will fall from the sky, and the heavenly bodies will be shaken.

Then will appear the sign of the Son of Man in heaven.
And then all the peoples of the Earth will mourn
when they see the Son of Man coming on the clouds of heaven,
with power and great esteem.

And he will send his angels with a loud trumpet call,
and they will gather his elect from the four winds,
from one end of the heavens to the other.[6]

We aren't getting ahead of ourselves, Avi. There is a day of great calamity coming. After that, the Messiah will regather the tribes from the ends of the Earth and return them to the land of Canaan. All the prophets have said the same.

Harry stood up and paced back and forth briefly.

Let's pick up the story line again, starting from when the Israelites inhabited Canaan. In less than five hundred years, the twelve tribes became a mighty kingdom under David's son, Solomon. Historians have often underestimated this period to the point of denying that there even was a tenth century kingdom. That denial ignores the cumulative evidence and the biblical record as actual history. As historian Steven M. Collins writes:

> The Bible tells us that King David subdued the Philistines, the Moabites, the Ammonites, the Edomites, the Amalekites and sufficient territory to reach the Euphrates River. (1 Chronicles 18:1-17) This area would roughly correspond to the modern nations of Israel and Lebanon together with much of Jordan, a sizable portion of Syria and a part of western Iraq. Israel's army, when fully mobilized, numbered 1,500,000 men! (1 Chronicles 21:5-6)[7]

My point is, Avi, that whatever number of Israelites left Egypt, their numbers had

6   Matthew 24:29-30.
7   Collins, *Israel's Lost Empires*, Bible Blessings publisher, 2002, p 10.

grown substantially in the five hundred years between the Exodus and Solomon. So
had the territory they occupied. It had grown from a part of the Nile Delta to a territory stretching between Egypt and the Euphrates River. Yet this is still a far cry from the
numbers that the Eternal One had promised to His friend Abraham for his posterity.

Nevertheless, the fulfillment of the Eternal One's promise was underway by the time
of Solomon. It is clear that by then the Israelites perceived themselves as a mighty nation,
and for good cause:

**Judah and Israel were many as the sand which is by the sea in multitude,
eating and drinking and making merry.
And Solomon ruled over all the kingdoms from the River [Euphrates]
unto the land of the Philistines, and unto the border of Egypt:
they brought tribute, and served Solomon all the days of his life....
For he had dominion over all the region on this side the River,
from Tiphsah**[8] **even to Gaza,
over all the kings on this side the River [Euphrates]:
and he had peace on all sides round about him.
And Judah and Israel dwelt safely,
every man under his vine and under his fig-tree.**[9]

It was a golden age for the Israelite nation under Solomon. A truly golden age! With
Phoenicia to the north and Egypt to the south as his willing allies, Solomon was at the
head of a vast empire. Tribute flowed into his treasuries, 666 talents of gold annually from
his vassal kings alone. With no serious military threats and unrivaled wealth, Solomon
could turn his attention to peaceful pursuits. Aside from Solomon's massive building
projects, there were exotic seafaring expeditions, international trade, and coloniza-
tion on a global scale. Consequently, "all the kings of the Earth sought the presence of
Solomon."[10] As Collins wrote, "Solomon's rule likely constituted the greatest golden age
in the ancient world."[11]

It was at this time that we begin to see fulfillment to the promise of multiplicity for
Abraham's seed. Solomon could rely on a sizable labour pool, and was able to export
workers for his construction projects and sailors for his Phoenician navy. More important, the Israelites began to populate other parts of the world as colonists. Solomon's
Red Sea fleet sailed east, reaching India and even China. Sailing west, colonies were

---

8   Tiphsah was an ancient city on the western bank of the Euphrates river that would now lie in modern
Syria or Turkey
9   1 Kings 4:20-25.
10   11 Chronicles 9:23-24.
11   *The "Lost" Ten Tribes of Israel...Found!*, p 41.

established in northern Africa, Spain, Great Britain and in the Americas. Herein we also see the prelude of the Almighty's plan to scatter His people throughout the nations to the very ends of the Earth. It would be as Moses said:

**And YHWH will scatter you among all peoples,
from one end of the Earth to the other,
and there you shall serve other gods of wood and stone,
which neither you nor your fathers have known.**[12]

Avi, I'll expand a little. There is much evidence for an ancient Israelite presence in the Americas. Steven Collins gives a long list of Israelite artifacts, inscriptions and structures in North America. So did the respected scholar and historian, Dr. Barry Fell, in his book *America B.C.* One example is the Los Luna inscription near Albuquerque, New Mexico. It dates to about 1000 BC, and on it are inscribed the Ten Commandments in ancient Hebrew. Another Decalogue Tablet was unearthed in Ohio in 1860 (*Decalogue* is a word for the Ten Commandments.). Similar inscriptions have also been found in South America. It's not even impossible, as some speculate, that Yeshuah also went to the Americas.

After the golden age of Solomon, his kingdom was torn apart. The ten northern tribes became the Kingdom of Israel, and the southern tribes of Judah and Benjamin, including many Levites, became the Kingdom of Judah. Both kingdoms eventually became victims of the political powers surrounding Canaan. Just five years after Solomon died, Egypt attacked Judah and looted Jerusalem of its gold treasures. In 734 BC, the Assyrians attacked the northern Kingdom of Israel and carried away a third of its population. In 597 BC, the Babylonians attacked the southern kingdom of Judah and took away ten thousand of its most prominent citizens. Both Assyria and Babylon dispersed their captives throughout the region of the Tigris and Euphrates in various cities.

That's the textbook version of how the Israelites of both kingdoms were dispersed among the nations, but it's by far not the whole story. Many Israelites of the northern tribes had already left as a result of a severe famine in the time of Elijah. Many more left their doomed nation prior to Assyria's last invasion in 721 BC. Since the Hebrews had collectively been a great maritime power under Solomon, the fleeing northern tribes had many possible destinations. Colonies had already been established in North Africa, Spain, Briton, Ireland and even North America. The historical evidence is often ignored, but many, many Israelites left their homeland voluntarily.[13] Again from Collins:

12 Deuteronomy 28:64.
13 Collins concludes in his book "that large contingents of the Israelite tribes of Dan and Simeon (the Danaan and the Simonii) sought refuge in Ireland and Briton after abandoning their old homelands to the Assyrians." See, *The "Lost" Ten Tribes of Israel...Found!*, p 125.

While sizable contingents of the tribes of Dan and Simeon fled by the sea to the British Isles, and other Israelites became Celtic migrants after the fall of Samaria [the capital city of the northern tribes in 721 BC], *there is historical evidence that the main body of Israelites fleeing the kingdom of Israel took an overland route to their new homeland.* They could not go east because of the Assyrian menace, there were not enough vessels to take everyone to new homelands via maritime routes to the west, and Egyptian forces were dominant to the south. This left the north as the only realistic land route out of Palestine, and that is exactly where historical evidence says they went. (*emphasis added*).[14]

Those Israelites leaving by an overland route were probably the largest contingent to emigrate from Canaan. One authority states that they left with an army of 120,000 horse-mounted and a hundred thousand foot soldiers.[15] This could easily mean that, in total, around a million Israelites fled northward. Tradition has it that they left so they could keep the commandments, which they had never been able to under Israel's wicked kings, and were miraculously assisted on their way in crossing the Euphrates. They ended their journey after a year and a half in an uninhabited region north of the Black Sea where they could dwell safely and grow in numbers.

But they took this counsel among themselves, that they would leave the multitude of the heathen, and go forth into a further country, where never mankind dwelt, *that they might there keep their statutes, which they never kept in their own land.*

And they entered into Euphrates by the narrow places of the river. For the Most High then showed signs for them, and held still the flood, till they were passed over.

For through that country [Armenia] there was a great way to go, namely, of a year and a half.... Then dwelt they there until the latter time. (*emphasis added*).[16]

The rest of this great story can only be told briefly. The region to which many of the Israelites and Jews were taken (from the Kingdom of Israel and the Kingdom of Judah) came to be known as Parthia. There the tribes of Israel prospered and grew in numbers. By around 100 AD, Josephus could write, "the ten tribes are beyond Euphrates 'til now,

---

14 *The "Lost" Ten Tribes of Israel...Found!*, p 125.
15 Gawler, Colonel J.C., *Our Scythian Ancestors Identified With Israel*, Edinburgh, 1875, p 9.
16 II Esdras 41-46.

and are an immense multitude, and not to be estimated by numbers."[17] Then, when Parthia fell to the Persians in 226 AD, it triggered the greatest migration of a people in all of history. During the next decades, a "mixed multitude" of Israelites migrated westward through Armenia to the region north of the Black Sea. There they reunited with Israelites that had already been there for nearly a millennium. For the first time since the united kingdom under David and Solomon, all the tribes of Israel were together again.[18]

The migration continued. With so many of the tribes together again, the pressure to continue expanding westward was greatly increased. In the period of 250-300 AD, various groups spilled chaotically and often violently into north-western Europe. They came as Teutons, Goths, Vandals, Saxons and other names. In a pivotal battle in 251 AD, the Goths routed a Roman army and killed the emperor Decius. More than a century later, Rome was sacked by the Gauls in 387 AD. In the course of those years, these groups – many of them descendants of the tribes of Israel – were able to settle themselves and become the population base for most of the modern Europeans nations.

The final episode in this phenomenal mass migration came in the nineteenth and twentieth centuries. Millions of Europeans emigrated from their home countries to new overseas homelands from countries such as England, France, Germany, Italy, Norway and Sweden. By the end of the nineteenth century, more than ten million Europeans had come to the United States of America. The momentum continued with the expansion of the British Empire. At its peak in 1933, nearly three hundred thousand left the United Kingdom for Australia, New Zealand and Canada. By 1921, 22% of Canada's population was foreign-born. This is not to exclude an eastward expansion as well. Beginning as early as the seventeenth century, several hundreds of thousands of Europeans immigrated to countries such as India, Singapore, Vietnam, Hong Kong and Macau. Today there is not one continent or country in the world that is without some element of European ancestry.

That is why Hosea could say prophetically:

Israel is swallowed up: now are they among the nations.[19]

Avi, the saying "swallowed up" might as well mean masticated. The seed of Abraham has been so thoroughly mixed with the seed of the gentiles that very few of us have any comprehension of who we are. To be certain, we would rather think of ourselves as gentiles than as Israelites or Hebrews. We even resist the idea that we might in some way be Jews. In that sense, we truly are the "lost sheep of the house of Israel." We are lost,

---

17   Flavius Josephus (37 BC - 100 AD), *Antiquities of the Jews*, Book XI (Ch. 5).
18   This part of the story is best told by Steven M. Collins in his, *Parthia: The Forgotten Ancient Superpower And Its Role In Biblical History.*
19   Hosea 8.8

forgotten, unnamed, and greatly in need of salvation.

Abraham, would you mind summarizing that story in your words?

Not at all. The story begins with Abraham. The Almighty Father promised Abraham that He would bless him, multiply his offspring, make out of him a great nation, and that through him all the nations of the Earth would be blessed. The nation that came forth almost a thousand years later was the united monarchy under David and later under his son and Solomon. That nation, as great as it was, lasted barely a hundred years before it divided into a northern and southern kingdom.

Both kingdoms almost came to an end under the regimes of Assyria and then Babylon. Their populations were dispersed or fled from their oppressors. Only ten percent of the tribe of Judah went back to Canaan around 537 BC. The rest of the tribes never returned and became known collectively as the Lost Ten Tribes of Israel. No doubt, the rest of Judah is among them to this day.

Many people claim that those Israelite tribes disappeared from history, but we know that they did not. The Lost Tribes reappeared later under various names in the early centuries A.D. – the Angles, Saxons, Goths, Vandals and Jutes for example. As they popu-lated most of northwestern Europe, they brought with them an odd mixture of ancient Hebrew customs and Christian traditions. Yet in many ways, they were hardly distinct from the nations of which they had become part.

I agree with you, Harry, that many of the tribes of Israel also migrated to the East. Ancient Hebrew customs have been noticed in India, China, Japan and Indonesia. You didn't mention South America, but there must be many Israelites there too. I know that a great number of Jews fled to many South American countries to escape the Spanish Inquisition in the sixteenth century AD. It must be that there's not a country in the world that doesn't have a meaningful Jewish or Israelite component.[20]

Actually, I know of a text in the Bible that says exactly that. Looking into the future, the author of Revelation wrote:

After these things I saw, and behold, a great multitude,
which no man could number,
out of every nation and of all tribes and peoples and tongues,

---

[20] From an article in a newspaper published in Israel (*Maariv*, Dec 31, 1974): "In 1587, a Jesuit Nicholas Delttsu was sent to South America by the king of Spain to convert the Indians. In Argentina, he found a tribe with Hebrew names, Abraham, David, Moshe, etc.. When he asked them if they were circumcised, they answered, 'Yes, just as our ancestors.'"

standing before the throne and before the Lamb.[21]

I've thought about it deeply, and I'm very sure it's not only the white, Anglo-Saxon Protestants that make up the seed of Abraham. I can agree that those countries have the highest concentrations of Israelites and Jews, but it's wrong to think of those countries as exclusive. The so-called "lost tribes" are now present in every nation in the world and in every race. I truly believe that.

I heard Harry exhale before he spoke.

That's powerful, Abraham. You said it so well.

Thanks. I'm going to be emphatic and I'm sure you'll agree. In the Father's plan of salvation, there's absolutely no room for racism. His plan is for every tribe and tongue and people. As I remember singing in Sunday school, "Red and yellow, black and white. They are precious in His sight." Personally, I have zero tolerance for racism of any kind, including anti-Semitism. Right, Harry?

Harry looked down at his feet.

Yes.

He said quietly before lifting his head.

Harry, I know from personal experience that within the modern messianic movement there's much evil spoken against the Jews and Blacks. It's most evident in the United States, especially in the southern states, but not exclusively. When it is evident, it goes from subtle to seething. I'm ashamed to say it, but it's true. I'm sorry too, but the Black race is not cursed, and the Jews are not Edomites. It's the people who say such things that have given themselves over to a perverse way of thinking.[22]

---

21 Revelation 7:9.

22 In the story of Noah in Genesis 9, the best explanation is that Ham had sexual relations with his mother ("saw the nakedness of his father"). Accordingly Canaan, Ham's son by his own mother, was cursed by Noah. The passage and curse cannot be applied to a whole race of people, the black race in particular.

A large majority of the Jews in the world today are of Eastern European descent. The ancestry of that majority can be traced to the Khazars, a powerful tribal kingdom and empire of the 10th century AD. In turn, the Khazars can be traced to the Parthian immigration to the region north of the Black Sea at the beginning of the 3rd century AD. As written earlier in this chapter, this is the same region and time when "all the tribes of Israel were together again!" That would make a significant number of the Khazars either Israelites or Jews. Given the nature of the national conversion of the Khazars in 740 AD, it's very likely that many of the original Khazars were from the tribe of Judah. Saying that the Khazars were all Edomites only demonstrates a very limited and prejudicial view of history.

I didn't want to say any more, and felt isolated myself. Then it came to me in an instant.

Harry, there's a passage in Isaiah that precludes prejudice against any people or race. I read it just the other day.

I found it easily and read it aloud:

And now saith YHWH that formed me from the womb to be His servant,
to bring Jacob again to Him, and that Israel be gathered unto Him...
Yea, He saith, It is too light a thing that you should be my servant
to raise up the tribes of Jacob, and to restore the preserved of Israel:
I will also give you for a light to the Gentiles,
that you may be my salvation unto the end of the Earth.[23]

That's it, Harry! The passage is prophetic, but the Almighty's plan of salvation is for the whole world, not for his chosen people only, not just for Israel and Judah!

I felt motivated to continue.

What's more, I know where you are going next with this great story. It has to do with the coming Kingdom of Heaven on this Earth.

Go ahead, Avi. You describe it.

All right. I've been reading the prophets a lot lately, particularly Isaiah and Jeremiah. It's all very plain in those books for those who care to read them.

To begin, Yeshuah was also a prophet. He said things at the very beginning and near the end of his ministry that made him a prophet too. Yeshuah began his ministry by quoting Isaiah:

"The spirit of YHWH is upon me;
because YHWH has anointed me to preach good tidings unto the meek;
he has sent me to bind up the broken-hearted,
to proclaim liberty to the captives,
and the opening of the prison to them that are bound;
to proclaim the year of YHWH's favor..."[24]

---

23 Isaiah 49:5-6.
24 Isaiah 61:2. This passage confirms that Yeshuah spoke the name of the Father, YHWH, in public.

Yeshuah was anticipating the time when there would no longer be any sorrow, spiritual bondage or oppression. That is why he went about healing the sick, the blind, and the lame, those possessed by evil spirits or in bondage to self-serving rulers. His miracles demonstrated the time when the Eternal One's spirit would be poured out universally. In that way, Yeshuah was announcing the coming kingdom of the Eternal One.

Near the end of his ministry, Yeshuah declared that angels would be sent out to gather his elect "from one end of Heaven to the other." His teaching was in accord with the prophets and Moses, that the Eternal One would return the tribes of Israel to their homeland in Canaan. This is a wonderful promise that the Eternal One's chosen people will be united again in the world that is coming.

The world that is coming is almost too good to describe. As far as nature goes, the whole Earth will become a Garden of Eden. The climate will be perfect everywhere. Deserts will be fertile, wastelands forested, and the amount of tillable land will be greatly expanded. The air will be clean and the water pure. Crops will flourish, and there will be an abundance of food for every living creature. Life spans will be longer again, and perfect health restored. It is said that a youth will die at the age of a hundred. All the Earth, and the life the Eternal One brought forth upon it, will be renewed to its original pristine condition.

Politically, humankind's long dream of a one-world government will finally come true. Jerusalem, at the geographic centre of the Earth, will be its capital city. All the nations will send their representatives there, and there will be a one-world language as well. The great cities of today will be decentralized into smaller more interactive communities. Individual freedom will be restored along with the private ownership of property. Everyone will feel secure. It will be a time of universal peace and prosperity.[25]

Spiritually, "the whole Earth will be filled with the knowledge of the Eternal One." There will be a time of unprecedented reeducation for every human being. Humankind will be healed from every emotional and mental disorder by learning to keep the commandments of the Almighty Father. Everyone will soon learn to keep the festivals introduced by Moses, the Feast of Ingathering for example. Whole families will be dancing in the streets and singing praises to the Eternal One. The Earth will be filled with righteousness, and everyone will be truly happy.

One thing makes the coming Kingdom of Heaven more distinct than anything else. With the Messiah's coming will be a great company of resurrected beings. These are the

---

25 And many peoples shall go and say, Come, and let us go up to the mountain of the Eternal One, to the house of The Mighty One of Jacob; and He will teach us of his ways, and we will walk in his paths: for out of Zion shall go forth the law, and the word of YHWH from Jerusalem (Isaiah 2:3).

righteous beings of the past who will be raised up from the dead and given eternal life. They will be kings and priests along with the Messiah. There will be two tiers of beings on the Earth, both mortals and immortals. There will be those who have been born naturally, and continue to be born naturally, and those who have been resurrected or born from above. Some of the latter have been mentioned by name: Abraham, Moses, Elijah, David, Daniel and the twelve apostles called by Yeshuah. Countless others, unnamed and often unrecognized, will also be resurrected and reign with them in the world that is coming.

That's about it, Harry.

I felt what my friend was thinking before I saw it. Harry was looking at me with a mixture of appreciation and perplexity. I wanted to laugh, but restrained myself.

Harry's look sharpened into awareness.

You've been studying.

We talked about this years ago. It's taken until now to blossom into my consciousness, although I've thought about it for a long time.

Harry gave out a long exhale.

We are a stubborn people, Abraham. In fact, we don't want to believe the truth about ourselves. We don't honestly want to know about the future either, as good as it is.

I've thought about that too. All this business about people spending eternity in Heaven or Hell is a pure fiction.

Harry sat quietly for longer than usual. He seemed to be adjusting to something internally. He looked at me again with a renewed appreciation.

Avi, the Scriptures are full of promises that the heavens and the Earth will be made new again. It's the Earth that was made for man to dwell on, not some other-worldly spiritual place. It also talks about the wicked being destroyed forever (whatever that means), not about them living forever in never ending torment. The greatest promise of all is that the Eternal One will dwell with His people on this Earth. Can anything be better?

Harry looked at me inquisitively.

May I sum up, Avi?

Sure.

I have three observations. The first has to do with the Eternal One's faithfulness. He made very specific promises to Abraham, and He has never relinquished on those promises. He remains faithful even though we have not.

As Isaiah wrote:

For as the new heavens and the new earth, which I will make,
shall remain before me, says YHWH,
so shall your seed and your name remain.[26]

The Eternal One has made His promise absolutely certain:

Thus says YHWH who gives the sun for a light by day,
and the ordinances of the moon and of the stars for a light by night,
who stirs up the sea, so that the waves of it roar;
YHWH of hosts is His name:
"If these ordinances depart from before me, says YHWH,
then the seed of Israel also shall cease from
being a nation before me for ever.

Thus says YHWH:
If heaven above can be measured,
and the foundations of the Earth searched out beneath,
then will I also cast off all the seed of Israel for all that they have done,
says YHWH.[27]

It's interesting how closely the creation of the whole universe is linked to Israel's permanence. The ordinances that sustain the universe will also sustain Israel. The continuance of both have been established by the Eternal One as permanent decrees by laws that He has ordained.

The second point follows from that. At no time did the Eternal One ever say or imply that He would replace Israel with another people, group or nation. It is a misconception that the Eternal One has replaced Israel with the Church. That lie is based on statements made by Paul, inferences by true Israelites who have forgotten who they are, and by the spiritualization of what was meant by the prophets to be literally understood. The Eternal

---

26 Isaiah 66:22.
27 Jeremiah 31:35-37

One's promises are for Israel, and to say otherwise is to charge the Eternal One with unfaithfulness. That's something that can never be said. The Eternal One will always be faithful to His Word.

Avi, the theory that the Almighty has replaced Israel with a new creation, the Church, is called *Replacement Theology*. The theory contradicts what Yeshuah taught. Recall the Parable of the Tenants. After the tenants beat, killed and stoned the owner's servants, they said to themselves about the owner's son: "This is the heir. Come, let us kill him and have his inheritance." The tenants were motivated by their desire to own, operate and profit from the vineyard themselves. In the parable, the vineyard represents Israel, and the tenants are the Church with its desire to rule over and profit from the Almighty's people.

The third point also follows. In the Almighty Father's wisdom, He scattered and mixed the seed of Abraham among the nations as a blessing. Also recall another of Yeshuah's parables where he said, "The Kingdom of Heaven is like leaven that a woman took and hid in three measures of flour, 'til it was all leavened." In that parable, Israel is the leaven and the three loaves are the world. Actually, Paul was close to the truth when he said, "For if their rejection means the reconciliation of the world, what will their acceptance mean but life from the dead?" The restoration of Israel that is coming will include a multitude of people and nations. The gentiles are included in the Father's plan of salvation.

This point needs to be emphasized. Moses made it clear to Israel from the start: they were never to treat the foreigner as different from themselves. As Moses reminded them, they were once foreigners themselves as slaves in Egypt, and that there was to be one law for all. Any non-Israelites who wanted to attach themselves to Israel were to have the same rights, obligations and promises as the rest of the nation. There was to be no inequality and no prejudice. None.

Avi, it's a mistake to think that Israel's designation as a chosen people was exclusive. The Eternal Father chose Israel as light for the nations, so that all of humankind would come to know Him and be blessed by Him. He truly loves all of His creatures: red and yellow, black and white. All of them.

Harry did his usual. He stood up, paced a bit, and sat down again.

Let's explore this just a little more. I have no strong objection to the gentile belief in Yeshuah as the savior of the world. That looks true from their perspective. However, Yeshuah did say that he came only for the lost sheep of the house of Israel. That term 'house of Israel' is unmistakably a reference to the Northern Kingdom of Israel or the Ten Lost Tribes. The term emphatically did not refer to the Kingdom of Judah. It was the Northern Kingdom that the Almighty sent packing with a certificate of divorce. The

House of Judah, although often guilty of the same sins, was never officially rejected. In the broadest sense, Judah remained faithful to the Almighty Father and retained its identity. It was only the Ten Lost Tribes that needed to be saved in Yeshuah's time.

That should give us a better perspective because in the narrow sense, the Messiah came only for the House of Israel. Keep in mind that it was to two of the Ten Tribes that the promise of multiplicity was given, to Ephraim and Menasseh. The promise to Abraham that his seed would be as sand of the sea would come through those two tribes, Ephraim especially. That's why the Messiah came for lost sheep of the house of Israel, because it was through the tribes of Israel that the whole world was to be saved.

Avi, the tribe of Judah makes up only one quarter of one per cent of the world's population. Admittedly, the Jews have had a positive influence in the world out of all proportion with their size numerically. We should look at their history with awe, and are missing something truly miraculous when we don't.[28] Someday, according to the prophets, the house of Israel and the house of Judah will be together again in harmony with each other. Nevertheless, it is through the Ten Lost Tribes, the House of Israel, that the salvation of the world will come.

This is the people and time that the prophet Hosea was referring to when he said:

Yet the number of the children of Israel shall be as the sand of the sea,
which cannot be measured nor numbered;
and it shall come to pass that,
in the place where it was said unto them, you are not my people,
it shall be said unto them, you are the sons of the living Mighty One.[29]

For a long, long time now, Christians have been said to be gentiles, and we have consistently called ourselves gentiles. Whether deliberately or not, calling ourselves gentiles is a rejection of our true identity. It's tantamount to saying that we are not Israelites, but according to the prophet Hosea, that will change. The Almighty's people will again be recognized and called "the sons of the living Mighty One." It's just as Jeremiah said:

Is Ephraim my dear son? Is he a darling child?

---

28 Historian Paul Johnson wrote: "My second reason [for writing *A History of the Jews*] was the excitement I found in the sheer span of Jewish history. From the time of Abraham up to the present covers the best of four millennia. That is more than three-quarters of civilized humanity.... The Jews created a separate and specific identity earlier than almost any other people, which still survives. They have maintained it, amid appalling adversities, right up to the present. When came this extraordinary endurance?" (Harper & Row, 1987, p 1.)

29 Hosea 1:10.

> **for as often as I speak against him,**
> **I do earnestly remember him still:**
> **therefore my heart yearns for him;**
> **I will surely have mercy upon him, says YHWH.**

Jeremiah also predicted:

> **With weeping they will come,**
> **And by supplication I will lead them;**
> **I will make them walk by streams of waters,**
> **On a straight path in which they will not stumble;**
> **For I am a father to Israel, and Ephraim is My firstborn.**[30]

Paul, thinking of himself as the apostle to the gentiles, misapplied the text from Hosea. There's no mistaking Hosea's meaning, however. In the next verse he predicted:

> **And the children of Judah and the children of Israel**
> **shall be gathered together,**
> **and they shall appoint themselves one head,**
> **and shall go up from the land;**
> **for great shall be the day of Jezreel.**

Avi, the word "Jezreel" comes from the combination of two Hebrew root words, 'to sow' and 'mighty.' The latter word is especially 'Almighty.' Put together, the two root words mean, "The Almighty will sow." The prophet Amos used the same metaphor to illustrate how the seed of Abraham would be sown among the nations. Every grain would be accounted for:

> **For I will give the command**
> **and will shake Israel along with the other nations**
> **as grain is shaken in a sieve,**
> **yet not one true kernel will be lost.**[31]

As I pointed out earlier, the prophetic books of the Hebrew Scriptures are clear on this subject for those who care enough to read them. All the prophets agreed:

> **Their seed shall become known among the nations,**
> **and their offspring in the midst of the peoples.**[32]

---

30 Jeremiah 31:20 and 31:9.

31 Amos 9:9

32 Isaiah 61:9

Avi, at the heart of this great story is a love like no other. The Mighty One of Israel wants His people to return to Him so that He can love them again as He did at first, that is, when He brought us out of Egypt.

If we can hear the Almighty Father's voice at all, then we can hear Him saying:

"Return, O backsliding children," says YHWH;
"for I am a husband to you.
I will take you, one from a city and two from a family,
and I will bring you to Zion."[33]

After those words, Harry and I sat for a long time without saying anything. My feelings were mixed. I fully understood the great plan of salvation, of how the Eternal One was going to renew the Earth, make His people great again, and bring all humankind into the knowledge of Himself. It had become so very real to me.

I allowed my intuitions to go where they wanted.

Harry, we need to be born again, don't we?

He didn't hesitate.

Yes, and that's what we will talk about next week.

I'm looking forward to it. I'm anticipating what we'll talk about.

I got up to go, looking at my friend. His eyes never wavered.

May Yah be with you, Harry.

And may He be with you, Abraham.

---

33 Jeremiah 3:14.

13. THE UNIVERSE IS NOT SERENE

On the next Sabbath, Harry greeted me with reserve and returned my gaze with reluctance. I had anticipated it, and shook his hand as warmly as I could.

Shabatt shalom, Harry.

Shabatt shalom, Avi.

Harry, I know that what we talk about today won't be pleasant. Please don't hold back on my account. I can handle it.

As soon as the words came out of my mouth, I knew something was wrong, and I was dumbstruck.

Harry nodded and began simply.

Avi, this is our ninth Sabbath together. From the beginning, we knew we would be talking about *eschatology*. This is the branch of theology concerned with the final events in the history of the world and humankind. Make no mistake, Avi, this present age will come to an end.

Harry paused only briefly.

Much of modern science leads us to believe that we have an infinite amount of time ahead of us. Supposedly, it took the solar system billions of years to coalesce into its present state, and presumably there are a few billion years more before it all ends. The stars and planets have stabilized in their present motions with little alteration expected any time soon. Modern science thinks everything will continue as it has for a very, very long time.[1]

---

1   In the mythology of science, in a few billion years the Sun will fuse the last of its hydrogen into helium,

Perhaps we can forgive their optimism. There have been many catastrophes in the last two thousand years, but they have been in the form of earthquakes, volcanic eruptions and tsunamis. In contrast, the number of catastrophes coming from the heavens has been few and comparatively minimal. In 1908, an exploding comet flattened some eighty million trees in Tunguska, a remote region of Russia. Fifty years earlier, the largest solar flare ever recorded struck the Earth and set many telegraph systems on fire. The Chinese observed a giant exploding star, a supernova, in 185 AD; and Johannes Kepler another in 1604 AD. In 1994, fragments of the comet Shoemaker-Levy collided with Jupiter in the first collision of two solar system bodies ever to be observed. Recently on February 15, 2013, a ten thousand ton asteroid exploded above the Russian city of Chelyabinsk, producing such a powerful shockwave that it raced around the world twice. Eyewitnesses felt intense heat from its fiery blast, and about 1,500 people were injured seriously enough to seek medical treatment. Scientists have much justification for seeing the universe as less than benign.

That was not the view of the ancients. When they looked up, they saw things that terrified them immeasurably. They described what they saw as fantastic beasts roaming the heavens: a dragon, a winged serpent, a winged bull, or a many-headed monster. They spoke of fire, lightning, molten rain, intense heat, thick smoke, loud and horrible sounds, and rumblings deep in the Earth. Those fantastic beasts brought disaster, chaos and universal destruction. The ancients feared the heavens more than anything else.

The ancients saw the planets in conflicting orbits, interacting in spectacular ways, and coming perilously near to the Earth. Saturn appeared as a brilliant orb, Venus as a giant veiled comet, and Mars as a fiery and two-horned behemoth. Those three planets dominated the skies, day and night, in their periodic visits. Their brilliance and trailing smoke made the rest of the sky invisible to the point of obliterating the sun and the moon. Such legends can be found in written records coming from the ancient Near East, China, India and the Americas. We can call them myths or legends, but they are too numerous and too consistent to be ignored.

Let's get some perspective. In our modern conception, all geological and cosmological events occur gradually over an exceedingly long period, but *catastrophism* has become acceptable again. The revival began when Immanuel Velikovsky wrote his now famous book, *Worlds in Collision,* in 1950. Mainstream scientists did their best to prevent the book from being published and to condemn Velikovsky's ideas. To this day in the hallowed halls of science, Velikovsky's name continues to be blasphemed. However, *Worlds in Collision* became very popular with the public, and Velikovsky soon became known as the Father of Catastrophism.

turn into a red giant, expand 250 times its current size – and that the Earth will be destroyed.

Immanuel Velikovsky had remarkable insight. As a Jewish man, he respected the Hebrew Scriptures, and accepted them as historical documents, but he went a step further. He made the astonishing conclusion that many of the local events depicted in the Hebrew Scriptures where actually global events. In his mind, the Great Flood was certainly a global event, but so were the plagues of the Exodus, the destruction of Sodom and Gomorra, Joshua's command for the sun to stand still, and other biblical events. What Velikovsky discovered through tireless research was that the memory of these events has been preserved by many non-biblical legends in many different locations worldwide. A variety of ancient cultures had recorded the same events from their perspective nearly everywhere in the entire world. Those legends not only confirmed the biblical accounts – they gave a much deeper insight into the nature of the various global catastrophes.

Velikovsky was not the first catastrophist, nor did he get everything right. However, he inspired and set the tone for the great body of research that followed. Therefore, to understand catastrophism, the place to start is with Immanuel Velikovsky.

With that, Harry picked up his copy of Worlds in Collision. *It was one of the books I had noticed in his library many weeks ago. It had been thoroughly annotated, and read more than once. It made me think back about how we had started and what my attitude had been then. I still wanted to listen and learn. I was prepared to change if I had to. I still had that attitude.*

Abraham, I'm going to paraphrase from *Worlds in Collision*, starting with the first chapter of Part II, and quote some parts of it. You can take my copy home with you later today if you want to, but I'll give you a pretty good summary right now. Keep in mind that I am going to interpret Velikovsky from a geocentric point of view. I won't be explaining celestial events in the way that Velikovsky did.

In the biblical account, before Joshua commanded the sun to stand still, great stones were cast down from Heaven. Velikovsky inferred that the sun's stoppage was not a singular phenomena, that something more was happening. Perhaps a large comet or even another planet was interacting with the Earth along with the sun. Such was the likely source of the falling stones. In the book of Joshua, tens of thousands were killed by large falling stones.

In the book of Jasher, describing the same incident, there was also an earthquake, a whirlwind, and the very Earth trembled. Indeed, all the kingdoms of the Earth tottered due to a multi-faceted event involving the sun, the moon and another very large celestial body. To corroborate this account, Velikovsky sought out how the event was perceived elsewhere on the Earth. On the opposite side of the Earth, there was a prolonged period of darkness instead of light: "In the *Mexican Annals of Cuauhtitlan*... it is related that during a cosmic catastrophe that occurred in the remote past, the night did not end for a long time." Sure, the sun had stood still for Joshua in Canaan, but only as part of a world-wide catastrophe involving other celestial events.[2]

Another worldwide calamity occurred about a half-century earlier, and is much better documented. We know it from the Scriptures as the ten plagues of Egypt. Other sources give more details. From Velikovsky:

> Ipuwer, the Egyptian eyewitness of the catastrophe, wrote his lament on papyrus: "The river is blood," and corresponds with the Book of Exodus (7:21): "All the waters that were in the river were turned to blood." The author of the papyrus also wrote: "Plague is throughout the land. Blood is everywhere," and this corresponds with the Book of Exodus (7:21): "There was blood throughout all the land of Egypt."

The *Manuscript Quiche* of the Mayans tells us how in the Western Hemisphere, in the days of a great cataclysm, the Earth quaked and the rivers turned to blood. So too the *Kalevala*, a Finnish poem of folklore, describes how, in a time of cosmic upheaval, the world was sprinkled with red milk. The Babylonians recorded red dust and rain falling from the sky.

Avi, let's remember how the seventh plague on Egypt was described:

And Moses stretched forth his rod toward Heaven:
and YHWH sent thunder and hail, and fire ran down unto the Earth;
and YHWH rained hail upon the land of Egypt.
So there was hail, and fire mingled with the hail, very grievous,
such as had not been in all the land of Egypt since it became a nation.

The text does not make it clear that the hail was ice. It may well have been stones accompanied by lightning and other electric phenomena. The stones were mingled with fire, according to the text. From Velikovsky:

> The Mexican *Annals of Cuauhtitlan* describe how a cosmic catas-trophe was accompanied by a hail of stones; in the oral tradition of the Indians, too, the motif is repeated time and again: In some ancient epoch the sky "rained, not water, but fire and red-hot stones," which is not different from the Hebrew tradition.

---

2   The following is from Part II, Chapter Two of *Worlds in Collision.*

There is also an ancient Hebrew *Midrash* that states naphtha, together with hot stones, poured down on Egypt: "The Egyptians refused to let the Israelites go, and He poured out naphtha over them, burning [blisters]." The population of Egypt was "pursued with strange rains and hails and showers inexorable, and utterly consumed with fire."

The ninth plague was a plague of unusual darkness:

And YHWH said unto Moses, Stretch out thy hand toward Heaven,
that there may be darkness over the land of Egypt,
even darkness which may be felt.
And Moses stretched forth his hand toward Heaven;
and there was a thick darkness in all the land of Egypt three days;
they saw not one another, neither rose any one from his place for
three days: but all the children of Israel had light in their dwellings.

This was a darkness that was so thick, it could be felt. Numerous rabbinical sources describe this intense darkness:

> An exceedingly strong wind endured seven days. All the time the land was shrouded in darkness. "On the fourth, fifth, and sixth days, the darkness was so dense that they [the people of Egypt] could not stir from their place." "The darkness was of such a nature that it could not be dispelled by artificial means. The light of the fire was either extinguished by the violence of the storm, or else it was made invisible and swallowed up in the density of the darkness. ... Nothing could be discerned. ... None was able to speak or to hear, nor could anyone venture to take food, but they lay themselves down ... their outward senses in a trance. Thus they remained, overwhelmed by affliction."[3]

Nations and peoples to the south, north, and west of Egypt have legends about a cosmic catastrophe during which time the sun did not shine. Other parts of the world also have legends where the sun did not shine for several days. The Peruvians tell of a time when the sun did not appear for five days. In one way or another, it seems that the entire world must have suffered from whatever was behind the ten plagues that fell on Egypt.

There must have been great earthquakes as well. Artapanus, a Jewish historian of the third or second century BC, was quoted by Eusebius. In the last night before the Exodus, there was "hail and earthquake by night, so that those who fled from the earthquake were killed by the hail, and those who sought shelter from the hail were destroyed by the

---

3   *Worlds in Collision,* p 75.

earthquake. And at that time all the houses fell in, and most of the temples." Saint Jerome also wrote in an epistle that "in the night in which Exodus took place, all the temples of Egypt were destroyed either by an earth shock or by the thunderbolt." Several Psalms say something very similar: "The voice of your thunder was in the whirlwind. The lightnings lightened the world. The Earth trembled and shook."[4] [5]

So far, we have rivers turning into blood, stones falling from above, thick darkness and earthquakes. To that, Velikovsky adds immense tides and electrical discharges. A great tide or *tsunami* explains how the Egyptian army was destroyed by a wall of water. Only a few weeks later, the thunder and lightning at Sinai can be easily explained as electrical phenomena. The same motif can be found in Greek mythology as Zeus throwing down thunderbolts.[6] Many of the Psalms commemorate these great electrical discharges.[7]

Avi, I want to step out of Velikovsky's shoes for a moment. To say that the ten plagues that fell on Egypt were natural phenomena does not make them any less miraculous. Keep in mind, the ancients did not think of the Earth as one small planet in an infinite universe. For them the heavens and the Earth were interconnected. What happened in the great expanse, or heaven, was concurrent with what happened on the Earth. They were not isolated from the heavens by billions of years of space and time. Those ancients attributed natural phenomena to divine interaction, even when they did not know the one true Almighty Creator. As Psalm 66:5 proclaims concerning the Exodus,

Come and see the works of the Almighty One:
He is terrible in his doing toward the children of men.

In chapter three, Velikovsky presents ideas that are difficult to imagine. The first is what he calls 'the collapse of sky.' Difficult or not, legends from around the world tell of a time when the sky appeared to come down. The Celti people on the shores of the Adriatic told Alexander the Great what they feared most was that the sky might collapse. The Ovaherero tribesmen of Africa said that long ago, the sky fell on the Earth, and almost all the people were killed. Another tribe, the Wanyoro, related that their god threw the firmament upon the Earth to destroy humankind.

Avi, there's also the biblical passage, "The Earth shook, the heavens also dropped at the presence of the Almighty." Can the heavens actually drop? A recent *National Geographic* article on solar storms said of the two Carrington flares in 1859:

---

4 Psalm 77:18 for example.
5 The following is from Part II, Chapter Three of *Worlds in Collision.*
6 Just as in Job 36:32, "He fills his hands with lightning and commands it to strike its mark."
7 Again as in Psalm 77:18, "Your thunder was heard in the whirlwind, your lightning lit up the world; the earth trembled and quaked." Notice the inclusion of high winds, another supernatural phenomenon.

Their combined impact squashed the Earth's magnetosphere - where the planet's magnetic field interacts with the solar wind - down from its normal altitude of 40,000 miles to 4000 miles, temporarily eliminating the Van Allen radiation belts girdling the planet. Charged particles entering the upper atmosphere set off intense auroras over much of the Earth. Some peoples thought their cities had caught fire.[8] [9]

Even more difficult to imagine is a time when the heavens were reversed, but there is testimony from all parts of the world that the side of the heavens that is now turned toward the evening once faced the morning. The Egyptians have a well-documented mythology that twice the sun rose in the east and twice in the west. In the *Papyrus Ipuwer* it is stated that "the land turns round as does a potter's wheel" and the "Earth turned upside down." In the tomb of Senmut, the architect of Queen Hatshepsut, a panel on the ceiling shows the celestial sphere with the signs of the zodiac and other constellations in "a reversed orientation of the southern sky." Apparently, "the southern panel shows the sky of Egypt as it was before the celestial sphere interchanged north and south, east and west."

Plato wrote of such a reversal in various places:

> The change in the rising and setting of the sun and the other heavenly bodies, how in those times they used to set in the quarter where they now rise, and used to rise where they now set... Of all the changes which take place in the heavens this reversal is the greatest and most complete... There is at that time great destruction of animals in general, and only a small part of the human race survives.[10]

It seems so unthinkable, and yet Velikovsky gave numerous examples of when the heavens were reversed:

> The Chinese say that it is only since a new order of things has come

---

8   See Psalm 68:8 and *National Geographic*, June 2012, p 48.
9   The following is from Part II, Chapter Five of *Worlds in Collision*.
10   In *The Statesman*, Plato wrote something remarkably close to what the Scriptures say: "There is a time when God himself guides and helps to roll the world in its course; and there is a time, on the completion of a certain cycle.... Hence there necessarily occurs a great destruction of them, which extends also to the life of man; few survivors of the race are left, and those who remain become the subjects of several novel and remarkable phenomena, and of one in particular, which takes place at the time when the transition is made to the cycle opposite to that in which we are now living.... And mark how consistent the sequel of the tale is; after the return of age to youth, follows the return of the dead, who are lying in the earth, to life; simultaneously with the reversal of the world the wheel of their generation has been turned back, and they are put together and rise and live in the opposite order, unless God has carried any of them away to some other lot."

about that the stars move from east to west.

The Eskimos of Greenland told missionaries that in an ancient time, the Earth turned over and the people who lived then became antipodes.

The Koran speaks of the Lord "of two easts and of two wests."

In *Tractate Sanhedrin* of the Talmud it is said: "Seven days before the deluge, the Holy One changed the primeval order and the sun rose in the west and set in the east."

Harry stood up and went for the teapot.

Avi. Please jump in here. I need a break.

I got up too and waited until my friend sat down.

It strikes me, Harry, that myths and legends are almost always overly simplified or exaggerated. How much can such colossal upheavals be exaggerated? Those 'myth makers' must have experienced something real. It's safe to say that what they experienced is no longer happening today, making it very difficult to comprehend.

I know a little about Velikovsky and his book *Worlds in Collision*. Velikovsky believed that the Earth has interacted with a very large comet on numerous occasions. Actually, he believed the comet was the planet Venus before it settled into its current orbit. The Earth was subject to Venus' gravitational pull and its huge comet tail of debris. Hence the Earth was besieged by red dust, great stones, darkness, high winds, tidal waves, earthquakes, and electrical storms. Such natural phenomena fit very well with the biblical descriptions of the Great Flood and the Exodus from Egypt.

I'm intrigued by the heavens' reversal. After all, science has never been able to explain how the sun could stand still at Joshua's command. How can the sun stop orbiting the Earth, or the entire cosmos in its daily rotation? Once stopped, how could they start moving again? There must have been a change in the structure of the universe as a whole. That makes the idea of the heavens shifting or the Earth turning over more plausible, and the sun's stoppage too. It's more holistic, just as the prophet said:

Ah, Master The Almighty One!
It is you who have made the heavens and the earth
by your great power and by your outstretched arm!

Nothing is too hard for you.[11]

I know of one thing that geophysicists often fear. It's a reversal in the Earth's magnetic field when the magnetic north becomes the magnetic south and vice versa. The consequences of a reversal in the Earth's magnetic field would likely be very serious. It could result in the destruction of the ozone layer with an increase in solar radiation and cancer rates. There could also be disruptions in the electrical grid, satellite communications and the migratory patterns of animal life. Apparently, previous reversals have not always coincided with the mass extinctions of the past, and most scientists believe we would survive another reversal. At the same time, these geophysicists are very certain that another reversal will occur.

Once again, it's the concept of time that becomes an issue. Magnetic reversals are said to happen every hundred thousand to one million years and the last one was 780,000 years ago. Conventional wisdom persists in making the Earth very old, and with it the belief in *gradualism*. Time, and lots of it, is needed to explain geological features like the Grand Canyon, the uplifting of mountain ranges, and how the continents have drifted apart. Most scientists are against the idea of *catastrophism*, although they have modified their belief with something called *punctuated equilibrium*.[12] Yet it's unthinkable in most scientific circles that such massive changes in the Earth's physical structure happened very quickly and only a few thousand years ago.

There's another type of polar reversal that is much more catastrophic. In this reversal, it is the Earth itself that wobbles back and forth on its axis and then turns upside down completely. Such a reversal could happen very rapidly, perhaps in as little as a few days. The consequences would be horrendous in the extreme, causing earthquakes, tidal waves and windstorms too massive to comprehend. There would be death everywhere for all life forms.

Harry, I've been pondering this for almost a month, ever since you mentioned that the Earth will be shaken according to the prophet Haggai. I made a list of similar references in the Scriptures. Actually, it's not only the Earth that will be shaken, the heavens will be too. I brought my list with me today.

Harry looked at me quietly.

---

11 Jeremiah 32:17.

12 *Punctuated equilibrium* is the theory popularized by Stephen Jay Gould in 1972 to explain the absence of transitional forms in the fossil record. Most organisms in the fossil record appear suddenly and remain unchanged for long periods of time. According to the theory, evolution (the appearance of new species) occurs in bursts too short to leave evidence in the fossil record.

Good, Avi. That's going to be very effective, more than anything else. What I'd like to do, however, is cover all the information that's not necessarily biblical first. Is that all right with you?

I concur, Harry. Please continue.

Thank you. Velikovsky did not think of the Exodus as a local event limited to Egypt. He perceived the biblical account in the context of a global catastrophe. For example, if the sun and moon were obscured by comet dust and debris, it would explain why the Israelites depended on pillars of smoke and fire for direction. Otherwise, they would have wandered aimlessly in the wilderness. It would also explain why the Almighty had to tell the Israelites when the new year began. The sun had not reappeared in its normal place and their calendar system was disrupted. So too the Almighty appeared to Israel at Sinai. The loud noise, smoke and fire came from an electrical discharge between the mountain top and the passing comet. Finally, how the entire Egyptian army was destroyed by a wall of water or a giant tidal wave.

Nor did Velikovsky believe the Israelites were immune to the worldwide catastrophe. He took Psalm 68:22 as an implication that many Israelites perished in the sea along with the Egyptians. There are also rabbinical traditions that only a small fraction of Egypt's Israelite population was spared from the global catastrophe of the ten plagues. Many legends tell us of a great destruction from which only a small part of the human race was saved.

Avi, it is hardly likely that 2.5 million Israelites wandered in the dessert for forty years. That would have been most of Egypt's entire population. This is another example of how the Bible is read uncritically, and how readers unwittingly accept traditional interpretations.[13] We know from the Exodus account that the Israelite population had grown large enough to be a threat to the Egyptians, but a recurring prophetic theme is that only a remnant will be saved. Therefore, if Moses led as few as seven thousand individuals out of Egypt, the number would be in harmony with the biblical pattern. This makes much more sense to me.

---

13   The Hebrew text of Exodus 12:41 which usually reads as "about six hundred thousand men on foot, besides women and children," can also be translated as "about six hundred chiefs (*eleph*) on foot are the warriors apart from the children." If it is assumed that each chief (head of a family) included a wife and five children, then only about 6,000 Israelites left Egypt. To that number can be added the "mixed multitude" or non-Israelites who went with them for a total of about 7,000 individuals.

Consider too, the logistics for 2.5 million individuals. That number would have required a camp of 3 to 5 square miles, and a daily or twice daily hike of a mile or two for obeying the commandment in Deuteronomy 23:12-13, "Designate a place outside the camp where you can go to relieve yourself. As part of your equipment have something to dig with, and when you relieve yourself, dig a hole and cover up your excrement."

It makes sense, but I'll add this – just because the ten plagues had natural causes doesn't take away from the miraculous. Even though the Israelites only saw the calamities as a local event, they saw them as judgements from their Mighty One, and attributed their deliverance to the Eternal One, the Almighty One of Israel. Their understanding was real and true.

I didn't hesitate.

I agree, Harry. The Israelites would not have known that what was happening to them was happening everywhere. All they knew is that they were being delivered from one terrible catastrophe after another. Neither did the Egyptians perceive their calamities as a worldwide event. They just wanted to rid themselves of the cause – the Israelite people.

Unbelievers can say what they want. The Eternal One, the Almighty One of Israel is behind all that happens in the heavens and on Earth!

I looked over at Harry, and knew that something had changed. Whatever faith Harry had acquired over his many years of study and mediation was now my faith too. Even though the strength of it had come belatedly, that faith was equally mine. In a fleeting moment, I thanked the Almighty Father for what He had given me.

Harry retuned my gaze, and seemingly read my thoughts.

That's all we need to come to, Avi. The Mighty One of Israel is the Mighty One of Heaven and Earth. It's the starting point for everyone who believes. That is the way the Eternal One frequently identifies Himself according to the Hebrew Scriptures.

Then Harry continued with his theme.

Others have followed in Velikovsky's footsteps. They too saw certain biblical events as global catastrophes. Let's take a look at *The Mars-Earth Wars* by Donald Patten and Samuel Windsor.[14][15] Their paradigm is that Mars was a rogue planet that did not assume its current orbit until the year 701 BC. Like Velikovsky they rely on legends that have been largely forgotten, but still retained in many ancient records, including the Bible. To that, they add what has been discovered by modern telescopes and exploratory satellites.

It has become obvious in recent times that Mars has gone through a cataclysmic

---

14 The book is subtitled, *Old Testament's Catastrophism, Christian Science & Archeology.*
15 Velikovsky blamed the direct impact of Venus with Mars for placing Mars on a collision course with the Earth some time in the first millennium BC. After that, according to Velikovsky, Mars had repeated close encounters with the Earth. Donald Patten and Samuel Windsor followed him in this vein.

process. Mars' southern hemisphere, the Clobbered Hemisphere, is heavily cratered by 355 cavities. Some are understatedly huge. The Hellas crater, despite being on a small planet, is the largest crater in the solar system. With a diameter of about 1400 miles, the crater would cover most of Alaska. Several other craters on Mars are also gigantic compared to the size of the planet itself.

The northern hemisphere, or Serene Hemisphere, has only twenty-five craters. Its distinguishing features are an immense bulge, a giant rift valley and the biggest volcanoes in the solar system. The bulge covers nearly twenty-five percent of the Martian surface, and the rift valley about nineteen percent of the planet's circumference. The caldera of the two largest volcanoes are sixty-five and fifty miles wide, respectively. By contrast, the Earth's largest volcano is on Hawaii and its caldera is only three miles wide.

Patten and Windsor have proposed that a planet-like body shattered in close proximity to Mars, and about 35% of its mass crashed onto the Martian surface. The crash resulted in a large number of craters on one side, and the bulge, rift valley and volcanoes on the other side. Some of the debris formed an asteroid belt around the planet. Patten and Windsor surmise this happened between 15,000 and 3000 BC, leaving Mars as the most scared and geologically active planet in the solar system.

In their proposal, Mars once had an orbit that took it very close to the Earth. The closest and most catastrophic approach was in 2484 BC, the date they give for the time of Noah and the flood. That approach took Mars to within fifteen thousand miles of the Earth. There was another encounter during the time of Abraham, and still another close one in Moshe's time. These flybys coincided with the Great Flood, the destruction of Sodom and Gomorrah, and the desolating plagues of the Exodus. The last approach of Mars was in 701 BC when the sundial of Ahaz went backward by ten degrees. Not all the flybys were of equal intensity.

Now consider how Mars would have appeared as it passed by the Earth. The moon's average distance from the Earth is about 238,000 miles, and Mars' distance only a small fraction of that. Mars also has a diameter twice the size of the moon's. Visually, Mars would have dwarfed the moon, and easily blocked the light of both the sun and the moon for many days. In the prolonged darkness, the lava flows of Mars' two giant volcanoes would have been highly visible, perhaps even spewing fire and brimstone on the Earth. In daylight, the sun would have been obscured by a dense haze of volcanic smoke, and the debris from the planet's asteroid belt. Mars would have appeared as the most dominant feature in the sky during the day, and especially at night as a fiery and two-horned behemoth.[16]

---

16 The Leviathan in the book of Job (chapter 41) is more likely the description of a celestial dragon, and not a crocodile or other earthly creature: "Its snorting throws out flashes of light; its eyes are like the rays of dawn.

The gravitational and electrical attraction between the Earth and Mars would have been intense. Again, those powerful forces would have unleashed great earthquakes, tidal waves and electrical storms, accompanied by loud and unnatural sounds from the Earth below and heaven above. One can only imagine the shaking and roaring that would have ensued from Mars' passing the Earth at such close range.[17][18]

Avi, I want to conclude this part of our talk by mentioning the Earth's axial shift, or a change in the position of the stars. Patten and Windsor mention it in relation to the shortened shadow of the sundial of Ahaz. In connection with that, the temple Solomon built has been shifted north by six degrees. You can visualize it by either the Earth shifting on its axis or a change in the orientation of the heavens. That includes the position of the sun, causing the shadow on the sundial to go backward and the east-west position of the temple to shift.

This implies that the stars can move from their fixed positions quite suddenly. Many ancient mythologies allude to that. One in particular comes from Jewish legends:

> The flood was produced by a union of the male waters, which are above the firmament, and the female waters issuing from the earth. The upper waters rushed through the space left when God removed two stars out of the constellation Pleiades. Afterward, to put a stop to the flood, God had to transfer two stars from the constellation of the Bear to the constellation of the Pleiades. That is why the Bear runs after the Pleiades. She wants her two children back, but they will be restored to her only in the future world.[19][20]

Avi, it doesn't matter if all the things that Velikovsky, Patten and Windsor tell us are accurate in every way, but we can't deny how frequent and consistent these legends are.

Flames stream from its mouth; sparks of fire shoot out. Smoke pours from its nostrils as from a boiling pot over burning reeds. Its breath sets coals ablaze, and flames dart from its mouth."

17 Sounds in space are transmitted electronically, and have been recorded by NASA... sounds of the planets, their rings and moons, the Earth and the sun. People all over the world have witnessed strange sounds seemingly coming from outer space. It has been proposed that some crop circles may have been formed by sound waves.

18 This sounds much like the description in Isaiah 29:6, "You will be visited by YHWH of hosts with thunder and with earthquake and great noise, with whirlwind and tempest, and the flame of a devouring fire." Notice especially the reference to "great noise."

19 Louis Ginzberg, *Legends of the Bible*, Konecky & Konecky, 1956, p 76. See also on page 74: In the days preceding the Flood, "the sun was darkened, and the foundations of the earth trembled, and lightning flashed, and the thunder boomed, as never before. And yet the sinners remained impenitent. In naught did they change their wicked doings during those last seven days."

20 "The Flood, of which you speak as of a fairy tale, has actually taken place several times. It has to do with a shift in the stars' course that actually took place" (paraphrasing Plato's *Timaios*, 22).

We can't dismiss them out of hand. Those legends are telling us something about the past.

I felt an urge to press a point.

Harry, I know why you have given these legends so much attention. It's because they match the biblical record of the same catastrophic events. Moreover, those legends parallel the end-time events that are depicted in the Bible.

Harry bowed his head.

What the Scriptures depict about the end-times is nothing short of horrific, Avi. There's no way to make it easy without being dishonest.

I pressed again.

The prophets didn't mince words about the end-times. They didn't hold back or sugar-coat their pronouncements.

My friend looked at me sharply.

Harry, I have seen your sorrow. I know you agonize over what has been said, but now it's time to be forthright. Sure, talking about the end-times is unpleasant, but this is not the time to refrain from speaking the truth because of your personal sorrow.

My friend looked at me again.

I don't want you to be like the preacher who tells his congregation only nice things. [21]

I opened my mouth to say more, and then shut it quickly. I couldn't say another word.

I obliquely turned my eyes on Harry. He was sitting there so calmly, and with such a sense of presence. If he had been chastened by my words, he didn't show it. If he was still in sorrow, it was not on display. In that moment, he looked so very alive and whole.

Abraham, we're talking about the destruction of the Earth and virtually the entire human race.

---

21 They say to the seers, "See no more visions!" and to the prophets, "Give us no more visions of what is right! Tell us pleasant things, prophesy illusions. (Isaiah 30:10)

The moment Harry said those words, I felt whole, too. It made me feel like a real person. Something felt complete.

This is strange, Harry. I don't understand my feelings.

Happy Harry stood up slowly in an act that seemed herculean.

Let's go for a walk again. I'll leave my notes behind, but please bring your list. Let's each take a bottle of water too. It's getting pretty warm.

I breathed easier as we began our walk. Harry had become such a good companion. I relished his friendship no matter what we were going to talk about. It was good just to be alive.

As I said, Harry, I began pondering a month ago because of what is written in the prophet Haggai. I made a list of similar passages. The one from Haggai 2:6 says:

> **For thus says YHWH of hosts:**
> **Yet once, it is a little while,**
> **and I will shake the heavens, and the Earth,**
> **and the sea, and the dry land.**

There are many similar descriptions:

> **The Eternal One, when you went forth...**
> **the Earth trembled, the heavens also dropped.**

> **The Earth quakes before them; the heavens tremble.**
> **The sun and the moon are darkened, and the stars withdraw their**
> **shining....**
> **And I will show wonders in the heavens and in the earth:**
> **blood, and fire, and pillars of smoke.**

> **The heavens and the Earth shall shake.**

> **Therefore I will make the heavens tremble,**
> **and the Earth will be shaken out of its place.**

**The Earth shall stagger like a drunken man,
and shall sway to and fro like a hammock.**[22]

I would be remiss, Harry, if I didn't quote similar passages from the Gentile Scriptures:

**The sun will be darkened, and the moon will not give its light,
and the stars will be falling from heaven,
and the powers in the heavens will be shaken.**

**And there shall be signs in sun, and moon, and stars,
and on the land is distress of nations with perplexity,
sea and billow roaring;
men fainting at heart from fear,
and expectation of the things coming on the world,
for the powers of the heavens shall be shaken.**[23]

Those texts are every much as explicit as the ones from the Hebrew Scriptures. I'll add one more that is specifically about the heavenly bodies:

**And all the host of heaven shall be dissolved,
and the heavens shall be rolled together as a scroll;
and all their host shall fade away,
as the leaf fades from off the vine, and as a fading leaf from the fig-tree.
For My sword has drunk its fill in heaven:
behold, it shall come down.**[24]

Harry my friend, I respect the wisdom you have acquired over the years. Please elaborate on what those verses mean.

All right. The place to start is in recognizing the Eternal One as Mighty One of Heaven and Earth. That's the way He frequently describes Himself, as the One who is so powerful that He controls the entire universe. The Eternal One determines the weather, causes earthquakes, makes the sun stand still, the stars to fall, and the Earth to tremble. Nothing is too difficult for Him, and we should not be surprised when He makes Himself known in His own creation.[25]

22 Judges 5:4; Joel 2:10,30; Joel 3:16; Isaiah 13:13; Isaiah 24:20; Isaiah 24:4;
23 Mark 13:24-25; Luke 21:25-26
24 Isaiah 34:4-5
25 He moves mountains without their knowing it and overturns them in his anger.

He shakes the earth from its place and makes its pillars tremble.

I like it, Avi, that you ended with a text about the heavenly bodies. That's what we have been talking about all along. I have been elaborating on the biblical texts with examples from ancient legends. The similarities are striking.

It may seem unthinkable that the heavens can be rolled back like a scroll, but recall how in the Egyptian tomb of Senmut, the heavens are shown in reverse. Imagining the heavens as a scroll that can be rolled closed is a fitting description. As the opposite scroll is unfurled, a new heavenly order is revealed. It also sounds like the legends of the Earth turning upside down.

It's the same for when "the Earth shall stagger like a drunken man." In this depiction, it's the Earth's motion that causes the sun to change its position. As the Earth totters back and forth, the sun rises and sets. Through the prophet Amos, the Almighty said that He will make the sun go down at noon, and darken the Earth during the day.[26] One can only imagine a heightened sense of drunkenness as the Earth reels out of the sun's path.

The Earth will reel, the heavens roll back, and the stars fall. The stars are the wandering stars, meaning the planets. They could also be comets, asteroids or some unknown interplanetary body. There's an ancient and modern belief about Nibiru, a large planet that comes close to the Earth every 3600 years. That such an interplanetary body could approach the Earth is supported by both the Hebrew and Christian Scriptures. Such an event would trigger the massive earthquakes and thunderbolts, fiery brimstone, piercing noise, smoke and intense darkness so frequently mentioned throughout the Bible.

One of the prophets asked why the people were looking forward to the day of the Master's coming. He asked why they didn't know that it was to be a day of darkness and not light. The most frequent description of that coming day is that it will be a time of intense darkness. Similar to the darkness of the plague on Egypt, the darkness will be so intense that it will be felt. In the midst of that darkness, there will be equally intense flashes of light and searing heat. Eye sockets will be burned out and human flesh consumed. The biblical description of the day of the Eternal Father matches the conventional imagery of Hell as a place of darkness, fire and death.[27]

He speaks to the sun and it does not shine; he seals off the light of the stars.

He alone stretches out the heavens and treads on the waves of the sea.

He is the Maker of the Bear, Orion, Pleiades and the constellations of the south.

He performs wonders that cannot be fathomed, miracles that cannot be counted.

Job 9:5-10.

26 Amos 8:9.

27 Small wonder that the "mighty ones" of the Earth will try to hide themselves in holes and caves. Luxury condos are being built into an abandoned missile silo to shelter fearful and wealthy people from the coming

At the end, very few of the Earth's population will be left alive. The Eternal One has said that He will make men more scarce than gold. There will be so few left that a child will be able to count them, according to the biblical terminology. Only a small remnant of the human race will survive.

According to one passage in Isaiah, the destruction will come upon the whole Earth. Yes, the Eternal One will spare a remnant of His people, the nation of Israel, but the day of darkness and death will come upon all of humankind, the righteous and the wicked alike. Many, many of the Eternal One's own people will not be spared, and their lives will be lost.

I'll paraphrase this particular passage:

> **The anger of YHWH is kindled against His people.**
> **He has stretched out His hand against them, and smitten them.**
> **The mountains tremble,**
> **and their dead bodies are as refuse in the streets.**
> **And still His anger is not turned away.**[28]

As soon as Harry finished, I knew that I was losing him. I could see it in his demeanor. He appeared to be drifting away, and no longer present. It was as if he had relinquished all the power of his being. Even his sorrow was gone.

I understood.

Harry was leaving me alone to make up my own mind about the end-time scenario that he had presented so vividly. He was certainly not going to persuade me by the strength of his personality. I could have resented that he was leaving me alone, but I took it as a compliment. I accepted his abdication as a vote of confidence.

We walked on in silence for a long time. Our silence was good. I felt no obligation to say anything, allow Harry into my thoughts, or confirm what had been said. We walked on and on, each of us alone in our beings. Then it came to me, that I was grieving too. I fully understood the enormity of our situation.

From that, I broke the silence, not caring about my friend's distance from me as a person.

---

doomsday. At a cost of $2 million per floor, the condos will keep their tenants safe, secure and fed for up to five years - supposedly. Search, "Doomsday shelters line Kansas missile silo."

28   Isaiah 5:25

We're going to have to talk about what this all means for us, and how it should affect our behavior, but for right now, the only question we need to ask is: "Is this for real?" Do the Hebrew Scriptures, as confirmed by Yeshuah, tell us that the Earth is going to be destroyed along with most of humankind? I've never heard anyone say this as plainly as you have today, but does your plainness match what the Scriptures tell us?

I'll answer my own question. As far as I'm concerned, that is exactly and plainly what the Scriptures say: the Earth will be destroyed - not completely - but certainly its inhabited surface. There is a terrible time coming, according to the prophets, when the Earth's face will be utterly obliterated along with most of its population.

Actually, Harry, you're not alone on this. I am reminded of something Isaac Newton said a long time ago. It's said to be one of his best known comments on biblical prophecy. I think I can remember it exactly:

> About the time of the end, a body of men will be raised up who will turn their attention to the prophecies, and insist upon their literal interpretation, in the midst of much clamor and opposition.

That being said, we still need to ask ourselves what our response will be. How should this affect our behavior? That is at least in part where our grief comes from. We know we have to do something. Otherwise, our grief will be nothing more than hopeless despair.

I'd like to take up that question next week, if it's okay with you.

There was no hesitation in Harry's answer, but as soon as he spoke, something delightful was confirmed to me. Harry accepted me as a person, a real person. No matter what he was dealing with internally, he did not allow it to affect who he understood me to be. I was a person in my own right. I couldn't help but admire his ability to be so unassuming about other persons, not just me.

That would be fine, Abraham. I agree with the question you posed about our behavior. Assuredly, we need to answer it. I had in mind to deal with the issue of Satan as a real being - the he is not a real being. Also, next Sabbath is *Shavuot,* or Pentecost. Shavuot commemorates the day our Almighty Father gave the Torah to the nation of Israel when they were assembled at Mount Sinai. Knowing that will be appropriate to our discussion.

All right then, Harry. I'm already looking forward to next week. It's always so good.

May the Eternal Father be with you, Avi.

237

May the Eternal Father be with you, Harry.

14. SATAN IS NOT A REAL BEING

It was the last day of July. The morning was sultry with a summer wind blowing. I marveled again at the seclusion of my friend's back yard with its protective trees and small rock strewn pond. The surrounding neighborhood could hardly be seen. Harry greeted me with his usual warmth.

Welcome, Avi. Happy Shavuot.

I nodded my head happily.

I don't get it, Harry. Here we are at the end of July and you're keeping Shavuot. I know Shavuot is the Feast of Weeks, better known as Pentecost, but Pentecost is usually celebrated in May. What gives?

I waited for my friend's answer.

It's well understood that Shavuot was originally a harvest festival – like the *Feast of Unleavened Bread* in Spring and the *Feast of Ingathering* in Fall. Shavuot or Pentecost should coincide with the summer harvest to be consistent, but it doesn't by the traditional count of fifty days. Therefore, I count seven weeks and then fifty days. The text in Leviticus 23 can be translated that way and sometimes is. There are also many indications in the Hebrew Scriptures that Shavuot was celebrated at the time of the summer harvest in late July or early August.

More important, Shavuot commemorates Israel's experience at Mt. Sinai exactly one hundred days after she left Egypt. The only way to link the two events is by counting the seven Sabbaths following Passover and then adding another fifty days.

Avi, it's so important to remember what Shavuot is all about. It commemorates the day on which the Almighty Creator gave His eternal laws to His people, and by extension to all people everywhere on the whole Earth.

239

All right, Harry, but among Christians, Shavuot or Pentecost is the day on which the Almighty's Spirit descended on the early church. Isn't that different?

Not really. Peter quoted the prophet Joel in Acts 2. There he linked the outpouring of the Almighty's Spirit with the coming day of signs upon the Earth with fire and smoke. That's reminiscent of what happened at Sinai:

> **And mount Sinai, the whole of it, smoked,**
> **because Jehovah descended upon it in fire;**
> **and the smoke thereof ascended as the smoke of a furnace,**
> **and the whole mount quaked greatly.**

Then Harry sat for a long while before saying more. Again, I waited.

I tremble too, Abraham. The truth is so powerful and yet so simple that we can miss it easily. Too often, we think it's what we believe that matters, or all that we really need is the Almighty's grace, but that's not the real truth. The truth is that we have a choice to make and what we do has infinite consequences. We can never understate what the Almighty Creator gave us at Sinai. It does make me tremble.

We tend to forget that long before the earliest Christians were persecuted by the institutional churches – Catholic, Protestant and Reformed (Calvinist) to name the main culprits – their persecutors were pagans and pagan authorities, the Romans in particular. That oppression came several centuries before the so-called *Apostles Creed* and the ruthless imposition of doctrinal conformity. Those early believers had a simpler code and more meaningful distinction. As quoted from *Fox's Book of Martyrs*:

> The whole account they gave of their crime or error (whichever it is to be called) amounted only to this—viz. that they were accustomed on a stated day to meet before daylight, and to repeat together a set form of prayer to Christ as a God, and *to bind themselves by an obligation—not indeed to commit wickedness; but, on the contrary—never to commit theft, robbery, or adultery, never to falsify their word, never to defraud any man*: after which it was their custom to separate, and reassemble to partake in common of a harmless meal. (*emphasis added*).[1]

Those early believers in Yeshuah were far more concerned with virtue and right behavior than they were with doctrinal correctness. That came later, "to a period when

---

1   From the letter of Pliny the Younger (ca 61 – 112 AD) to Trajan on page 7 of *Fox's Book of Martyrs*.

persecution, under the guise of Christianity, committed more enormities than ever disgraced the annals of paganism."[2] It was by their virtuous conduct that the early followers of Yeshuah made themselves known to the pagan world around them. Their good behavior made them stand out uniquely, and brought to them the wrath of pagan authorities.

My friend put his head down and sat quietly and nearly a minute went by.

Abraham, here is another aside. If ever there was an indictment against the Catholic Church, it's surely found in *Fox's Book of Martyrs*. The atrocities recorded in that book, and committed against the Almighty's people, are in themselves an abiding condemnation of that evil institution. No power from above could ever have conceived or perpetrated so many acts of cruelty against so many innocent people. It was during that time of persecution, commonly known as the Inquisition, that the Catholic Church began to be called the Anti-Christ and the Beast. Rightly so.

I saw Harry breathing deeply, keeping himself composed.

To the lasting shame of the protesting reformers, they soon proved themselves to be her offspring, and committed the same evil deeds. In the Book of Revelation, they're appropriately called Jezebel's children. The Protestant churches have their own legacy to contend with and, like the Catholics, have never repented of it. They can't repent of course without acknowledging that it's a fraudulent institution, and that they love their lies more than the truth.

Harry looked at me with quietness in his eyes.

The moral of the story is that we're all individually responsible. Each of us needs to decide the truth for ourselves in our personal relationship with the Almighty Father. During the time of the Inquisition, it was the conscience of individuals that empowered real believers with so much courage, and they understood it was their right to decide for themselves who or what they were going to trust. That's the conclusion we need to make, Avi, each of us individually.

When he looked up, it was with vigor and confidence. The sorrow that seemed so much part of Harry's being was gone. In its place was unfathomable hope.

Avi, it's all so simple as we come to a conclusion. We have a decision to make, one with everlasting consequences. However, first let's talk about the being we call Satan. It's a related issue in the choice we need to make.

---

2   *Fox's Book of Martyrs*, p 43,

Let's start with the Tanak or what is commonly called the *Old Testament*. There the Hebrew word *sawtawn* is an adjective referring to humankind's evil inclinations. In the Greek language, however, that adjective is extended into a proper noun. This is a recurring problem when translating from Hebrew to Greek and then to English. What begins as a metaphor becomes literal and then is objectified. In this instance, the metaphor for our proclivity toward sinful actions has become a real being called 'satan' - from the Hebrew word *sawtawn*. Our English translations have retained the Greek meaning of Satan as a proper noun.

The same usage goes for the word 'demon.' In the Hebrew or Aramaic language, the counterpart words for demon such as 'evil spirit' or 'unclean spirit' meant something very different. A demon was a human infirmity, a disease of some sort, or an unhealthy state of mind. It could also have meant that a person was choosing to do things that were unclean according to the Law of Moses, and thereby having an unclean spirit.

One biblical scholar puts it this way:

> In spite of the translations, there is no word in Hebrew equivalent to the English word "demon," nor any word that communicates the same meaning that the term communicates in English as a malevolent being in the service of the devil out to destroy humans. That idea today has been shaped by the imagination of medieval writers and popularized in the modern church in terms of evil beings against which Christians need to wage "spiritual warfare." Yet, the ancient Israelites lived in a world in which that view of "demons" was not part of their culture or way of thinking.[3]

I had lunch with a Jewish man some time ago, who said it perfectly. In his words, "God has no adversary." In the Hebrew mind, there is only one Almighty Being – not two or three. For my lunch companion, there is no other powerful being that the Almighty needs to contend with, certainly no other being that is also immortal or indestructible. There is only one Creator and Mighty One.[4]

There are no passages in the Hebrew Scriptures or *Tanak* that unequivocally refer to an archangel who once inhabited heaven, rebelled against the Almighty, and then was

---

3   Dennis Brattier, *Demons in the Old Testament: Issues in Translation*, crivoice.org/demonsot.html

4   Much to their credit, the Jews have remained staunchly monotheistic. Their unwavering witness or *Shema* is: "Hear, Israel, the Lord is our God, the Lord is One." The Shema is the most important element in their prayer services, and it's a *mitzvah* or religious commandment for all Jews to repeat it twice daily, morning and evening. It's a tradition for Jews to say the Shema as their last words, and parents teach their children to say it before they go to sleep at night. The Shema is an abridgment of Deuteronomy 6:4-9.

cast down to the Earth. The main passages used to endorse Satan as a being are about the King of Tyre and the King of Babylon - two real life, historical human beings. More about that later.

In the earliest books of the Tanak or *Old Testament*, the term for Satan appears quite often. There the term means 'to oppose' or to be an 'adversary.' A satan is a person sent by the Almighty and allowed to speak in opposition. From the beginning, the Eternal One has given humans a choice, including the choice of being against Him. That choice, however, does not come from a third party:

I am YHWH and there is none else.
I form the light and create darkness.
I make peace and create evil.
I, YHWH, do all these things.

That's from Isaiah. A similar statement is found in Lamentations:

Who has commanded and it came to pass, unless the Master has ordained
it? Is it not from the mouth of the Most High that good and evil come?

During the three centuries before Yeshuah's birth, the portrayal of an adversary to the Almighty's purpose underwent a major change. The Persian concept of dualism began to appear in Jewish writing. The Almighty was looked upon as wholly good, and Satan as profoundly evil, and Satan was no longer the Almighty's representative as the choice between good and evil. Satan was now the Almighty's arch rival and humanity's greatest enemy.

As one well-read author writes:

> Prior to this statement by Carus in his work, we are given a sizeable
> treatise on the Persian religion of Zoroaster. We are shown how this
> ancient religion was a primary catalyst for religion to move towards
> a two-God philosophy. Zoroastrianism remains known as the most
> consistent form of dualism. This Persian dualism, we are taught,
> is intricately connected to major religions today by the nature of a
> philosophy of an evil, supernatural being, and a good supernatural
> being.... Much of common religion has conformed to the Persian
> philosophy with the most notable of the conformists being found in
> Christianity. A religion that has turned the Persian good God and evil

God into the entities that are called God and Satan.[5]

It's easy to see why Ezekiel 28 is used as a proof text for Satan:

Son of man, take up a lamentation over the king of Tyre,
and say to him, Thus says the Master YHWH:
You seal up the sum, full of wisdom, and perfect in beauty.
You were in Eden, the garden of Elohim;
every precious stone was your covering,
the sardius, the topaz, and the diamond,
the beryl, the onyx, and the jasper,
the sapphire, the emerald, and the carbuncle, and gold:
the workmanship of your tabrets and of your pipes was in you;
in the day that you were created they were prepared.

The passage is written in exceptionally figurative language. Nevertheless, it is addressed to the king of Tyre, and it expressly states that the one being addressed is a man. Furthermore, the figurative language is appropriate for an exalted and proud leader who is both king and priest for a very powerful nation. The imagery is of a man living at the height of luxury, bearing the signet rings of kingship and the jewelry of priestly garments. In his heart of hearts, he has exalted himself as if he were the Almighty Himself. Nowhere in the passage is there an explicit reference to Satan.

Isaiah 14 is more interesting, and may have a double meaning:

And it shall come to pass in that day...
that you shall take up this parable against the king of Babylon, and say...
How you are fallen from heaven, O day-star, son of the morning!
how you are cut down to the ground, you that did lay low the nations!
And you said in your heart, I will ascend into heaven,
I will exalt my throne above the stars of Elohim;
and I will sit upon the mount of congregation...
I will ascend above the heights of the clouds;
I will make myself like the Most High.

The passage is addressed to the king of Babylon and the all the chief ones of the Earth. The name Lucifer appears in the passage. Lucifer is a Latin word meaning 'phosphorous,' and it's the Roman name for the planet Venus. The Hebrew word is *helel* which is linguistically related to the Assyrian *Mushtilil*, an epithet for Venus. Venus is also called the

5   James R. Brayshaw, *Imagine There's No Satan*, SCOG Publishing, 2010, p 23.

'morning star', which is how most translators now render the passage.

Harry turned to me.

Avi, you might want to read the passage in Isaiah for yourself. It fits with what we talked about last week. The planet Venus was once the most terrifying object in the sky. Its appearance made the kings of the Earth tremble fearfully in their impotence. After, when Venus had settled in its current orbit and became just another planet, Isaiah could say, "The whole Earth is at rest, and is quiet." Let's recall, the last known celestial catastrophe was in Isaiah's time when Hezekiah's sun dial moved back ten degrees. That was in 701 BC. No celestial body has threatened the Earth and its kings since that time.

My purpose today is to focus on the consequences of not believing in Satan, and on the future of evil in the world. I have a colleague who has written two excellent books on the subject of Satan. My colleague and fellow Canadian is James R. Brayshaw. In his second book, he wrote this:

> Imagine if you will, there is no Satan. Imagine that the teachings on Satan we received from religion and from culture as simply not true. Is it possible that religion has made a mistake in this area? Imagine that a lie has been told so long that it has become the truth and now it is time to right it. It is time to place the satan of tradition back into the place he came from. Believe it or not, we can take Satan out of our belief system, place him back into the creative mind of man where he came from, and still recognize the sovereign God of the Universe for who He or it is. That is a God who makes alive, and a God who shares the cosmos with no other supernatural being.[6]

However, Brayshaw's momentous conclusion came in his first book:

> Probably the most serious repercussion of a culture coming to terms with the non-existence of a cosmic Satan is the impact this information will have on the individual when they fully realize what it is they are responsible for. By there being no "Satan," you and I are then left as the party who must take the full responsibility for sin. We can then dismiss the idea that an evil influencing force has secretly introduced sin to us and we are hapless participants in behavior that is not approved by the Almighty.

---

6 *Imagine There's No Satan*, SCOG Publishing, 2010, p 6.

> The fault for evil then is not laid on a supernatural, mind controlling, satanic spirit; the fault lies with the individual who submits to the original propensity to choose sin, which is a potential that is inherent in the human psyche.[7]

Now Abraham, I'm not going to give this subject the coverage it deserves. Not that it's so very difficult or even questionable. I'm making the point that Satan is not a real being. 'Satan' is an allegory for evil and the human inclination to disobey the One who made us. 'Satan' is also an accusing spirit for those with a righteous conscience, and there's lots of that in the world![8] Anyway, people like James Brayshaw have written very well on the subject in a way that even lay-readers can easily understand. I expect, Avi, that you'll study it for yourself.

I nodded my headed vigorously without interrupting my friend.

Once again, here's the issue. If Satan is not a real being – and he is not – than we are autonomous as human beings. That is, we are free to make our choices without coercion. There is no external being out there who can oppress, harass or pester us into making a bad decision. At the risk of being misunderstood, let's also imagine that there is no Mighty One. To that there's momentous conclusion – the conclusion that we are fully responsible for the decisions we make, and accountable for our own future welfare.

I submit, Avi, that that's exactly how the Creator made us, as autonomous beings and fully accountable for our own welfare and the future of the world. Yes, it's up to us to turn the Earth into a paradise. The decision is ours and it is only us, as human beings, that can bring it about.

In this context, Abraham, there is no satanic being that has power over us, and our Almighty Father will not coerce us into doing what is right. Therefore, it is uniquely up to us to make the right decision and take the right course of action. That's what the Almighty wants us to do, but he won't do it for us. It's up to us by His design.

I can't think that it's otherwise. Surely, we can't wait for the Almighty to make us perfect or wait for Him to establish His kingdom on the Earth. Not only does such an approach fail to recognize who we are as human beings, it reduces us to mere pawns and puppets in the Eternal Father's plan. It's unthinkable to me that the future doesn't depend on us and our choices.

---

7   *Satan: Christianity's Other God*, iUniverse, 2009, p 1. A highly recommended book. A must read.

8   No doubt one accusation will be that we've been deceived about Satan. After all, if there really is a Satan, he would be doing his best to convince us that he doesn't exist. How ironic. Obviously, Satan has been a miserable failure because all of Christendom believes in the Devil.

Just consider that when the religious leaders accused Yeshuah of claiming to be divine, he threw it back at them by quoting the Scripture, "You are gods." That we are beings made in the Creator's image must be inclusive. Human beings surely have the power to determine their own future and the future state of the Earth. Yeshuah even said that we will do even greater works than his.

Truly, truly, I say to you,
whoever believes in me will also do the works that I do;
and greater works than these will he do,
because I am going to the Father.

Is it not plain in your face, Avi, that Yeshuah was going back to the Father, and was leaving it up to us to carry on? That it's up to us to see that the Almighty One's kingdom really does come to the Earth? John the Baptist said it too, for he was:

the voice of one crying in the wilderness,
Prepare ye the way of the Master,
and make His paths straight.

I know Harry. I've been following along just as if I'd been saying it myself.

Harry, all this multitude of people who are waiting for the 'second coming' aren't helping in the least. They're thumb twiddling at best. At worst, they may soon be the initiators of the very tribulation they're hoping to be spared from. That's the price of doing nothing.

Harry gave me that look of his – a look somewhere between being startled and knowing what was coming.

It has become obvious to me that there are tensions or conflicting ideas in the Bible. Some of them have been resolved internally. For example, the Almighty does not want us to bring sacrifice to Him. All He really wants is for us to be humble and genuine towards him. The prophets and Yeshuah resolved that tension.

However, the conflicting tension that's the most germane to all our conversations has to do with the future. On the one hand, the Bible teaches that there's a Day of Wrath coming and it's imminent. On the other, the Kingdom of Heaven is also near. Both expectations can be real, but which one is coming?

Harry, I've thought about this a lot. All those things about the Earth being shaken, the sun being darkened, and the stars falling from heaven don't have to happen. They will happen if we as human beings stay on the course we are now on. That's a certainty, and maybe it's already too late to prevent entirely, but our situation can be reversed if we change our course. That's a certainty too. Maybe it sounds bizarre, but our behavior has a direct bearing on how the universe unfolds. We can, in biblical language, liberate the world from the tyranny of sin and death.

I bowed my head. I didn't want to say any more.

Harry didn't feel the same way.

That's right, my friend. Human nature can be changed. So can animal nature, and even the nature of the material universe. Even now, the Almighty Father is telling us that there will be a new Earth and a new Heaven. Those of us who can hear His voice are paying close attention. We can initiate the paradise that was lost.

I looked at Harry with renewed confidence.

I know what the issue is, Harry.

Go ahead. Say it.

We have to stop killing and eating animals.

I saw again the impenetrable discernment in Harry's eyes.

Harry, the first instruction that ever came out of the Creator's mouth, after He had blessed and empowered both men and women, was to eat from every plant and every tree that bears fruit. Physiologically, we are vegetarians. That's the way He made us, and the way our bodies function best.

Do you know something, Harry? The Creator spoke with animals before He spoke with us. He blessed them and told them to fill the Earth with their kind. As you repeatedly said many weeks ago, "animals are living, breathing creatures too." They have all the five senses we have, and an equal ability to experience pleasure and pain. We have no right to take away their life and their happiness. They have been blessed by their Creator. Thanks be to Him.

I paused to collect my thoughts.

I'm not going to elaborate on the subject, Harry. There are now a host of witnesses confirming veganism as a way of life, but I want to make the point that veganism is the issue of our age, and there is no other issue of comparable significance. If we want to change the world and usher in a new age, veganism is the place to start. I'm thoroughly convinced.

That's all I want to say, Harry, except for this – it's not what we believe that will save us, it's what we do.

In my inner spirit, I knew we were on the right track.

That's good, Avi. I agree that we won't repeat all the evidence against the killing of animals for human consumption. The economic, environmental and psychological cost of consuming animal flesh is too high to be sustainable. Never mind the terrible cruelty involved and the critical issue of human health. All those issues have been thoroughly dealt with in a wide range of studies. The literature is abundant, conclusive and irrefutable. It's readily available for anyone who cares enough to investigate it for themselves.[9]

I also agree that veganism is the unique issue of our time.

Harry fell into the topic so easily, as any man would who had spent so many years pondering his life and the world around him.

The term *vegan* (pronounced vee-gan) was coined by a British woodcutter named Donald Watson in 1944. By the time Watson died in 2005, at age 95, there were at least 250,000 vegans in Britain, and two million in the United States. Now there must be at least six million vegans in the US alone. The number of vegetarians avoiding eggs and dairy products is growing rapidly: "The science of nutrition, the mechanization of labor, and the availability of synthetic products are all 'signs of the times': they give notice that the age of the unthinking abuse of animals is coming to an end."[10]

Most vegans would consider their lifestyle as ethical, and rightly so. Vegans aren't particularly religious, even though they have a keen sense of right and wrong, but the deeper issue is spiritual, and that's what we need to grapple with. Yeshuah was bang on when he reputedly said, "The children of this world are in their generation wiser than the children of light."

Let's go for a walk, Avi. I want to summarize all that we've talked about during the last three months. Besides, I want to enjoy the Sabbath in your company.

9   May I recommend the e-book *God's Covenant with Animals* by the late J.R. Highland. She quotes Genesis 9:16 on the title page, "Whenever the rainbow appears in the clouds, I will see it and remember the everlasting covenant between God and all living creatures of every kind on the earth."
10   Quoted from *God's Covenant with Animals,* p 66-67.

That sounds good to me. I feel complete today, and for now, all I want to do is enjoy what I've learned. My mind is at ease.

That was my mood as we headed toward the river again. Harry spoke on in his easy and concise manner, but I was only half listening. He began with how uniquely special the Earth is: the only place in the whole universe inhabited by sentient beings. I heard him saying how "the life is in the blood" in both humans and animals, and how it was Paul who developed the Christian doctrine of atonement. Dimly I heard him say how much he appreciated the Hebrew and Greek Scriptures, even after having come to terms with their pervasive errancy.

He repeated again his theme that science has led us astray just as religion has. Both have invented realities that defy our common sense and everyday experience. The history of the Earth and humankind can never span millions of years any more than a man can also be God. Vaguely I heard him say that we all have the right to follow our own conscience, and that each of us has enough innate intelligence to know when we are being lied to.

When it came to Harry's vision of the future, his words shimmered with hope. There will be another paradise on the Earth that we can all be part of even if the Almighty Creator of all has to bring us back from the grave. Even the animals will revert back to their original forms, and there will no longer be any death for all of His creatures. I heard it even in my half-attentiveness.

Yet, my ears perked up when I heard my friend talk about our human responsibility. Yes, the Almighty Father will freely forgive our sins or failures as He still loves His people from long ago, but it's up to us to be obedient to what we know is right. The choice is ours because that's how He has made us. It's who we are, and our power as human beings. It's our priceless gift to choose rightly.[11]

Perhaps I stopped listening after a while. I don't know because I was too intent on what I already knew, what was true and real. The walk along the river was engaging and my memories pleasurable. It seemed fitting for the day of Shavuot. All too soon, we were back in Harry's private yard.

I asked the question that had been formulating in my mind.

---

11 As J.R. Highland wrote on page 96: "Throughout the Bible, there is the explicit teaching that women and men are capable of choosing between good and evil. They can manifest the violence and aggression that brings destruction in its wake, or they can manifest the goodness and compassion that can bring about the peaceable kingdom."

What kind of opposition can we expect? After all, we'll be going against the powers that be. That's Big Government, the economic and educational systems, the Church – not to mention human nature.

Hah... Avi.

I took that as a laugh from Happy Harry.

Your question is fine, but let's get all those ideas about persecution and tribulation out of our minds. Nothing can stand in the way of the truth. Nothing.

Why are you so sure, Harry?

Because it can't be any other way. Our Almighty Father has promised to be with us if we keep His commandments. That's the thing about real truth. We can manifest what the Eternal One is doing when we walk in His way. We can do it.

I felt no resistance to what my friend was saying.

I agree. Our hope for the future has precious little to do with the powers that be. Sure, our governments and churches can start acting responsibly, but the real power is with us as individual people. It's a choice that each of us has to make, becoming more and more effective as our numbers increase. This has to be a grass-roots movement, independent from the leadership of institutions. It's more realistic that the church and big governments will have to follow in our wake.

I still believe we are the very people that the Eternal One appointed long ago. We can see ourselves as the promised seed of Abraham or as human beings created for a purpose. Either way we have a destiny – or should I say predestination. It's just as Yeshuah the Messiah said to his disciples, **"You have not chosen me, but I have chosen you."** This is our calling once again.

We sat quietly for some time, each of us in our own domain.

Then I looked at my friend as if for the first time. I had come to know Harry as a man who was equally reflective and considerate of others. Was there a line between his search for wisdom and the need for companionship? Harry was anything but a lonely man.

Then I saw it – the smile that spread across his face and demeanor. It came from deep within, from wherever all his mediations had taken root, and now unreservedly displayed in the garden where we were sitting. What made the smile so new was its playfulness. Through all our dialogues and their momentous conclusions, Harry had never made himself the subject of attention. In this smile, I saw that he could have a good time without taking himself too seriously. In a manner, he had enjoyed being provocative and not overly concerned with the outcome. He was being himself, enjoying his hard won knowledge and the camaraderie that came with it. My friend was a happy man.

On this day, Harry had drawn our many weeks together to a singular conclusion. It's up to us as created beings to determine the future for good or for evil. Far from being religious, philosophical or mystical, Harry had laid out a simple formula. Humankind must return to the vegetarian diet that humans were designed for. In our present context, that means veganism. For Harry, that one simple reality was the starting point for all humans on their path to a full and happy future.

I looked at my friend again. In all honesty, that was his opinion, and just one of his opinions among all the others. He was convincing enough for sure, and had no lack of confidence, but would anyone else adopt his simple solution? Time would tell, but at the very least, I was convinced.

Thanks, Harry. I'm going to be on my way. May our Father be with you.

And may our Father be with you, Abraham.

EPILOGUE.

I will end as I began, with something of myself and the way I think.

My subtitle, "a believer's guide to reality" is much more inclusive than it may seem. In my mind, a believer is any person who has a measure of common sense, good judgment, and intuitive wisdom. In addition, a believing person has sound moral principles, a steadfast sense of purpose, and overriding good will toward all other living beings. Finally, and without reservation, a believer has a genuine hope for the future, both personally and for mankind.

A believer is any person who can transcend the narrow confines of his or her own being for the sake of the big picture when all living beings will have been released from their current bondage.

Without apology, I'm still very much a Biblicist. Even when I'm not reading the Book of Books, I'm habitually meditating on its precepts. That much is clear from how often I quote in bold print from the Hebrew and Christian Scriptures. For me, those Scriptures are the written result of mankind's dialogue with the one and only Creator and Primary Being. Regardless of whether they were written by a man or a woman, our Scriptures are the collective results of their courage and willingness to reach into the unknowable and grasp what they could concerning the nature of the One who created us from His own being. Without disparaging history's other great spiritual texts (Hindu, Buddhist, Islamic, etc.), our Hebrew-Christian Bible is unique in its record of mankind's dialogue with the Creator, and – for those who have come to know Him – the Father of us all.

More than any other sacred text, the Bible is a record of real people and real events, from their abject failures to their spectacular triumphs. (Moses forfeited entering the Promised Land where Joshua commanded the sun to stand still.) And yet, from within our supposedly inspired Scriptures, it's readily apparent that the Almighty's people and all of mankind have failed miserably in coming anywhere near what those sacred texts require and promise. The human dimension in the Book of Books makes it all too clear that human beings have a proclivity to reject the Creator for the sake of their own self-centered independence. Scarcely anyone said it better than the prophet Isaiah in the third verse of the book bearing his name:

253

**An ox knows its master, the donkey its owner's manger,
but Israel does not know, my people do not understand.**

Too often the objection has been made that there is no historical record of Yeshuah's life and deeds outside the Christian Scriptures. What is overlooked is the reason why there is so little. Simply put, Yeshuah never sought fame, wealth, power, or any lasting tribute to himself. The Scriptures say that "his voice was not heard crying in the streets," and "a bruised reed, he shall not crush." Throughout his life, Yeshuah made himself small and became a servant for the sake of those who were too weak to help themselves. He served the lonely, the poor, and the powerless. That the Almighty Father exalted him afterward – and his own people made him into an idol – is quite another matter. Yeshuah never sought to establish himself as a historic personage.

The reason he did not is obvious. Yeshuah saw the present order of Earthly reality as a passing phase in the Almighty's purpose. It was Yeshuah's mission to introduce a new and ultimate reality for all of mankind, a new order called the Kingdom of Heaven. In that new order, all suffering would come to an end, the Earth would be filled with happiness, and human beings would receive eternal life. It was Yeshuah's mission to show the way forward for humanity's entrance into the Kingdom of Heaven. There would have been no point in establishing his name or position in an Earthly realm that was soon to pass away.

The Messiah had a very different perception of human nature and capacity than we commonly have today. Typically, we associate human nature with weakness, proneness to error, and innate limitations. In religious parlance, human beings have a sinful, or more extremely, depraved nature. Accordingly, by their very nature, human beings will go on sinning, making mistakes, and having only limited success. Therein lies the Messiah's ultimate purpose: he came to liberate humanity from failure, bondage, and extinction, or in scriptural terms, from sin and death. For Israel's Messiah, all humans have the potential of overcoming the world and becoming fully transformed beings.

Here is a question that has confounded all great thinkers, philosophers, and theologians down through the ages. If the Almighty Creator is all-knowing and all-powerful, why does He allow evil to continue? Why doesn't He instead set everything right, and make everyone happy? The answer is simply this: the future is up to us. In His unsearchable wisdom, the Creator has given every human being the capacity to choose between good and evil, fulfillment and failure, utopia and annihilation. This is our lot as human beings, and we have no one to blame for the continuation of evil in the world except ourselves, individually and collectively. The choice is ours alone, not one the Almighty Father will make for us. What more can be said about the stature of human beings than that we are endowed with such a capacity? And why have our thinkers altogether missed it?

Recall how Yeshuah the Messiah answered his accuser's claim that he was making himself out to be equal with the Almighty Father. He quoted Psalm 82:6 where the Almighty declares:

> **I said, you are gods [mighty ones],**
> **and all of you sons of the Most High.**

Recall too how Yeshuah the Messiah summarized the beatitudes after assuring his audience that not one jot or tittle would fall from the Almighty Father's immutable laws?

> **You therefore must be perfect,**
> **as your heavenly Father is perfect.**

The biblical premise is that the Almighty has made us in His image, which means to be like Him. From that we can conclude that we share many if not all of the Creator's attributes. This is not something we need to strive for. We already are like Him, and even more so potentially. We have at least some idea of what we will become from the witness of the Christian Scriptures regarding the resurrected Yeshuah. Ultimately we are to be eternal beings, each of us with our own body and personal identity.

I find it inconceivable that if the Almighty One created us in His own image, He would not also have given us the wherewithal to enter into eternal life. This may be hard to fathom, so I'll put it this way: It is within our capacity as human beings to bring about the Kingdom of Heaven. I truly wonder if this was not the Messiah's essential message as he went about doing good and announcing the coming new order. The same message came through John the Immerser when he quoted the prophet Isaiah:

> **For this is he that was spoken of through Isaiah the prophet, saying,**
> **The voice of one crying in the wilderness,**
> **Make you ready the way of the Eternal,**
> **Make His paths straight.**

This of course flies in the face of our Christian tradition in which the so-called Second Coming will change everything. In that tradition, all that a believer needs to do is wait patiently for a salvation coming down from heaven at some indeterminate time in the future. In such a framework, whatever a believer does now has no bearing on when the Messiah will return, and there is no direct connection between the actions of human beings and the timing of the kingdom of heaven. In my mind, that is little more than spiritual thumb twiddling. Worse yet, it contradicts the biblical premise that we have been made in the likeness of our Creator.

It contradicts the evolutionary view of mankind as well. If we really are the result of a random sequence of events, then what we will be is beyond anything that we can determine for ourselves. Whatever will be, will be, not by any human ability or potential, but by whatever time and chance may bring. Even if we are to believe in our continuing evolvement toward a higher order of being, the theory of evolution offers us no means of active participation. All we can do is hope that our evolvement will be for the better, and twiddle our thumbs along with our second-coming counterparts. In either view, we human beings have no effective role in bringing about a better world for mankind.

(There are differences, however. Believers in the Second Coming have someone to talk to while they wait. Evolutionists in their loneliness will have to wait a lot longer, perhaps thousands or millions of years.)

I shouldn't be facetious while trying to make my most important point. But our identity as human beings has been lost in the welter of religious and scientific dogmas. Thinking that we are ultimately responsible for the welfare of the Earth, its living inhabitants and all future beings, is nowhere to be found in religion's other-world destiny or science's come-by-chance future. Conventional religion and science have each in their own way distanced themselves from any crowning hope for Earth and its inhabitants. Both have a definition of what it is to be a human being that precludes mankind from generating a better and even perfect world, which all humour aside, is my point.

My assertion is simple though far-reaching in magnitude. If we were to collectively apply any one of the Almighty's moral laws – whether we believe they come from Him or not – we would change the world in a very short time. Any one of the great commandments would do the job if enough of us applied it consistently; the commandments against adultery, stealing, and lying for example. A world based on such commandments would surely move humanity towards perfection.

I have broadened the meaning of "Thou shalt not kill" beyond its literal meaning in the biblical text. If my reasoning was not clear from chapter 8, I believe the injunction was originally intended to safeguard animal life as well as human. From the beginning, according to the Bible, the life-force or energy is "in the blood" for all living beings. We should not be butchering animals, and certainly not eating them for their lifeforce.

Countless others have spoken out against killing animals and for the beneficial outcome of not using animals for food. These fervent souls were often secular or non-religious. A list of their names would include Socrates, Plato, Leonardo da Vinci, Benjamin Franklin, Abraham Lincoln, Mahatma Gandhi, Robert Louis Stevenson, George Bernard Shaw and Isaac Bashevis Singer. Albert Einstein said what I and many others are proposing:

> Vegetarian food leaves a deep impression on our nature. If the whole world adopts vegetarianism, it can change the destiny of humankind.

To illustrate our human role in the world, let's imagine just for a moment that there is no G-d, no Creator, no Everlasting Father. The secular and scientific world is in effect asking us to do just that. So whether or not such an effort even qualifies as true imagination, let's give it a try. In daring to imagine there is no G-d, and before the panic begins to take hold, we can at least for a brief moment feel being totally and utterly alone. There is only *me,* or only *us* as human beings, and we have none but ourselves to live with, no one else to depend on, no one else to solve our problems; and no one else to assure our future continuation. Whatever the future holds, whatever problems we have, and whatever uniqueness we feel, we have no one but ourselves to be with and place our confidence in. Through such an imaginative exercise, all we know is the stark reality of being completely alone, as if we ourselves are the only beings in existence.

Why this exercise in imagination? Because it may actually be real. Not real in the sense that there is no Almighty Father to help us. But very real in the sense of who we are as created beings. The Creator has made us fully independent and completely autonomous. We have been made responsible for our own well-being, the welfare of all life on Earth, and even the very stability of the cosmos. As mind-boggling as it may sound, our Almighty Creator has made humans to have dominion over all that He created. It is in that sense that we truly are the one being to inhabit the universe and be responsible for it. We are indeed gods, as in Psalm 82:6: "I said, You are gods, and all of you sons of the Most High."

I can say that based on two other equally sufficient biblical texts. The first, from Genesis 1:26, tells us that human beings are to have dominion over the entire natural world of animals including the fish, birds, and cattle:

And the Mighty One said,
Let us make man in our image, after our likeness:
and let them have dominion over the fish of the sea,
and over the birds of the heavens, and over the cattle,
and over all the earth.

The other is from a vision of the future in Daniel 7:13-14. It's not an easy passage to translate or interpret. But it does show that a son of man (a *human being* in the Aramaic), along with the clouds of heaven (a great host of fellow human beings) will eventually have dominion over the Earth in a kingdom that will never pass away:

In my vision at night I looked,
and there before me was one like a human being,
coming with the clouds of heaven.
He approached the Ancient of Days and was led into his presence.
He was given authority, esteem and sovereign power;
all nations and peoples of every language served him.
His dominion is an everlasting dominion that will not pass away,
and his kingdom is one that will never be destroyed.

As a vision, the text may be depicting the Messiah specifically or the whole of mankind in a future where all the evil of the world has been overcome. A similar interpretation can be gleaned from another text. Paul, a visionary in his own right, writes in Romans 8:19-21:

**The creation waits eagerly for the sons of the Mighty One to be revealed;
for the creation was made subject to frustration –
not willingly, but because of the one who subjected it.
But it was given a reliable hope that it too would be
set free from its bondage to decay
and would enjoy the freedom accompanying
the esteem that the Almighty's children will have.**

According to Paul, there will be a time when nature and human beings are set free from the bondage of decay. Elsewhere, Paul alludes to something even more astonishing. He says that the last enemy to be abolished will be death (1 Corinthians 15:25-28.) Clearly there is a process in overcoming evil in which death will be the final evil to be vanquished. The victory over death is here synonymous with the revealing of the sons of the Almighty One. By implication it is the sons who will overcome death.

As the passage continues:

**And when all things have been subjected unto [the Almighty One],
then shall the Son himself also be subjected to [the Almighty One]
who did subject all things unto [the Messiah and Mankind],
that [the Almighty One] may be all in all.**

Surely, this passage speaks of a time when nature and mankind will be whole again. All things will one day be in subjection to or in harmony with the Creator and Almighty Father. The Messiah, and by extension all human beings, will be complete and no longer subject to aging, deterioration and death. Death will have been conquered according to the Scriptures, and the Almighty One will be all and in all.

How long will it be? One generation? Two? Many? There are absolute signs that unless something is done very soon, the present world order will continue its downward spiral toward oblivion. The environmental signals alone are unmistakable. Both on land and in the sea, the life of the Earth is seeping away. It is for this reason that mankind's responsibility for our well-being and the welfare of life on Earth is so paramount. The decision as to whether we continue on the path to destruction or begin moving towards the time when all beings live in harmony with the Creator is entirely in our hands. The time is short, and the cost of doing nothing unthinkable.

I have already given a non-theological definition of the Messiah, the one who will bring about the salvation of the Earth. At the heart of my message is the belief that this role is within reach for every one of us:

A messiah is any person who can transcend the narrow confines of his or her own being for the sake of the big picture when all living beings will have been released from their current bondage.

May the Almighty Father be with us all.

BIBLIOGRAPHY

Arndts, Russell T., *Geocentricity, Relativity And The Big Bang: Was Copernicus Wrong?*, Lindquist Books, 2008.

Asher, Shmuel, *The Land of Meat & Honey*, Amazon CreateSpace Publishing, 2011.

Asher, Shmuel, *The Greater Exodus: An Unfolding Prophecy In Our Time*, Amazon CreateSpace Publishing, 2012.

Astronomy Before the Telescope, edited by Christopher Walker, St Martin's Press, 1996.

Aveni, Anthony F., *Empires of Time: Calendars, Clocks, and Cultures*, Tauris Parke, 2000.

Bajgent, Michael and Leigh, Richard, *The Dead Sea Scrolls Deception*, Corgi Books, London, 1991.

Barbour, Julian, *The End of Time: The Next Revolution in Physics*, Oxford University Press, 1999.

Baeck, Leo, *Judaism and Christianity*, Meridian Books 1958.

ben-Mordechai, Uriel, *IF: The End of a Messianic Lie*, Uriel ben-Mordechai, 2011.

Bjerknes, Christopher Jon, *The Manufacture and Sale of Saint Einstein*, on-line PDF, 2006.

Berlinski, David, *The Devil's Delusion: Atheism and its Scientific Pretensions*, Crown Forum, 2008.

Branley, Franklyn M., *The Milky Way, Galaxy Number One*, Thomas K. Crowell, 1969.

Brayshaw, James R., *Satan: Christianity's Other God*, iUniverse, 2009.

Brayshaw, James R., *Imagine There's No Satan*, SCOG Publishing, 2010.

Bright, John, *A History of Israel*, Westminster Press, 1959.

Brown, Walt, *In The Beginning: Compelling Evidence for Creation and the Flood*, 2001.

Bouw, Gerardus D., "A Geocentric Primer: Introduction to Biblical Cosmology," *The Biblical Astronomer,* Cleveland, 2004.

Cahill, Thomas, *The Gift of the Jews: How a Tribe of Desert Nomads Changed the Way Everyone Thinks and Feels*, Nan A. Telese/Anchor books, 1998.

Collins, Steven, M., *Israel's Lost Empires*, Bible Blessings, 2002.

Collins, Steven, M., *Parthia: The Forgotten Ancient Superpower And Its Role In Biblical History*, Bible Blessings, 2004.

Collins, Steven, M., *The "Lost" Ten Tribes of Israel...Found!*, CPA Books, 1992.

Collins, Steven, M., *The Origins and Empire of Ancient Israel*, Bible Blessings, 2002.

Davidovits, Joseph, *Why the Pharaohs built The Pyramids with fake stones*, 2009.

de Santillana, Giorgio & von Dechend, Hertha, *Hamlet's Mill: An Essay Investigating the Origins of Human Knowledge and Its Transmission Through Myth*, Publisher David R. Godine, 1969.

DeYoung, Don, *Thousands... Not Billions: Challenging an Icon of Evolution, Questioning the Age of the Earth*, Master Books, 2005.

Dictionary of the Bible, edited by John L. Mackenzie, Simon and Shuster, 1995.

Dimont, Max I., *Jews, God and History*, New American Library, 1962.

Dingle, Herbert, *Science at the Crossroads*, Martin Brian & O'Keeffe, 1972.

Discoveries and Opinions of Galileo, translated by Stillman Drake, Doubleday Anchor Books,1957.

Ehrman, Bart, D., *Lost Scriptures: Books that did not make it into the Bible*, Oxford University Press, 2003.

Ehrman, Bart, D., *The Orthodox Corruption of Scripture: The Effect of Early Christological Controversies on the Text of the New Testament*, Oxford University Press,1993.

Ehrman, Bart, D., *Lost Christianities: The Battles for Scripture and Faiths We Never Knew*, Oxford University Press, 2003.

Eusebius, G. A. Williamson translation,*The History of the Church: From Christ to Constantine*, Penguin Books, 1965.

Haigh, Paula, "Galileo's Heresy," on-line PDF.

Friedman, Richard Elliott, *The BIBLE with Sources Revealed*, HarperOne, 2003.

Friedman, Richard Elliott, *Who Wrote the Bible?*, Harper Collins, 1989.

Ginzberg, Louis, *Legends of the Bible*, Konecky & Konecky, 1956.

Gruber, Dan, *The Church and The Jews: The Biblical Relationship*, Elijah Publishing, 1991.

Hanson, James N., *The Bible And Geocentricity*, THe Association of Biblical Astronomy, 2005.

Highland, J.R., *God's Covenant with Animals*, Lantern Books, 2000.

In Six Days: why fifty scientists choose to believe in creation, edited by John F. Ashton, Master Books, 2001.

Johnson, Paul, *A History of the Jews*, Harper & Row, 1987.

Johnson, Phillip E., *Darwin on Trial*, IVP Books, 2010.

Johnson, Phillip E., *Reason in the Balance: The Case Against Naturalism in Science, Law & Education*, InterVarsity Press, 1995.

Jones, Floyd Nolan, *The Chronology of the Old Testament*, Master Books, 1993.

Kelly, Al, *Challenging Modern Physics: Questioning Einstein's Relativity Theories*, Brown Walker Press, 2005.

Koestler, Arthur, *The Watershed: A Biography of Johannes Kepler*, Anchor Books, 1960.

Liechty, Daniel, *Andreas Fisher and the Sabbatarian Anabaptists*, Harold Press, 1988.

Lubenow, Marvin L., *Bones of Contention: A Creationist Assessment of Human Fossils*, BakerBooks, 2004.

McCabe, Robert V., "A Defense of Literal Days in the Creation Week," on-line PDF.

Mathisen, David, Warner, *The Mathisen Corollary: Connecting a Global Flood with the Mystery of Mankind's Ancient Past*, Beowulf Books, 2011.

Merkley, Paul Charles, *Christian Attitudes towards the State of Israel*, McGill-Queen's University Press, 2001.

McEvoy, J.P., *Eclipse: The Science and History of Nature's Most Spectacular Phenomenon*, Fourth Estate, 1999.

Moore, Patrick, *Watchers of the Skies*, G.P. Putnam's Sons, 1973.

Navas, Patrick, *Divine Truth or Human Tradition?*, Author House, 2007.

Olson, Ross S., "Young Earth Creation: The Scientific Evidence," on-line PDF.

Patten, Donald W. and Windsor, Samuel R., *The Mars-Earth Wars*, on-line PDF.

Perry, Marvin and Schweitzer, Frederick M., *Anti-Semitism: Myth and Hate from Antiquity to the Present*, Palgrave Macmillan, 2002.

Pitman, Sean D., "The Geological Column," on-line PDF.

Popick, Jeff, *The Real Forbidden Fruit*, VeganWorld Publishing, 2007.

Prager, Dennis & TeLushkin, Joseph, *Why The Jews: The Reason For Antisemitism*, A Touchstone Book, 2003.

Radcliffe, Hilton, *The Static Universe: Exploding the Myth of Cosmic Expansion*, C.

Roy Keys Inc., 2010.

Rempel, Abraham, "The Earth is NOT a Planet," on-line PDF

Rubenstein, Richard E., *When Jesus Became God*, Harcourt Inc, 1999.

Sachar, Howard M., *A History of Israel From The Rise of Zionism To Our Time*, Alfred A. Knopf, 2001.

Schiaparelli, G., *Astronomy In The Old Testament*, Oxford, 1905.

Scranton, Laird, *The Velikovsky Heresies: Worlds in Collision and Ancient Catastrophes Revisited*, Bear & Company, 2012.

Snobelen, Stephen D., "Isaac Newton, Socinianism and "The One Supreme God,"" on-line PDF.

Stott, Philip, *Vital Questions*, Reformation Media Press, 1998.

Tabor, James D., *Paul and Jesus: How the Apostle Transformed Christianity*, Simon & Schuster, 2012.

Thiede, Carsten Peter, *The Dead Sea Scrolls and the Jewish Origins of Christianity*, Palgrave, 2001.

Toulmin, Stephen and Goodfield, June, *The Fabric of the Heavens: The Development of Astronomy and Dynamics*, Harper Torchbooks, 1961.

The International Encyclopedia of Astronomy, edited by Patrick Moore, Orion Books, 1987.

The Rotating Earth.. Theory, Fact or Fiction?, on-line essay.

Thiel, Rudolf, *And There Was Light*, A Mentor Book, 1957.

Thirring, Hans, "The Effect of Rotating Distant Masses in Einstein's Theory of Gravitation" (Translated from the *Physicalische Zeitschrift*, **19**:33-39, 1918)

Thompson, Bert, "Biological Evolution," on-line PDF.

Velikovsky Immanuel, *Worlds in Collision*, Paradigma Ltd., 2009.

Vujicic, John, "Did Abel or Cain Offer a Lamb in Sacrifice to God?", on-line paper.

Wells, Jonathan, *Icons of Evolution: Science or Myth?*, Regency Publishing, 2000.

Williams, Alex, and Hartnett, John, *Dismantling The Big Bang: God's Universe Rediscovered*, Master Books, 2005.

Wilson, Marvin R., *Our Father Abraham: Jewish Roots of the Christian Faith*, William B. Eerdmans, 1989.

Witham, Larry, *The Measure of God: Our Century-Long Struggle to Reconcile SCIENCE & RELIGION, The Story of the Gifford Lectures*, Harper Collins, 2005.

Wycliffe Bible Encyclopedia, Moody Press, 1975.

INDEX

Abib (see, Aviv)

Abraham 33, 105, 115, 174, 182, 191, 200, 207-209, 213-216

Adam 27, 29-30, 80, 125

Adoption 83-85

Airy, George Bidel 16n

Alexandria 49, 54n, 55, 112

Alexander the Great 57, 224

Anglo-Saxon 209

Anti-Christ 187, 241

Annals of Cuauhtitlan 221-222,

Antisemitism 81n

Apostles Creed 240

Arian Catholic Church 51

Artapanus 223

Arp, Halton 148n

Asher, Shmuel 110

Assyria 158, 205-206, 208

Astronomical 76, 120, 141, 167

Astronomers 147, 148, 162, 171n, 175

Astronomy 14, 124, 137

Athanasius 49

Atomic dating 64, 73

Atonement 105

Australia 63, 66n, 156, 207

Aviv 174-176

Barley 175-177

Bible 27, 80, 109-110, 113-120 passim, 128, 145-153 passim, 185, 247, 253

Bio-rhythm 166, 176

Babylon 25, 53, 141, 157, 205, 208, 222

Big Bang 17, 63n, 140

Black race 209

Black Sea 206-207, 209n

Blood 31, 40, 83, 90, 95, 99-105 passim, 107, 111, 114-116, 201n, 222, 224, 233, 250, 256

Boscovich, Ruggiero 16n

Bouw, Gerardus D 19n, 155n

Brahe, Tycho 20

Brayshaw, James R 245

Calendar 157-158, 162, 165, 168, 176-177

Cambrian period 70, 76

Canaan 200-203, 205-206, 208, 211, 222

Canada 1, 207, 63n, 74n, 245

Canon 45, 48-51, 58

Carbon-14 71

Catastrophe 74-75, 200, 220-223, 228-229, 245

Catastrophism 220-221, 227, 229n

Catholic Church 110, 161, 241

Celestial Sphere 14, 15, 137, 225

Chelyabinsk 220

China 121, 204, 208, 220, 225

Church 55, 56, 83, 90-91, 105, 161,
　　213-214, 251

Church fathers 26, 54-55, 84

Clementine Homilies 40n, 53, 112

Clement of Alexandria 112

Collins, Steven M. 201, 203-5

Colonies (Ancient Hebrew) 204-205

Constellation 173-175, 225, 231, 235n

Constantine the Great 161

Copernicus, Nicolaus 16, 62, 152-152, 174

Copernican Principle 147

Coriolis Effect 19

Cosmology 17, 62, 145-146, 155n, 174n

Covenant 30, 113, 160, 249n

Christianity 25, 43, 53, 55, 83, 103, 189,
　　241, 243

Clementine Homilies 40, 53, 112

Creation 65, 67-70, 75-76, 95, 120, 135,
　　139, 142-143, 148, 157, 168, 173-174,
　　213-214, 234, 258

Cro-Magnon 123

David 33, 87-88, 93, 100, 140, 152, 201n,
　　203, 207-208, 212

Day of Wrath 75, 200, 247

Dead Sea Scrolls 58, 71, 159

Dead 3, 23, 24, 31n, 33, 88-89, 122n, 212

Death 23-24, 32-33, 75, 88-89, 103-104,
　　107, 126n, 227, 236, 248, 250,
　　254, 258

Deception 9, 28, 91, 113, 120-121, 150

Demon 242

Documentary Hypothesis 111

Dualism 243

Earth 2-4, 10-11, 14-21 passim, 33, 61-77
　　passim, 113, 124, 133-154 passim,
　　159, 169, 171-174, 200-205, 208,
　　210-213, 217-240 passim, 243-248,
　　250, 254-258

Earth's age 70-75

Ebionites 53n, 84n, 195-196

Eclipse 14, 72n, 120, 172

Edomites 203, 209

Ehrman, Bart D. 40n, 84-86, 92

Einstein, Albert 17-18, 64, 137n, 155n, 256

England (see Great Britain)

Ephraim 201, 215-216

Epiphanius 195, 196n

Equinox 162, 166, 172, 174-176

Eschatology 7, 25, 199, 219

Europe 29n, 126, 207, 208, 209n

Eusebius 58n, 69, 195, 223

Evolution 61, 68, 72, 77, 119, 121-123,
　　127-130, 141

Exodus, the 204, 221-230 passim

Festivals 157-158, 167, 170, 211

Fingers of God 148

Firmament 135-137, 148, 231

First visible crescent 159, 166

Flood (see Great Flood)

Forgiveness 99-103 passim, 107, 111, 183,
　　186, 194, 250

Foucault 19, 155

France 207

Galileo 134, 148, 150

Garden of Eden 27, 114, 117, 211, 244

Gauls 207

Genesis 29-30, 67-69, 76, 79n, 111, 119-
120, 135-137, 143, 148, 153, 257

Gentry, Robert 66n

Germany 207

Geocentricity 19, 141, 146, 153-155

Geological column 70, 72

Giza (see, Great Pyramid)

Globular clusters 76

Gnosticism

Good News 3, 33n, 48, 54-55, 89

Golden Age 204-205

Gordon, Nehemia 160

Goths 207-208

Gould, Stephen Jay 1-2, 127-128, 227

Gradualism 227

Grand Canyon 70, 73-74

Gravity 64-65, 72, 76, 133

Great Britain 65, 121, 205-207, 249

Great Flood 30, 66n, 73-75, 125-126, 221,
226, 230, 231n

Great Pyramid 123-127

Gregorian calendar 161, 163, 167-168,
177n, 182

Gregory XIII 162, 164, 167n

Ham 209n

Hamlet's Mill 129

Hatshepsut, Queen 225

Heliocentric 15n, 19, 20n, 153

Holy Spirit 58, 90, 134, 150, 186, 195-196

Hoyle, Fred 15n,

Hubble Constant 62n, 63n

Hubble, Edwin 146-147

Human being 2-3, 17, 26-27, 58-59, 75-76,
79n, 82, 84, 87, 89-91, 94-95, 97, 127-
128, 148, 150,   164, 167, 178,
211, 243, 246-247, 250-251, 253-258

Immortal beings 33, 95, 106, 117, 184,
211, 212

Incarnation 91-92, 94, 96-97, 104,
119, 122-124

India 182n, 204, 207-208, 220

Instruction 41, 53n, 103, 109, 184, 187, 248

Intercalation 171

International Date Line 163

Interpretation 4, 59, 91n, 119, 135,
148n, 237

Inquisition 208, 241

Ipuwer 222, 225

Isaiah 58, 79, 114, 169, 189, 236

Islam 171, 253

Israel 31, 89, 107, 113-114, 158, 167, 177,
201, 204-07, 211, 215-217, 229

Israelite 102, 204, 205, 208, 228-229

Jasher, book of 124, 221

Jerome 224

Jerusalem 38-43, 55, 89, 159-160, 177,
205, 211

Jesuit 208n

Jews, Jewish 25n, 26, 81, 105, 177, 208,
215, 242n

Joseph of Arimathea 182

Josephus 125-126, 206-207

Joshua 140, 173, 192, 201, 221-222, 226, 253

Judah 87, 201, 204-210, 214-216

Judaism 55, 110

Julius Caesar 162

Jupiter 11, 65n, 74, 140, 220

Justification 56, 104, 189-190, 195

Karaites 160, 177

Khazars 209n

Kingdom of Heaven 49, 106, 183, 191, 210-211, 214, 247, 254-255

Kingdoms of Judah and Israel 205-206, 214

Koran 171n, 226

Lateran Council 26

Law (Scientific) 17-19, 145, 213

Law (Biblical) 28, 33, 40-42, 58, 101-102, 106, 112-113, 161, 167, 184-185, 189-196 passim, 201-202, 211n, 213-214, 239, 242, 255-256

Lawlessness 40-41

Law of Moses 101, 102, 184n, 191, 242

Lense and Thirring 18-19, 137

Levites 201, 205

Lie 10, 27, 28, 53, 81, 105, 150-151, 154, 182, 184, 241 (see, Three Great Lies)

Lord's Supper 103-104, 115

Lost Ten Tribes 201n, 205n, 206-208, 214-215

Lucifer 244

Lunisolar 157, 165, 171

Luther, Martin 26, 32, 83n, 189

Magnetic field 225, 227

Maimonides 111, 116, 144

Manuscript Quiche 222

Mars 2, 11, 14n, 17, 65n, 74, 151, 220, 229-231

Mars-Earth Wars, The 229

Menno Simons 189n

Messiah 3, 33, 39, 48, 52, 58-59, 79, 87, 94, 165, 184, 189, 191, 195, 215, 251, 254, 257-258,

Metonic cycle 171

Michelson and Morley 17

Moon 2, 17, 63n, 72, 74, 135-137, 140, 143, 163, 167-168, 171-173, 220-221

Moses (Moshe) 24n, 26, 31, 41, 55, 103, 111, 112, 167, 184-185, 192

Muslim 28, 29n, 58, 162, 164

NASA 14-15, 141-142, 171n, 177, 231n

National Geographic 71n, 121, 224

Nazarenes 195-196

Nazareth 87, 89,

Neanderthal 121-123

Nebraska Man 121

Newton, Isaac 29, 69, 81, 237

New Moon 34, 59, 61, 159-160, 169, 172, 175-176

New Zealand 207

Nibiru 235

Nicea, Council of 51, 90, 92, 163n

Noah 74, 125-126, 209n, 230

North America 23, 71, 205

OOPArt 71

Origen 25, 54

Papyrus Ipuwer (see Ipuwer)

Parallax 153, 174n

Parthia 182n, 207

Pentecost (see, Shavuot)

Persia 243

Pharaoh 95-96, 124, 186

Piltdown Man 121

Plato 25, 32, 57, 225-256

Pope Gregory XIII 162, 164, 167n

Pre-existence 91-92

Precession 174,

Physics 19, 64, 66, 145, 155n

Pleiades 231, 235n

Polar reversal 227

Precession 174

Prophets 28, 44, 52, 75, 113-116 passim,
181-182, 185, 191, 195, 199, 201, 203,
210-216 passim, 232, 235, 237, 247

Protestant 28, 161-162, 209, 240-241

Punctuated equilibrium 128, 227

Pyramid 126-127, (see, Great Pyramid)

Radiometric dating 63-64, 76

Redshift 62

Reggio, Archbishop of 161

Religion 1-2, 23, 25, 28, 43, 81n, 111-
112, 256

Religious 4, 10, 27-29, 49, 56, 109-110, 150,
242n, 247, 256

Repentance 55, 74-75, 81n, 87, 107, 187,
194, 241

Replacement Theology 213-214

Resurrection 3, 26, 89, 32-33, 225n

Revelation 103, 115, 134, 148, 154n

Ritual 103-104

Rome, Roman 54, 71, 94, 161, 207, 240

Russia 66, 164, 220

Sabbath 59, 61, 108, 130, 156-170
passim, 177

Sacrifice 39, 99-101, 105-106, 111-
115, 247

Sagnac, Georges 17n

Saturn 220

Saxons 207-209,

Science 4, 14, 62n, 67, 123, 127, 137, 143,
145, 150, 153, 167, 219, 226, 249,
250, 256

Scientists 15, 16-19, 68, 73, 120-121, 128,
130, 137, 141-142-149 passim, 154,
220, 227

Scripture 29, 31, 41, 48-55 passim, 86,
91-92, 108-110, 113, 115-117, 134-
136, 140-145, 161, 170, 232-237

Scopes Monkey Trial 121

Sent 235

Septuagint 54, 58, 69

Seth 125-126

Shavuot (Pentecost) 89, 237, 239-240

Shoemaker-Levy 220

Sin 57, 99, 100-107, 183, 245-246, 248, 254

Sodom and Gomorrah 221, 230

Sosigenes 162

Sola Scriptura 161

Solomon 110, 120, 203-205, 207-208, 231

South America 126, 182n, 205, 208

Spain 205, 208

Sphinx 125

Stars 14, 16, 18, 135, 141n, 143, 144, 147, 151, 167-168, 173, 234, 247

Stone Age 123, 126, 158n

Sumerians 157, 171n

Sun 2, 17, 20, 72n, 113, 134-137, 140-141, 143, 148, 152, 155n, 167, 170, 172-174, 213, 219n, 223, 225, 233-235, 245

Sundial of Ahaz 230-231

Tabernacle 110, 143

Tesla, Nikola, 143

Theologians 28, 152, 254

Theology 43, 83, 214, 219

Thirring, Hans 18n, 137 (see, Lense and Thirring)

Time 2, 62, 63n, 64-67, 75

Time dilation 64-65

Tithe 110, 201

Torah 24n, 26, 28, 31, 41, 53n, 108-115, 160, 184n, 185, 191, 237

Tractate Sanhedrin 226

Three Great Lies 26-27, 80-81, 185

Tractate Sanhedrin 226

Tradition 28, 48, 85, 90-91, 161, 166n, 177, 245, 255

Tree of Life 117

Trent, Council of 161,

Trinity 90-94, 97, 182

Tunguska 220

Tyndale, William 26

Uniformitarianism 62, 73

United States of America 207, 209, 249

Ussher, James (Bishop) 69, 77, 119-120

Vandals 207-208

Veganism 156, 248-249, 252

Velikovsky, Immanuel 220-228

Venus 11, 14n, 74n, 220, 226, 229n, 244-245

Vernal equinox 166, 176

Virgin birth 56-59

Water 73, 135-137, 140, 143-144, 231

Watson, Donald 249

Week (lunar) 130, 157-159, 165, 168, 175

Week (seven-day) 164-165

World Calendar 163-164

Worlds in Collision 220-221, 226

Zodiac 173, 225

Zoroaster 243

Zeus 224

CONTACTING THE AUTHOR:

Abraham Rempel

Mail:
P.O. Box 29020
St Catharines, ON L2R 7P9
Canada

Email:
bookofnots@cogeco.ca

Telephone:
905-682-1970

Website:
www.mennoniteisrael.org